The 7th Python

A Twat's Tale

--

By Mark Forstater

Featuring the court testimonies of Michael Palin and Eric Idle

©Mark Forstater 2015, 2020
Irregular Features
London UK

****

June 17 2014 Time Out- Ben Williams:

I start with the big question: why re-form at all? 'We need the money!' says Terry Jones. Eric Idle explains why: 'We were meeting last August in gloomy circumstances because we had just been sued by this twat,' he says. The 'twat' is Mark Forstater, co-producer of 'Monty Python and the Holy Grail', who claimed he was underpaid royalties from Idle's 'Spamalot' musical. The Pythons lost the court case, and it left them with a hefty legal bill.

June 29 2014 Eric Idle on Imagine, BBC 1

"We've been involved with this idiot who was one of the producers on Holy Grail and he has spent seven years suing us. So what it meant was it cost us a million quid to defend ourselves."

November 13, 2014 The Meaning of Live, Gold TV

Michael Palin: "We got ourselves into a law suit which was to do with royalties on merchandising for a man who had been one of the producers on Holy Grail."

Eric Idle: "Seven years he's been pursuing us, seven years; it's cost us a million quid, with lawyers, just to turn up and say no, that's not true, to defend yourself."

John Cleese: "And we were kind of laughing about it, you know, nobody was in despair. We just... just what, it's insane- Why didn't we settle 5 or 6 years ago?"

For my mother
Dorothy Forstater
who taught me to stand up for
myself- and to seek justice

Table of Contents:

Acknowledgements: 1

Preface: The Twat's Journey 2

Chronology is Always Useful 5

PART ONE: The Tale of a Twat 6

PART TWO: The Twat From Hero to Zero 46

PART THREE: Caught in the tentacles of the law 91

PART FOUR: The Trial: The law is an ass (or a twat 196

Appendix 1: Cross Examination of Eric Idle by Tom Weisselberg 293

Appendix 2: Cross Examination of Michael Palin by Tom Weisselberg 321

Acknowledgements:

I have to thank David Cohen for encouraging me to write this book. After 7 years of dealing with this case I was in no mood to re-visit it, but he persisted and after a year, I felt able to deal with recounting these episodes in my life.

Harry Pepp, Ruth Blair, Dan Weinzweig, Miranda Watts, Bob Storer and Susie Stables all read the first draft and their comments helped shape the final version. Thanks to Oween Williams for the amusing cover and to John Mackay for the bar charts.

David Morgan was kind enough to allow me to quote extensively from his book Monty Python Speaks for which I am grateful. I want to thank Gerry Harrison for the account of his experiences working on the Holy Grail, Lawrence Abramson for his account of meeting up with Simon Olswang and Tom Weisselberg QC for sharing some of his thoughts about dealing with the case.

Alan Weitz sent me some 50 year old photos which are priceless. Carol Cleveland allowed me to use one of her wedding photos for which I thank her. Thanks to Ray Buckland for the typesetting.

I spent a lovely day with Neil Innes talking over old times. He reminded me that I once said in an unterview that his music for the Holy Grail was 'lousy'. He suggests that I meant 'not appropriate.' He was right. I put it down to my ignorance and stupidity, Sorry, Neil.

Preface: The Twat's Journey

Eric Idle called me an idiot on Imagine on BBC 1 and a twat in Time Out - all because I successfully sued the Python group for reneging on a deal we had made in 1974 when I produced Monty Python and the Holy Grail. What follows is this twat's account of his dealings with the Monty Python group, first in 1973-75 when I produced the film, and again in 2005-2013 when I was in dispute with them over my share of royalties from Spamalot, the musical based on the film. Seven years of dispute and litigation came to dominate much of my life.

I never wanted to go to court, and did everything I could to settle the dispute. There were a number of times when I thought a settlement was possible, but in each case I was rebuffed. I assumed that the Pythons would prefer not to fight this out in public, since the battle of these cultural legends versus a loser (as Eric Idle tweeted about me) was sure to generate negative publicity for them. Yet, to my great astonishment and disappointment, we did end up in the Court of Chancery, like characters in Dickens.

I can't answer the obvious. Why couldn't we settle and why did the Pythons allow the dispute to go on for so long? There are two classic explanations. First, once a group of performers is successful for a long period of time, their wealth and fame often insulates them. Managers act for them and deal with all the mundane and messy aspects of life. Was I a mundane and messy twat or flea that they really didn't think they had to bother with? The second explanation is more brutal, but the history of show business is packed with monsters. One example: when Alexander Salkind, the producer of Superman died, he was being sued by his son.

At least I wasn't related to the Pythons but I was a friend of most of them and worked with all of them when we made the Holy Grail. The film is now a classic, and has earned many millions of pounds of profit. It is the most successful independently produced film ever made in the UK. When producing the Holy Grail, I made it my aim to be certain that the Pythons owned and controlled the copyright in the film through their own company, which gave them ultimate artistic and financial control. This was in contrast to the unhappy experience they had on their first film - And Now For Something Completely Different - which was owned and controlled by the financiers.

The Pythons made about £ 6000 profit each from their first film, whereas on Holy Grail each Python has received over £ 1.5m into their bank accounts. The success of the Holy Grail allowed the Pythons to make Life of Brian and inaugurated the directing careers of Terry Gilliam and Terry Jones. The Holy Grail is also the basis of Spamalot, another huge money spinner for them. They did well from my efforts on their behalf. But 30 years later they had forgotten what I had done for them, and instead used their powerful position as sole owners of the film against me.

This was a bitter, shocking seven year long experience. Yet even as I was suffering the hardship and insults that accompany litigation, I wonder if the Pythons were aware of what their manager and lawyers were trying to achieve. I wrote a number of times to Michael Palin to make certain he was informed of what was happening, but in the end we faced each other in court. Perhaps, as that wise Professor Freud might say, a group that calls themselves Monty (after the Field Marshal who won El Alamein) and Python (after that wrap around snake) may have an instinct to squash, strangle or crush.

The title of the book - The 7th Python – is a bit of a joke, and a provocation. At the trial I claimed that during the making of the film I was being treated financially as a 7th Python, since my fees, profit share and financial responsibilities were the same as the six Pythons. Our sensitive comedians, however, took offence and assumed I was suggesting that I was claiming to be a 7th Python i.e. - a member of the group who could write sketches and make jokes; I never claimed any such thing.

This is in many ways a sad story, one of friendships ending, and of goodwill eroded - a tale of greed and hope, of desperation and negligence. I exclude Graham Chapman of any blame, of course; he died back in 1989. No one wins in litigation except the lawyers; Dickens famously wrote in Bleak House about the fictitious case of Jarndyce vs Jarndyce, which meandered through the Victorian law courts for generations. Although I was once a student of English literature, I never read Bleak House. Perhaps if I had I would have taken to heart some of Dickens' warning, and not proceeded down the legal path:

"This is the Court of Chancery, which has its decaying houses and its blighted land in every shire, which has its worn-out lunatic in every madhouse and its dead in every churchyard, which has its ruined suitor with his slipshod heels and threadbare dress borrowing and begging through the round of every man's acquaintance, which gives to monied might the means abundantly of wearing out the right, which so exhausts finances, patience, courage, hope, so overthrows the brain and breaks the heart, that there is not an honourable man among its practitioners who would not give- who does not often give- the warning, "Suffer any wrong that can be done you rather than come here."

Well, this twat went there, and this is the story of that journey.

***

Chronology is Always Useful

1973   Fund-raising for Monty Python and the Holy Grail
1974   Production and post-production of Holy Grail
1975   UK and US releases of Holy Grail
2005   Spamalot opens on Broadway
2006   Dispute Year 1
2007   Dispute Year 2
2008   Dispute Year 3
2009   Dispute Year 4
2010   Dispute Year 5
2011   Dispute Year 6
2012   Dispute Year 7 - Trial
2013   Judgement

****

PART ONE: The Tale of a Twat

The Pythons: An Idiot's Guide

Monty Python was formed in 1969 when five writer-performers from Oxford and Cambridge, and an American illustrator and animator, were brought together to do a series of 13 comedy half hours for the BBC.

The five writers were three Cambridge graduates- John Cleese, Graham Chapman and Eric Idle - and two Oxford graduates- Michael Palin and Terry Jones. Terry Gilliam was the lone American. Cleese and Chapman had been writing partners on shows like The Frost Report and Marty, and Cleese had become well known for his appearances on Frost, making him the 'senior' figure of the group. Palin and Jones were also writing partners and had worked with Eric Idle and Terry Gilliam on Do Not Adjust Your Set, a much liked children's programme. Gilliam had met Cleese in New York when he was working for Help!, a satirical magazine started by Harvey Kurtzman, famous for Mad Magazine.

The group produced a second series of 13 shows and in 1971 produced a short series of six episodes, but without Cleese.

The success of the Holy Grail gave the Pythons the chance to make a bigger budget epic- Life of Brian, which was financed by George Harrison's company Handmade Films.

In 1980 they performed Monty Python Live at the Hollywood Bowl, and, two years later, produced their third and relatively disappointing film The Meaning of Life.

In 1989 Graham Chapman died. In 1998 there was an HBO reunion (with Graham as a cardboard cut-out) in Aspen.

Since 1982 diehard Python fans have been desperate for more Python shows, but few of the Pythons wanted to regroup. It was only due to my legal persistence that the Pythons were forced to perform together again - at the London 02 arena shows in 2014. I hope that Python fans appreciate my sacrifice on their behalf.

***

Even Legends Were Once Unknowns, So Here Is A Thumbnail of Their origins

John Cleese – The Headmaster - famous for silly walks, *Fawlty Towers*, and marrying tall blondes.

John Marwood Cleese was born in Weston-Super-Mare in 1939. Father Reginald was an insurance salesman and mother Muriel a housewife. His father changed the family name from Cheese when he served in the First World War, which was helpful to John when he befriended a boy called Barnabus Butter at school.

I wonder if Cleese's sense of humour would have been different if he had grown up as John Cheese? -and sometimes I refer to him by his original name.

As a child Cheese loved soccer and cricket, and supported Bristol City FC and Somerset County Cricket Club. He went to St. Peter's Preparatory School when he was eight and later attended Clifton College, when he left in 1958. By the age of 12 Cleese was already 6' tall and had acted in a school production, but he dreamed of becoming a professional athlete.

Cheese watched American comics like Jack Benny and Phil Silvers on TV and was an avid fan of The Goons. He studied law at Downing College, Cambridge, intending to become a solicitor.

At Cambridge Cheese joined the Footlights Dramatic Club, writing and performing alongside Bill Oddie and Tim Brooke-Taylor, as well as his future writing partner Graham Chapman. The success of the revue A Clump of Plinths (renamed Cambridge Circus) brought Cleese to the West End, New Zealand and Broadway. Later he wrote for BBC radio – I'm Sorry I'll Read That Again, a hit show. David Frost then asked Cleese and Chapman to write for The Frost Report. Cleese and Chapman later went on to work on At Last the 1948 show with Marty Feldman.

At this point the Monty Python group was formed to do the first series for BBC TV. After that, Cheese wrote Fawlty Towers with his wife Connie Booth, and also played the rage repressing Basil Fawlty. He went on to write and act in a successful film- A Fish Called Wanda, but a follow up - Fierce Creatures - was a disaster. This was Cleese's first failure. After this, he seemed to avoid taking on larger projects and increasingly acted in other peoples' films, TV commercials, and, later, put on a one man show to raise alimony.

Connie Booth had introduced Cleese to psychotherapy, and he eventually wrote two books on the subject with Dr. Robin Skynner – Life and How to Survive it and Families and How to Survive Them. Cleese shares with the Royal Family the possible identity confusions that come if you change your name. During the 1914-19 war George V decided his family could no longer be called after a German cake since the country was at war with the Huns. So the Teutonic Battenbergs became the English Windsors. Dropping the family name Cheese is curiously not a subject raised in the books Cleese co-wrote.

Eric Idle- Nudge nudge, wink wink – Is that a chip on my shoulder?

Eric Idle was born in 1943 in South Shields, County Durham. His mother was a nurse and his father a Sergeant in the RAF who was killed on Christmas Eve 1945 while hitch-hiking home on compassionate leave. As a young child Eric lived with his aunt in

Manchester, and then with his mother in Liverpool. When he was seven he was sent to The Royal School Wolverhampton (called The Ophany) for boys who had lost their fathers in the war. Influenced by Elvis mania, Idle bought a guitar when he was twelve and his grandmother bought him a typewriter. He had everything he needed to write and compose songs too. Perhaps his finest lyric is One Foot In The Grave, the theme song of the TV series. Idle went to Pembroke College, Cambridge, to read English Literature.

In 1964/5 Idle was President of Footlights and changed the rules to accept women members, the first of whom was Germaine Greer. He toured in the Footlights Revue, My Girl Herbert, which also ran at The Lyric, Hammersmith. After a season in rep at Leicester, he started to write: for radio, I'm Sorry I'll Read That Again and television's The Frost Report.

In 1968 Idle wrote and acted in the children's TV hit, Do Not Adjust Your Set, with Michael Palin, Terry Jones and Terry Gilliam. It was at this point these four joined with Cleese and Chapman to form the Monty Python group.

After Python, Eric co-created The Rutles (with Neil Innes), did the Greedy Bastard tour, and wrote Spamalot.

Michael Palin- The nicest man in the world - a National Treasure,

Michael Edward Palin was born in 1943 in Sheffield, West Yorkshire, the son of an engineer and housewife. He was embarrassed by his parents' relative poverty, and later ashamed to discover that half his father's salary went to pay for his public school fees. He was educated as a boarder at Shrewsbury School (following his father), and went to Brasenose College, Oxford, to read Modern History. Palin was influenced by the Goons and listened to Radio Luxembourg. At Oxford he joined forces first with Robert Hewison and later Terry Jones to write and perform revue material.

After University Palin was a presenter on a comedy pop series called NOW and he soon re-united with Terry Jones to write material for TV, eventually joining the writing team on The Frost Report. This was the first time all the British members of the future Python team worked together, since other writers included Eric Idle, John Cleese and Graham Chapman.

Palin and Jones then worked together on the TV series Twice a Fortnight, and on Do Not Adjust Your Set, collaborating with Eric Idle, Terry Gilliam and Neil Innes from the Bonzo Dog Doo-Dah Band.

After Python, Palin and Jones wrote Ripping Yarns. Palin also co-wrote and acted in Time Bandits with Terry Gilliam, and wrote and starred in The Missionary. In 1984, he reunited with Terry Gilliam to star in Brazil, and also appeared in A Fish Called Wanda, for which he won the BAFTA Award for Best Actor in a Supporting Role. His stammering brother was superb – and who can forget the scene in which he bulldozes Kevin Kline to death at Heathrow airport. Was the role made for Palin? A nice man with a ruthless streak? He also starred in Alan Bleasdale's series G.B.H.

Palin has gained a new audience recently by making travel documentaries and writing books based on them. He has also published his Journals.

Terry Gilliam- The angry iconoclast.

Terence Vance Gilliam was born in 1940 in rural Minnesota. His parents were religious; at one time he wanted to be a missionary. He (and possibly Africans) were saved from this fate by his talent. His father worked on building the Alaska Highway, became a coffee salesman and finally a carpenter. His sister's health forced the family to move to Panorama City California, where Terry became the student body president, king of the senior prom, head cheerleader and Valedictorian at his high school. He was also a good track athlete.

After college Gilliam worked at a children's' theatre building sets, and sent his cartoons to Harvey Kurtzman at Mad Magazine. When Gilliam came to New York Kurtzman gave him a job on Help! and he studied film-making at a night course at CCNY, which is where we met. He later worked at an animation studio.

Gilliam was angry at the state of race relations in the US and the country's involvement in the Vietnam War. He left for Europe in 1967, and got a job doing animated spots for the kids' show Do Not Adjust Your Set, where he met the other Pythons- Palin, Jones and Idle.

After Python, Gilliam became an internationally recognized film director, making Jabberwocky, Time Bandits, Brazil, The Fisher King, 12 Monkeys, Baron Munchausen, Fear and Loathing in Las Vegas, The Brothers Grimm and others. Recently he has begun directing operas for the English National Opera.

Terry Jones- The passionate Welsh medievalist.

Terry Jones was born in 1942 in Colwyn Bay. His father served with the RAF in India and later became a bank clerk. His family moved to Claygate in Surrey when he was four and Jones attended the Royal Grammar School in Guildford. When he was seven he decided he wanted to be an actor and also began writing. He was a big fan of The Goon Show. Jones went to St. Edmund Hall, Oxford, where he read English and History.

At Oxford Jones joined the Experimental Theatre Club, and later he and Palin acted together in The Oxford Revue. After university, he again collaborated with Palin and wrote and appeared in the television series Twice a Fortnight, as well as The Complete and Utter History of Britain. He also wrote for The Frost Report and joined Palin in Do Not Adjust Your Set.

After Monty Python and the Holy Grail, Jones directed Life Of Brian and The Meaning of Life. He later directed Personal Services, Erik the Viking, The Wind in the Willows and Absolutely Anything.

He also wrote and presented television documentaries, especially about the medieval period.

Graham Chapman- On his own planet, alas.

Graham Chapman was born in 1941 in Wigston Fields, near Leicester, the son of a policeman and his was the great tragedy of the group. He was educated at Melton Mowbray Grammar and took a degree in Natural Sciences at Emmanuel College, Cambridge; he also studied medicine at St. Bartholomew's Medical College, but he never practiced.

Chapman was influenced by The Goon Show and other radio comics; he once said he wanted to be a Goon. At Cambridge he acted in revue by appearing at a Pembroke Smoker, where would- be performers appeared in front of the members to try to entertain them sufficiently to be admitted. Chapman got in and later joined Footlights. There he met John Cleese and they began writing together.

The Cleese/Chapman writing team took the Frost Express from Cambridge to the BBC to work on the satire shows of the day. Graham also wrote for other comics, singers and for the Doctor series. In 1966 he celebrated coming out as gay with a party for his friends.

Chapman played the lead in the Holy Grail and Life of Brian. After Python, he starred in and co-produced (with me) The Odd Job. He published his autobiography- A Liar's Autobiography - in 1980. In 1982 he starred in Yellowbeard, which he co-wrote with Bernard McKenna. Drinking was a severe problem for him. He died far too young - when he was 48 years old - in 1989 - of throat cancer.

How They Got Together

There are two versions about the group's genesis. Barry Took, who was a comedy adviser for the BBC at the time claims that he originated the idea of introducing Cleese to Palin with the aim of their collaborating on a new TV series. Cleese claims that he rang Michael Palin to suggest the same thing. However it came about, the BBC did give the group a 13 part series, on the basis that it would be new, fun and exciting. It was a rare period of television freedom. The group did not have to present even an outline to get the commission from the BBC. They had a free hand to do what they liked.

The BBC had written a working title - The Flying Circus - on their internal accounts, so when the series was greenlit, they asked Barry Took if they could please keep the name so that they could avoid the bureaucratic hassle of re-writing the schedules. Being a galley slave is easy compared to being a BBC-crat. So the Pythons added Monty Python's to The Flying Circus and Monty Python's Flying Circus became the name of the series, and Monty Python the name of the group.

David Morgan in his book, Monty Python Speaks, collected quotes in which different members of the group described and dissected each other. He has kindly allowed me to use some of his quotes, including a few from Carol Cleveland, the one and only female Python.

John Cleese:

On Palin: Michael's great aim in life is to be affable. And this makes him enormously pleasant and enormously good company, but infuriating if he doesn't want to do something, or if he disagrees with something, because it's almost impossible for him to say so at the time.

On Idle: Eric is much more a loner than the rest of us, and it suited him to write on his own. I thought his analysis of comedy was always very good. Eric was the one I could work with most easily.

On Jones: Terry Jones and I were the most powerful personalities, or the most argumentative, or the most stroppy- you could put it lots of different ways, positively or negatively.

Carol Cleveland on Cleese: The most logical, definitely moody, like all comic geniuses a complex man but he was the only one who really changed during the course of Python. When he was going through his questioning period with his psychoanalysis, he was actually at times quite unpleasant to be around. He was unfriendly and difficult.

Eric Idle:

On Palin: Michael is a selfish bastard.

On Cleese: Cleese is a control freak.

On Gilliam: Gilliam is one of the most manipulative bastards in that group of utterly manipulative bastards.

On Jones: Jonesy is shagged out and now forgets everything.

On himself: I am the only real nice one.

Carol Cleveland on Idle: The only one I never felt close to was Eric. Eric always seemed a little distant, rather aloof. He in my opinion was the most serious of the lot, and the most business-like. He was the one that always had his head together as far as the financial side of Python was concerned

Michael Palin:

On Cleese: John is a very strong forceful character and within the group he was probably the one who would have the most obsessive desire for structure, both within the sketches and in the way we wrote, the way we worked.

On Jones: Terry was always positive about what Python could achieve. I always say Terry was like the conscience of Python. Terry had a doggedness which sometimes was very useful and sometimes could be an irritant to other members of the group. Terry argued for too long. Terry was the one who least accepted compromise.

On Idle: Eric was always a slightly cheeky chap. He could catch a tune which none of the rest of us could do at all, so musically he made a strong contribution.

Carol Cleveland on Palin: Michael has never changed, and he remains the same charming, shy, sweet, helpful person that he is, and he is of course the only one who's actually quite shy, and that's very appealing, which is why all the women adore Michael.

Terry Jones

On Gilliam: I think Terry G was a great fighter.

On Cleese: When it came to dealing with the BBC, we always felt they took John seriously. Partly because he was best known; it's partly his personality as well. Everybody always feels that John's really the Prime Minister in disguise.

Carol Cleveland on Jones: Very excitable, being a Welshman, very emotional, quite fiery at times. I was never present at the writing sessions.. but I'm told he was the one that had been known to throw things.

Terry Gilliam

On Palin: Mike's gift was his ease with dealing with things. Essentially I think Mike was the one that everybody liked, he was the one we could agree on that we could like, because he was the easiest to work with.

On Idle: Eric's strength is sharpness, I suppose; his quickness, his ability to do one-liners, fast things. He should have been the manager of the group, he was the one who got things started.

On Cleese: John loves manipulating and controlling; he's only comfortable when he's doing that.

On Jones: Terry's passion, his enthusiasm, his crusading zeal.. it's just his passion for things. When somebody is so enthusiastic and so convinced of something, I tend to think that's probably a good way to go.

Carol Cleveland on Gilliam: Also very excitable, very visual, very loud! And you never quite knew what was going on in his head, until you actually saw the animations you really got quite worried about what was going on there!

On Graham Chapman, who died in 1989:

Terry Jones: Graham always played everything as if he didn't think anything was funny, (as if) he didn't see the joke in anything, really, which was just wonderful.

Michael Palin: Graham as a performer had a quiet intensity which, if you look at all of his performances, quite unlike any of the rest of us, is very convincing whatever he does.

John Cleese: But to understand Graham you have to realise he didn't really work properly. If he was a little machine, you could take him back and somebody would fiddle with it, and then it would come back working perfectly. So he was a very odd man.

John Cleese: We all wanted to check a point in the script, and none of us could find a copy, and Michael said, "Oh, Graham's got a script in his briefcase." And Michael opened the briefcase, took the script out, then did a double-take, because there was a bottle (I think of vodka) in the briefcase. And Michael looked absolutely stunned, and somebody said, "What's the matter?" And Michael said, "That was full when we left this morning," and it was like quarter past ten, and the bottle was half empty.

Terry Jones: When he was drinking the worst thing would be he couldn't remember his lines.

Terry Gilliam: He was genuinely mad. He was probably the only one who was really living at the edge in some strange way. We just played at it, we just wrote it, he lived the stuff.

John Cleese: Graham was just on another planet at times.

Carol Cleveland: Graham always did everything to excess, everything he did: obviously his drinking, and the way he flaunted his homosexuality, which wasn't the done thing in the early seventies. He was a lovely man.

Eric Idle: Graham as you know is still dead

The first series of Monty Python's Flying Circus was broadcast in late 1969 and had some terrible scheduling problems. It was only seen in certain parts of the country and its time in the schedules kept changing. The critics initially didn't know what to make of it, but people who stayed up late- students and intellectuals, according to Michael Palin, appreciated it very much. It gathered a cult following, and this was good enough for the BBC to commission a second series of 13 which was broadcast the following year. Cleese's Fawlty Towers too was not appreciated by the critics at first.

The popularity of Monty Python led Victor Lownes, then head of the Playboy Club in London, to propose a film based on the group's best sketches. He loved Python humour and thought it would travel. He agreed to put up 50% of the finance and found the other 50%. The film made in 1970 was not a success and the Pythons were not pleased with the experience.

A third series of Monty Python's Flying Circus was made in 1971, but, by this time Cleese felt he had had enough; he thought they were repeating themselves and it was getting less interesting.

In 1973 the Pythons did a live tour of the UK, and continued to produce books and records. In 1974 we made Monty Python and the Holy Grail of which much more later. The film was a huge success in the US because the Public Broadcasting Network had started to show the TV series, first in Dallas of all places, and then in most cities in the US. This created a huge cult following among a young audience who were ready to greet the Holy Grail

****

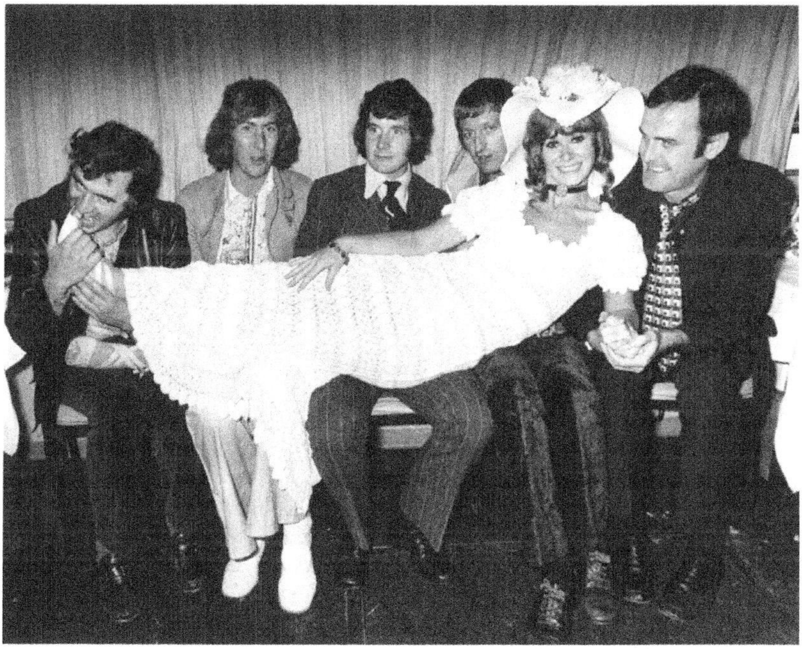

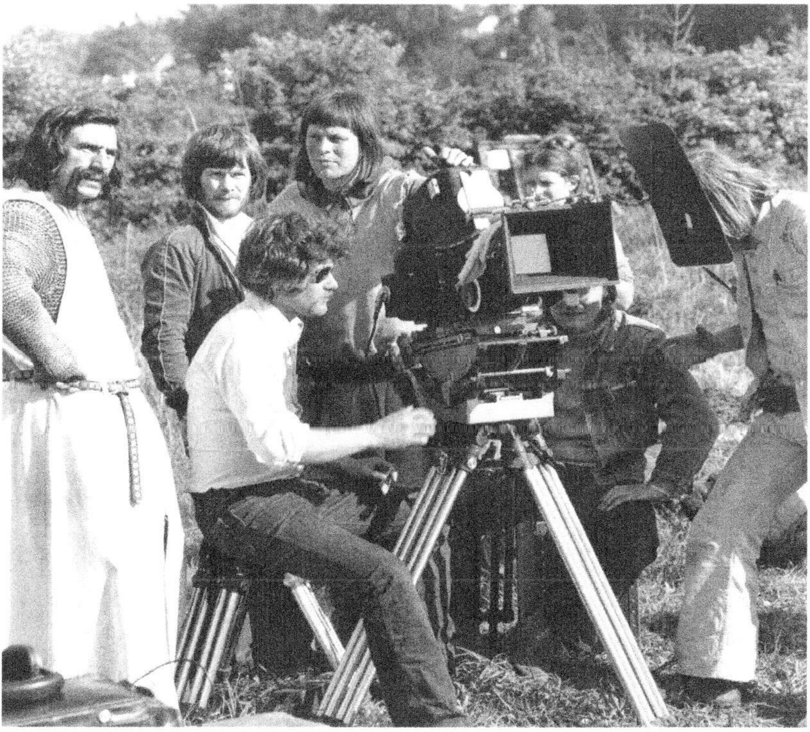

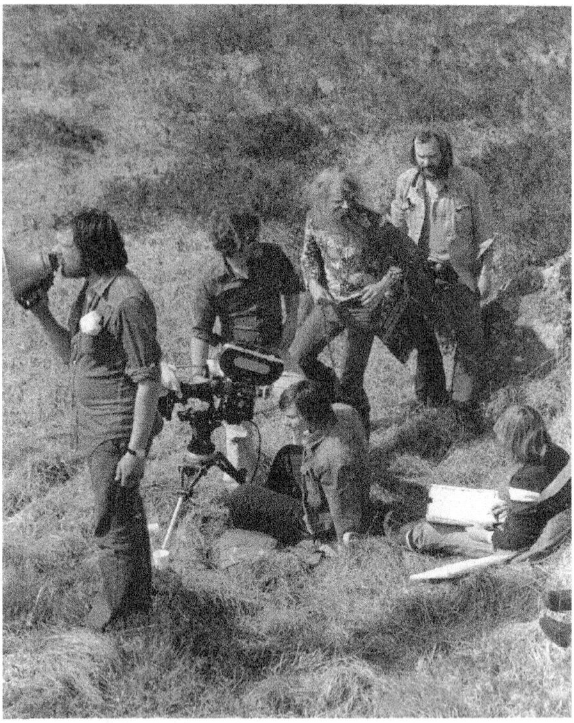

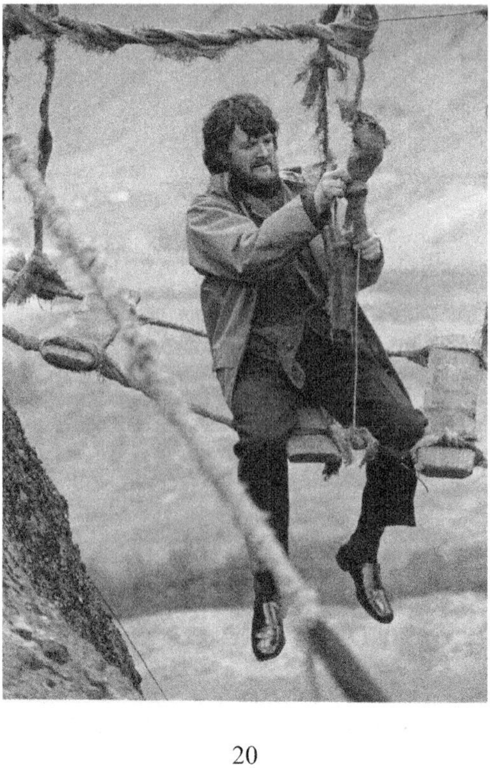

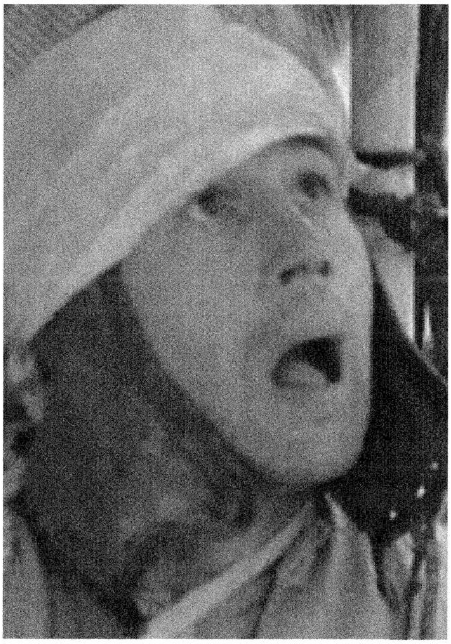

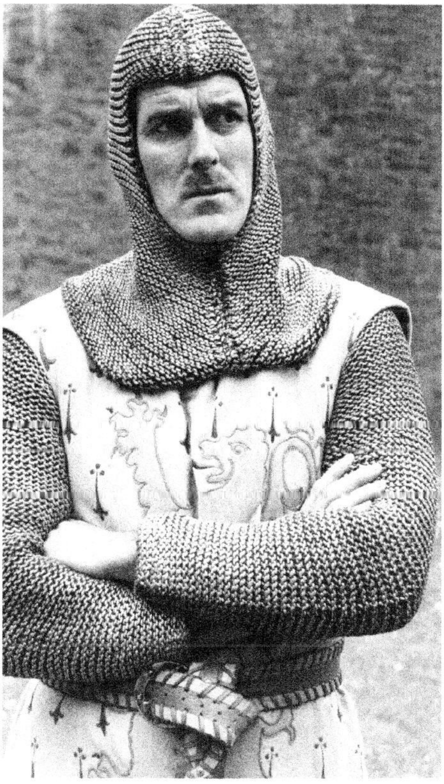

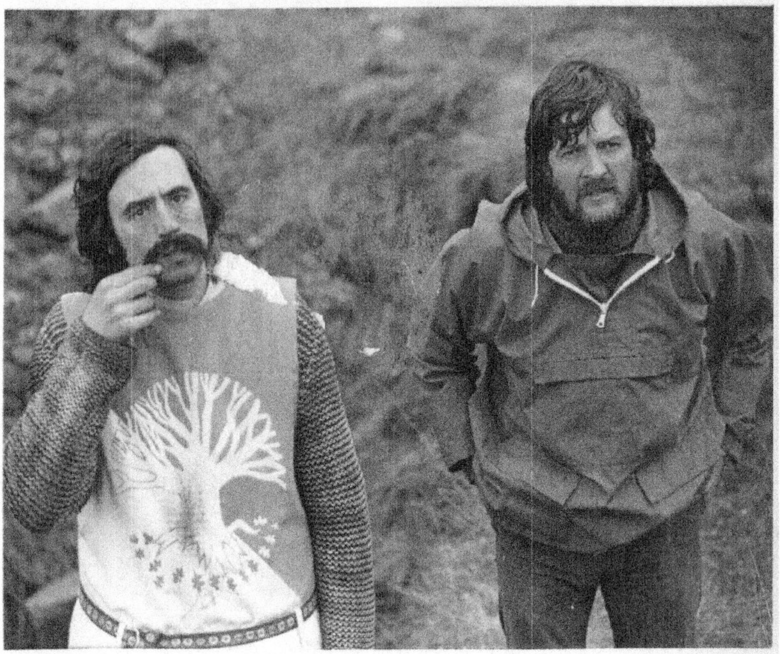

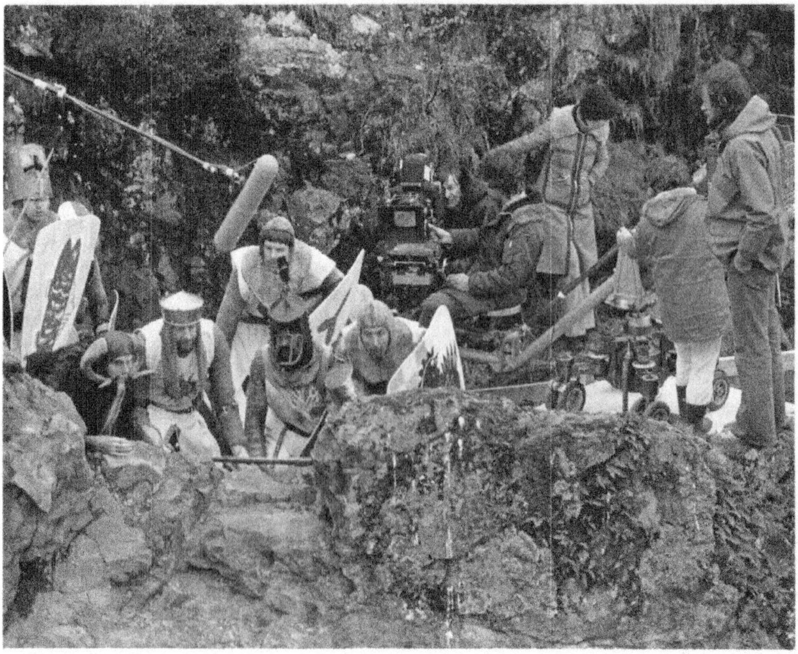

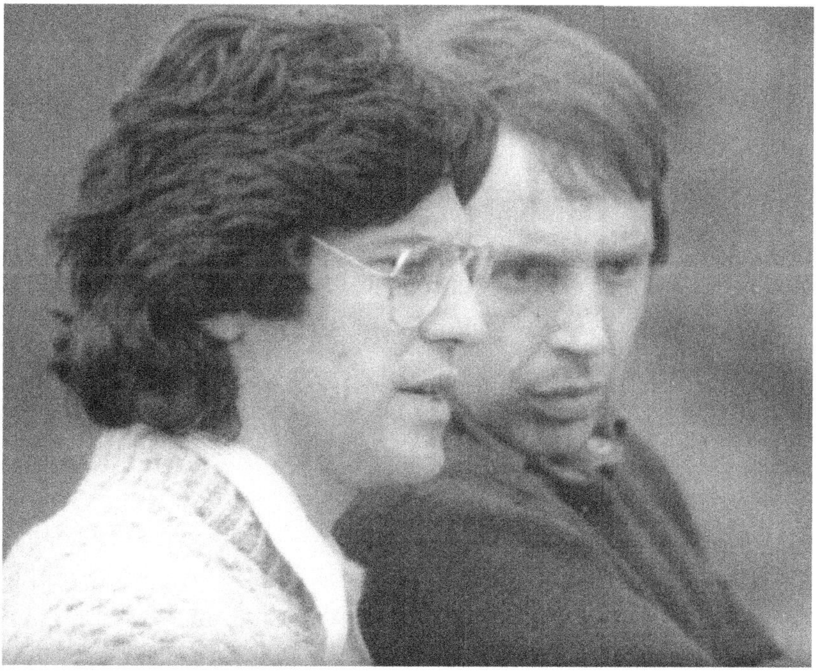

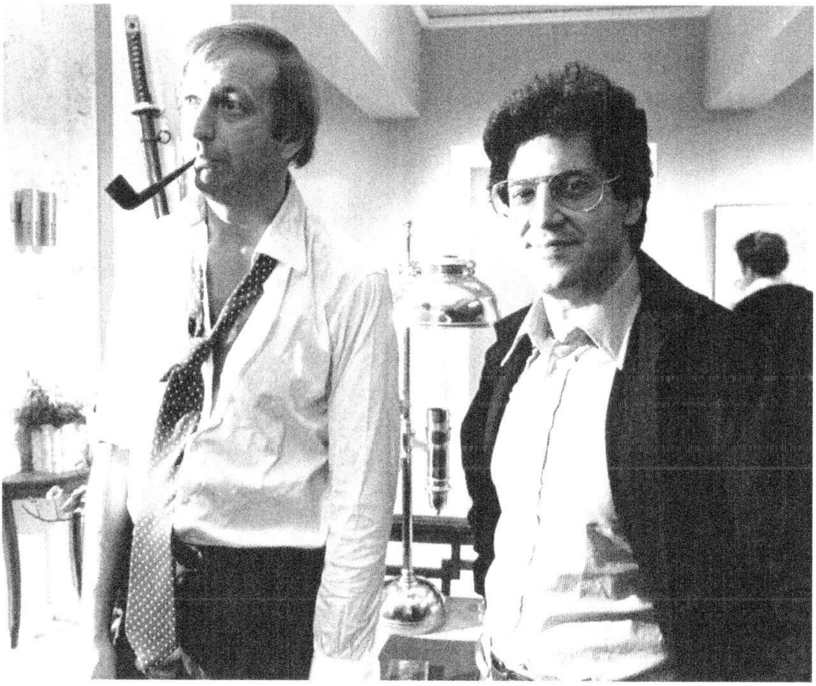

And Now for Something Completely ... umm, Similar?

The Pythons' first film, And Now For Something Completely Different (1971), was based on the sketch based material from the first (and part of the second) TV series. The film was made to introduce Python to US audiences, especially to the college circuit but it didn't work there. Its limited success was in the UK.

The only difference between the sketches on TV and in the film was that the film was in colour. Iain MacNaughton, who directed the TV series also directed the film, which was shot in an abandoned dairy.

The Pythons didn't like Lownes, who insisted they cut Michael Palin's character Ken Shabby out of the film. When Terry Gilliam designed the opening credits, he illustrated the names of the Pythons in blocks of stone. Lownes insisted his Executive Producer credit be displayed in a similar manner but Gilliam refused. Eventually Gilliam was forced to give in, but then created a different style of credit for the Pythons so that in the final version of the film Lownes' credit sticks out as the only one that appears in stone.

Working with a producer who owned the film and exerted too much control made the Pythons aware that in future they needed to have more artistic and commercial control.

****

Dire films, Wacky TV- British Comedy in the 70s

Python humour did not emerge from a vacuum. It came from two distinct sources: the radio series The Goon Show and the TV satire/sketch show boom of the 1960s. Both influenced the Pythons.

The Goons pioneered off-the-wall British humour in a BBC radio series that lasted from 1951-1960. The inspired maniac who conceived Goon humour was Spike Milligan.

Milligan was the main writer on The Goon Show, which mixed ludicrous plots with surreal humour, puns, and catchphrases. His TV series Q5 showed the Pythons that sketches did not need to link neatly and that ideas could free-flow one into another without any rational connection. Their famous tag line was 'And now for something completely different' – and their brand of 'stream of consciousness' comedy had at its best a surreal logic.

The Pythons did not do political satire, but were influenced by shows like That Was the Week That Was (TW3), (1962-3) a sketch show presented by David Frost. John Cleese and Graham Chapman were among the writers. This was followed by Not So Much A Programme More A Way of Life (1964-65) presented again by Frost and Willie Rushton, and then The Frost Report (1966-67), on which all the Pythons (save Gilliam) worked as writers and John Cleese as a performer.

British comedy films of the 1970s, unlike the TV shows, were pretty awful. Most were spin-offs of successful TV series, made for quite low budgets. If a hit show had 15-20 million people watching it regularly on TV, you would only need a fraction of that audience to come to the cinema to make a modest profit. These films were largely for UK audiences and could only be exported to countries where the TV series had found a home.

Examples of these cheap and cheerful films are Doctor in Trouble (1970), Dad's Army (1971), On the Buses (1971), Steptoe and Son (1972), Bless This House (1972), Nearest and Dearest (1972) and Love Thy Neighbour (1973). These films carried on from the Carry On series, where flat overall lighting was used to give the actors as much freedom of movement as possible, but also to avoid major lighting changes between set-ups. The Pythons' first film And Now For Something Completely Different (1971) fell into this category.

When we came to make Monty Python and the Holy Grail our approach was entirely different. We wanted to make a comedy but we also wanted to make it look like a dramatic film, one which took into account aesthetic considerations. This is why the lighting and sets of the Holy Grail are more like The Godfather than a Carry On film. The people making the film were ex-film students and film enthusiasts who took film aesthetics seriously.

****

And now for something deeply personal: how I got involved with the Pythons

How I came to produce Monty Python and the Holy Grail is a serendipitous and almost magical story. But perhaps every event, when looked back on years later, looks rather magical and serendipitous. My Python story starts in 1963 in New York City.

My editor insists that I go back to my birth, even though my memory of that event is not at all clear. However my mother told me that I was so eager to get into the world that I began to emerge in the lift leading to the maternity ward. Whether I was actually born in the lift is not certain, but made a good story. This was at 4.0 or 5.0 am on November 10, 1943 in Philadelphia.

My parents were both good and honest people, hard-working and with a great sense of duty. My father had to quit school in the 5th grade to go to work so his seven younger siblings could get an education. My mother finished school in the 9th grade to go to work. In their early 20s they had to endure the financial crash of 1929, and the scarcity of money and jobs left an indelible imprint on them.

I was preceded in life by my brother Art, born 1940, and followed by Paul in 1946. For the first ten years of my life we lived in a small terraced house in North Philadelphia, a mainly Jewish area called Strawberry Mansion. It is now a decaying black neighbourhood.

My father was a men's clothing salesman until he saved enough to start up his own store, which was successful. However he decided to start a second shop (with a dodgy partner) in Pottstown Pa., a mining town. Why my father thought that miners would appreciate or afford the stylish clothes he was selling I don't know, but both shops soon had to close, leaving him bankrupt.

He wanted to pay off all his creditors and to do so he worked three jobs - managing a store during the week, working in the post office on Saturday, and selling clothes on Sunday. The stress of losing all his savings, the punishing work schedule, his smoking, lack of exercise, and diet of heavy Jewish food brought on a massive heart attack from which he died aged 49. I was 10. This loss changed our lives forever. Although there was enough money in his last few years (although he had to sell our car), we now had to become much more frugal, and my brother tried to step up as head of the family. My father's absence weighed heavily on all of us. We had to move home, gone were holidays, and the car was a dream of the past. He was a good man and I miss him. I'm sorry that he never managed to see how we got in in the world.

I had worked part-time from quite a young age. My first job was delivering newspapers when I was 8 or 9, a job that my older brother Art found for me, since he had already started a paper round a couple of years before. After my father died, I always found holiday work, initially as a bus boy (waiter's assistant) and later as a waiter at hotels and restaurants in places like Atlantic City. All three of us went to University, and it's a testament to my mother that she managed to achieve this.

I became interested in films in 1958 when an art house cinema (almost the first of its kind in Philadelphia) called the Wayne Avenue Playhouse opened a couple of miles from my house. It was here, from when I was 16, that I and a few of my friends started to see films that were completely different from the Hollywood movies we had grown up with. Hollywood films of the late 50s were largely an uninspiring mix of the bland leading the bland - family-friendly Doris Day comedies and biblical epics prominent. There were some good American films, especially those made by directors like Hitchcock, Elia Kazan and Billy Wilder, but most studio fare was undemanding. The Playhouse, on the other hand, had a mix of European films - British, French, Italian, Japanese, Swedish, Polish - interspersed with American classics like the Marx Brothers, WC Fields, Chaplin, Preston Sturges and Orson Welles.

It was here that I first saw those modern now classic European films: Godard's Breathless, a funny, smart movie that invented a new and free screen language, Truffaut's 400 Blows, a moving portrait of alienated youth, Bergman's The Seventh Seal, whose unique and striking images made the metaphysical real, Kurosawa's Rashomon, where four differing viewpoints of a violent rape showed how the truth can dissolve into nothingness the closer you approach it. I also saw there Resnais' mystifying Last Year at Marienbad, Visconti's Rocco and his Brothers, a powerful family saga of poor Sicilians trying to make it in Milan and Fellini's poetic and decadent La Dolce Vita, which made Rome seem the age-old capital of every vice, physical and spiritual.

These films had no equivalent in contemporary American studio productions. They were artistic and interesting, dealing with real issues and confronted sexuality and politics. Some were raw and powerful, others polished and mysterious, but they all took their craft and their audience seriously. I was hooked.

My family owned a black and white 17" TV set. When I was growing up, late night TV showed old black and white movies on the three channels that existed at that time- ABC, NBC, and CBS. They raided the libraries of the film studios for non prime-time viewing. It was late at night in my living room that I first saw Orson Welles' Citizen Kane, Fritz Lang's American films, Josef Von Sternberg's Marlene Dietrich films, Carol Reed's The Third Man, and all the old Universal and RKO horror films- Frankenstein, Dracula, The Mummy, King Kong and so on. I stayed up as often as I could to catch these classics.

There were also exciting films being made on small budgets outside the studio system like John Cassavetes', Shadows and Shirley Clarke's The Connection. I was entranced by them, and wanted to know how it was possible to make them. I had no idea how to make films, and being an unworldy kind of guy I didn't think about getting a job in the industry but thought that the best thing would be to go to a film school. The most obvious way seemed to be to travel to California and enrol at either the USC or UCLA film schools. But California was 3000 miles away, I had no car, no money, and knew no one on the West Coast. Even if I got there how would I survive? So I looked for an alternative. I had heard of the famous Polish Film School at Lodz, and it sounded like an exotic place to go and study. You had to spend the first 6 months learning Polish, and then you could enter the film academy itself. I applied, but I can't remember if I was accepted or not.

I had started reading books on film theory (unfortunately stealing some from the library - so guilty, so Jewish) and took out a subscription to the American Cinematographer. It might have been from an ad in the magazine that I found out about the City College of New York course on film making. I was attending Temple University in Philadelphia at that time, and was bored. I was living at home, and the hour long commute by bus and subway to and from campus every day felt like an extension of high school. I didn't feel I was experiencing campus life, and wanted a change.

I applied to the City College Of New York (called CCNY) and was accepted. I made the move from Philly to Manhattan with a friend and we took a small apartment on the Upper West Side. My Uncle Dave was a bond dealer on Wall Street and my mother asked him to try to find me a job. My plan was to work days and study nights. My uncle contacted bankers he knew and arranged meetings for me, but I didn't feel that banking was for me, and didn't take up the offers. Since I hadn't graduated University, the jobs on offer were low paid clerical jobs. I sometimes think if I had taken one of those jobs my life would have been completely different. I might have become one of those fat cat Wall St bankers who oversaw the banking meltdown, but also made themselves immensely rich. I see this as My Alternative Destiny number 1.

I eventually found a simple clerical job at an insurance company (Mutual of New York). Their skyscraper was at 55th St and Broadway so it was close to my new flat on 74th St and a short subway ride to Harlem. The job was boring, but paid enough to keep me alive and to pay for cinema tickets. At work I found time to read and generally was a reluctant employee.

Nights and weekends were spent watching films, sometimes as many as four in a day, as I used the great movie resources of the city to catch up on hard-to-find films that I had missed. My usual haunt was the Thalia, a rep theatre that had a huge turnover of programmes. I was also a regular at the Museum of Modern Art's cinema, and the Bleecker St Cinema in Greenwich Village.

Terry Gilliam and I met at CCNY. It was a part-time night course that the college put on at their Harlem campus in upper Manhattan. It was not a great time for white people to be roaming around Harlem. One night I had to run from some stones that were thrown at me. To get to the campus I took the subway (The famous A Train) from mid-town to Harlem, and it was the walk from the station to the campus that was the worry. Apart from this one incident I didn't have any other trouble. I can't remember a thing about the film course, other than that one of our fellow students whose name I can't remember made one of the first black indie films in America,

After the course ended in June 1963 I moved out of my apartment and moved in with Terry, who had a place on Madison Avenue in the East 70s. Terry was three years older than me and he was already working at Help! Magazine. We both took the course because we wanted to learn how to make movies. I spent that summer in New York and remember watching the March on Washington with him on TV. I have no idea why I didn't make the trip to Washington, since I supported the cause. Maybe I was broke, which was often the case in those days

In September I returned to Philadelphia to resume my studies. One reason was that the draft for the US Army was in force and as a student I could defer being called up. More and more American soldiers were being poured into Vietnam. I didn't want to join them so I returned to get my degree. It was on Temple's campus that I heard the news about President Kennedy's assassination.

As war fever increased in America, I began to feel extremely alienated. I opposed the war and felt oppressed by the jingoism in the media and in society. Like many of my contemporaries, I didn't want to fight for a war I could not understand. The government tried to convince people that there was a domino theory: if Vietnam fell to the Communists, then Laos would too, and so on, each falling country leading to another communist victory. Most Americans had no idea where Vietnam even was, much less why we were killing these farmers with Agent Orange and massive bomb strikes. The phoney attack at the Gulf Of Tonkin was the pretext for incensing the American public against the Vietcong and for the war. I thought seriously about becoming a conscientious objector or even leaving the country.

At around this time I bumped into Harry Pepp, the older brother of my good friend Richie Pepp, and Harry told me that he was just about to go to Europe to spend a year studying at Sheffield University in England. I asked him how he managed this. He explained that all I had to do was to visit the library, find a reference book of British Universities, and write a letter to any I fancied, stating that I wanted to spend a year abroad studying. It sounded too simple to be true.

But it was true. I wrote and sure enough letters arrived from Sussex and Manchester inviting me to spend a year studying English Literature from fall term 1964. Since the only person I knew in England was Harry, I chose Manchester as it was closer to Sheffield. Before leaving, I spent the summer in NYC with my friend Richie, bumming off friends and eventually staying at his cousin Rose's house in Brooklyn while her family was on holiday. The house was a big brownstone that was built in the 1850s in an area called Cobble Hill. At the time, the neighbourhood was a mix of Italians who had lived there for generations, poor newcomers from Puerto Rico, and a few young families, artists and professionals who needed cheap living space. The houses were big and could be bought for very little money. Now this area is completely gentrified, and nearby Smith Street is known as 'restaurant row'.

When Rose, her husband Mike, and their three sons returned from Massachusetts, I met Mike's adopted sister. She was born in Japan to a Japanese mother and an American soldier and was brought up in an orphanage in Yokohama. Mike's parents lived in fashionable Bucks County, Pennsylvania, where they were friends of the writer Pearl S. Buck. Mrs. Buck won a Nobel Prize for her novel The Good Earth about Chinese peasants, and adopted a large number of orphans from the Far East. She encouraged Mike's parents to adopt and they thought it would be good to have a young oriental girl around the house, so they adopted her when she was 11 years old.

The adopted girl did not find it easy to adapt to American life, and was sent to Switzerland to be educated (or finished, as they used to say). When I met her, she was 16 and very beautiful; her photo had appeared in a magazine as one of the 10 most beautiful women in the world. We were attracted to each other at once and started hanging out in Greenwich Village, seeing films and roaming the city. I was planning to leave soon for England and I asked her if she wanted to join me. She did, but her parents wouldn't let her travel unless we were married.

I met her parents at their Greenwich Village apartment, where they had lived since the 1930s. Getting married was not something I anticipated. I was only 20. I was willing to do it, but I had to tell my mother (or work out how to tell her) and also figure out how to get married. Because of my bride's age, the only state that would marry us was North Carolina. Her parents said that if we wanted to move to Mexico instead of England they would be happy to make introductions for us. They had many friends there in artistic circles, as the portraits of their sons by Diego Rivera hanging on the wall were proof. In the end I decided to continue with my plans, thereby leaving My Alternative Destiny number 2 behind - the Mexican one.

I was more worried about my mother. After my father died, she had started working at Strawbridge and Clothier, a big department store in downtown Philly. She sold shoes in the bargain basement for many years, paying the bills that kept her three sons in food and in school. I met her as she was leaving for the day, and I told her in the street that I was going to get married, and that my wife-to-be was not Jewish. It was cowardly to tell her like this, but my mother had a fierce temper and I knew that she wouldn't explode in the street, but would have to keep her cool. She stopped walking and was visibly disturbed as I explained the situation. Eventually she agreed to meet my bride to be and wanted me to introduce her to my Grandfather Chiel, who was living in a Jewish geriatric home.

My grandfather lived on the 10th floor of a high rise home, and as we made our way to his room I wasn't sure how he would react. Not only was my wife to be not Jewish, she was oriental as well. When we entered his room, he was seated in a comfortable easy chair reading Moby Dick (in English), something which, for an uneducated 82 year old Polish immigrant was impressive. He told us about his life in the home, and showed me letters he had published in their newsletter. Eventually I got around to explaining the reason for our visit, that we were planning on getting married and to leave for England in a few weeks, thereby reversing the voyage he had made from the old country to America in 1904. I didn't realise it at the time, but we were actually seeking his blessing for our marriage.

He told us, in his still heavily accented English, that when he made the decision to leave Poland and come to America, that it was to a new land, and that all the old ways would have to change. So if I wanted to marry a non-Jewish girl that was not a problem for him. I'm crying as I write this, because I really loved that man, and I was so impressed with his open and loving attitude. He wanted us to be happy, that was his only concern.

Having done my family duty, the only thing left was to fly to Raleigh, the capital of North Carolina, where in 1964 there was a drive-in marriage service. A cab from the airport took us to the State Capitol building, where we registered and took a blood test (for VD). They told us to come back in two hours and if the test was OK, they would summon a witness (a local drunk from the park) and perform the ceremony. It was a warm September day and we decided to take a stroll around the city. We didn't go more than a few paces when the traffic slowed to a halt. Drivers and passengers stopped to gaze in amazement at this lightly bearded man walking hand-in-hand with an oriental woman. It wasn't so much racism (I don't think), even though we were in the south, as the extraordinary and uncommon sight we offered on the lily-white streets of Raleigh. We high-tailed it to the nearest lunch counter and waited till we could return to the office. Having passed our VD tests with distinction, we were presented with a marriage certificate, and a taxi and airplane returned us to civilised Manhattan.

Two weeks later I was in Manchester.

****

Sunny Manchester

I flew first, with my new wife following a few weeks later. In case you're wondering, my first wife does have a name, but she doesn't want me to use it in this account. It's a pity, because her memory is so much better than mine, and these pages would have been much richer if she had been willing to take part. Instead I will have to refer to her with any number of words, but no name. Sorry for the mystery.

The idea of travelling separately was that I would settle in, register at the University, find us a flat, and she would come after. As part of my economy drive, I flew Icelandic Airways from New York to Glasgow, via Rekyavik. I'm really sorry I didn't get off at Rekyavik to sample the hot springs, but at the time I didn't even know they existed. From Glasgow I took the Manchester train, arriving late in the evening. The streets around the station looked like a shambles, so I wasn't surprised to discover that this was indeed the name of the district, which had many old crooked red-brick Victorian buildings, dimly lit by yellow sodium lights. There was even some fog to add to the Dickensian atmosphere, so I really felt I had travelled back in time. I found a cheap B and B and next day went to the University to register.

Manchester folk were kind to me. I didn't know how to use the buses, or how to work out where they were going. I didn't know there was a usually friendly conductor on board. It was easy to hop on a bus through the open back, but where did you get a ticket? Finally a conductor asked where I was going, took my money, gave me a punched ticket and told me when to get off. People in Manchester were unbelievably friendly, polite and easy-going, and I liked being called 'luv'. The university was a small collection of mainly Victorian buildings, and was in fact called The Victoria University of Manchester. I re-visited Manchester a couple of years ago when my daughter was thinking of going to Uni there. I couldn't believe the number of students in the city- every educational establishment had expanded, and new ones had been created - so it really is a city of students.

My new in-laws had asked me how I planned to survive in Manchester. Although there was no tuition fee, I had to buy books, food and rent a place to live. I told them that I was planning to find a part-time job, and they kindly volunteered to send us a monthly stipend so that I wouldn't have to work and could just study. That was very generous of them.

I found a centrally-heated flat for 5 guineas a week (a fortune in 1964) and met my wife at the airport when she arrived. So we started our married life together. I think we were happy, although my memories of those days are so vague that it feels as if my life just drifted by in a haze. I remember when she cooked a curry for the first time and I couldn't eat it; I was not very pleasant to her, but her cooking did improve. As an unreconstructed male of the time, I never did learn to cook properly, although I am better now. I spent time at the University attending lectures and tutorials, and started to meet some fellow students. My wife spent a lot of time with me at the Student Union cafeteria and bar. Then she found a job at the laundry of the Manchester Royal Infirmary. She took to riding a bike to work, and unfortunately broke her leg when she was knocked down by a British Rail van. So instead of being a worker she became a patient. She had to keep the leg in traction for weeks, so I decided to move out of our flat in Didsbury and move in with a few friends I'd made- Alan Weitz, Peter Neumann and Mel Marcus. I had a single room without a window for three months while she recovered. I met many of their friends, almost all Jews from Northwest London, and settled in to my work.

I studied English Literature, and enjoyed the lectures and tutorials. Frank Kermode and Brian Cox (not the physicist - he wasn't born then) were two of my teachers. I realised pretty quickly that my education in the US was somewhat incomplete, especially compared to the Grammar school educated students around me. I tried to make up for it by reading deeply. I studied Shakespeare, Ben Jonson and the other Elizabethan playwrights, Jonathan Swift also, but I can't remember the rest. I know I spent a lot of time reading poetry, especially Auden, Eliot and Pound.

There were a few other American students there. One guy left after a few weeks, saying the place was antediluvian and he had to get back to civilisation's comforts. I must have been an Anglophile, since I found the customs charming, and I liked being a fish out of water. When I was in high school, my English teacher made fun of the English eating cucumber sandwiches, but in Manchester I heard more jokes about chip butties. A few Americans, like Maurice 'Socky' O'Sullivan and Fred Steinberg stayed the course. Fred bought himself a green MG sports car and started hanging around in pubs with a young footballer named George Best. Fred drove me to my first Manchester United match and I was amazed to see Best's skill, the ball seeming to stick to his boots like glue while he danced around defenders.

I had never been to London, so one weekend Alan Weitz drove a few of us down to the Smoke in his 1934 Rover, nicknamed Phoebe. As we made our way through North West London, I was amazed to see Peter Neumann ducking his head down so that no one would see him being driven in a car on Friday night. We had to let him off a few blocks from his house so he could walk home, which is what his family expected on the Sabbath. I had never grown up with Jews who were so *frum,* (observant). To me Friday night was a night to go out, but for my friends it was time to be with their family having a Shabbas dinner. It's a good ritual, one that I appreciate, though I have never brought it into my own life.

I wrote essays and took exams, and ended the year in June 1965 with a 2.1, which I was pleased with. But I had to return to Temple University to finish my degree. If I went back to the US and didn't attend school I was liable to be called up for the draft.

We returned to Philly and I finished my last year at Temple, gaining a BA in English. To survive we got a student job as caretakers at an apartment house, which gave us free rent and a small salary. It was a perfect job for a student. My caretaking skills, however, were imperfect, and I almost set fire to the place when repairing an electrical socket. My best friend Carl's father gave us his old blue and white Chevy Impala when he bought a new car. One Friday we drove down to Atlantic City for a beach weekend, and when we got back to the building found that all the power had gone out. The residents, though happy to finally see us, were not very pleased at the level of service. My boss fired me, so we had to move in with my mother.

I decided to apply for a post-grad course in England. Sussex accepted me and Manchester even offered me a scholarship of £ 500, so we decided to go back North for another year. In 1966 the Vietnam War had intensified, and I found the blind patriotism of the country oppressive; the media and most people were totally gung-ho in supporting this immoral war. I was glad to leave. I didn't realise that I would never return to live in the US again. Did I ever regret it? Sometimes. I was sorry not to see my family as much as I would have liked. I also think that my taste in films and style of producing would have made me a lot more successful in the US than in the UK, but I have had a good life in London and raised two wonderful families, so I try not to look at what might have been. I look on regrets as the corpses of old desires. I suppose going back to the US is My Alternative Destiny number 3.

I was considering becoming an academic. I did the course work for my MA pretty well, but when it came time to write a dissertation on Tristram Shandy, a book I loved, my heart just wasn't in it. I never completed the MA. Instead, in summer 1967 I tried to get a traineeship at Granada TV. I didn't make the grade, so instead started teaching at a secondary modern school in Salford. But I still wanted to pursue film, and decided to go back to film school. I applied to the London School of Film Technique and was accepted for the autumn 1968 term.

Before starting at the school, my wife and I made a trip to Southern France, to stay at the hilltop town of Mirmande, in the Drome, an area famous for its cherries and peaches. It was also a place where artists like André Lhote had lived and worked in the 30s. Her family had owned a simple house there since that time, so we had a place to stay. We got work on one of the peach farms, where we could pick in the morning and pack in the afternoon. Pay was not great, but you could eat as many peaches as you liked; I also learned some French by picking on one side of a tree while the farmer worked on the other. My French had a distinctive Southern accent. We then travelled on to Italy before returning back to London to start film school.

We moved into a bed-sit in Wandsworth. Twice a day Young's Brewery would bubble up with an awful smell of fermentation which puked up the neighbourhood. I commuted to the film school and my wife got a job at the Westminster Library on the Marylebone Road. After one term I ran out of tuition money and decided I had to drop out. I had been voted class representative, so at the Christmas party, and when looking through the pigeon holes for my mail, I came across an envelope addressed to the Student Council. I opened it to find a letter from Anglia TV asking if any student was interested in taking a holiday job with the company. I decided that as a representative of the student council it would be correct of me to put the letter in my back pocket and check out the job offer on Monday. Which I did. Director Stanley Joseph explained to me that it was an assistant editing job for a few weeks with the Survival team, a famous unit that specialised in animal documentaries.

I got the job, and soon convinced Stanley that Survival needed a full time assistant and I was happy to volunteer for the job. Anglia was good enough to apply for a work permit for me, and it shows how full employment was in those days that the permit came through in weeks. I never returned to school, but used my time at Anglia to help some of my friends make films using some of Anglia's editing facilities. I produced a film directed by Joel Tuber called The Great Wall of China very loosely based on the story by Franz Kafka. We shot it in 16mm colour, and edited at Anglia. My share of the production finance came from a begging letter that I wrote to my Uncle Al in Detroit.

Later, with Barry Salt, I produced Six Reels of a Film to be Shown in any Order. This was shot in 35mm black and white. After I left Anglia I had the chance to produce a short film for the BFI Production Board, which was headed by Australian Bruce Beresford, who later became an accomplished director. That film was cut at the BFI, and the late Tony Scott was in the next door cutting room finishing his first film after leaving the Royal College of Art.

Now I was freelance, but there didn't seem to be many jobs around. I became worried about how we were going to survive. My wife continued to work at the Westminster Library, while I tried to work out ways of earning a living. Again Stanley Joseph came to the rescue, asking me to help him make a short corporate film for one of his friends. I brought in Julian Doyle, a film school friend. Together we shot and edited the film, and the sponsor was very happy. Stanley said that he would try to get other corporates to make, and Julian and I set ourselves up as Chippenham Films.

****

Spiritual Matters

My editor suggested I write something about my interest in Taoism, since I refer to Taoist books and ideas later in this book, and I used them to keep my balance as the dispute came to dominate too much of life.

Sometime in the early 1970s my wife started to work at Acumedic, which was one of the first places in London to offer Chinese medicine and treatments. Acumedic's bookshop now is a large well stocked room but then it consisted of two revolving book stands which could hold a few paperbacks including the Chinese classics (in translation). I worked my way through The Analects of Confucius and The Book of Mencius before discovering the quirky and original world of the Taoists: Lao Tzu, Chuang Tzu and Lieh Tzu.

From Confucius I learned that seemingly archaic ideas and values could still change lives. At the time I felt little respect for the way my older brother was living his life. But Confucius tells us that the younger brother must have respect for his elder brother, no matter what his character or life is like. So I decided to follow this principle and changed my attitude and behaviour towards my brother, offering him the respect due to age. And after I did this, interestingly, I noticed that he seemed to change in small ways that earned my real respect. The Confucian way of family relations contained a truth that I had not expected or believed in, but I discovered its relevance by putting it into practice.

I also loved Mencius and his belief in the innate goodness of people; his search for the true heart of humanity I found inspiring. One year I sent out a Xmas card quoting his story of Ox Mountain:

> *There was a time when the trees were luxuriant on Ox Mountain. But as it lies on the outskirts of a great city, its trees are constantly felled by axes. Is it any wonder that they are no longer fine? With the rest they get by day and night, and moistened by the rain and dew, there is certainly no lack of new shoots rising up, but then cattle and sheep come to*

graze. That is why it is as bald as it is. And people, seeing only its baldness, tend to think that it never had trees.

But can this possibly be the nature of a mountain? Can what is in man be completely lacking in moral inclinations? A person's letting go of his true heart is like the case of the trees and the axes. When the trees are lopped day after day, is it any wonder they are no longer fine? If, in spite of the rest a person gets by day and night, and of the effect of the morning air, scarcely any of his likes and dislikes resemble those of other people, it is because what he does in the course of a day once again dissipates what he has gained. If this dissipation happens repeatedly, then the influence of the night air will no longer be able to preserve what was originally in him, and when that happens, a person is not far removed from an animal. Others, seeing this resemblance to an animal, will be led to think that he never had any human endowment. But can that be what a person is genuinely like?

Hence, given the right nourishment there is nothing that will not grow, and deprived of it there is nothing that will not wither away. Confucius said, "Hold on to it and it will remain; let go of it and it will disappear. One never knows the time it comes or goes; neither does one know the direction." It is perhaps to the heart that this refers.

But it was Taoism that really spoke to me, and I thought it answered many of the spiritual questions I had. I tried to understand the depths of the Tao Te Ching, was enchanted by the humour of Chuang Tzu, and mystified by the sagacity of the I Ching. I would return to these books again and again when I felt that I was losing my way, and needed some guidance. Among the Taoist teachings that I tried to live by, I thought that "Treat the things of the world lightly" among the simplest and best of advice. For when we lose attachment to things, and realize there is no need to get upset over worldly concerns and problems we gain a more objective and calmer view of life. We learn to cope with whatever life throws at us, not swinging wildly between hope and despair, or failure and success.

In the late 1980s my second wife Jo encouraged me to learn to meditate and to take up yoga. This blossomed into an interest in Buddhism, especially Zen and Chan Buddhism, which is so close to Taoism. A number of years ago I decided to put my Taoist interest into practice and learn Tai Chi Chuan.

In 1997 I did an audio recording of the Tao Te Ching, and this led almost directly to my writing The Spiritual Teachings of Marcus Aurelius. Hodder Audio asked if I had any other ideas for audio books. I suggested the Meditations of Marcus Aurelius, and decided to write my own version for recording, since I thought the existing translations seemed old-fashioned. I also saw in the stoic thinker Marcus Aurelius affinities to Buddhist ideas, and wanted to bring this out in my translation. This eventually became a book and audio and led to my writing a series, culminating in The Spiritual Teachings of Yoga. To write four books in as many years, I had to put aside my film and TV work, and concentrate on writing. The writing gave me a very concentrated education in let's call it living philosophy and spirituality, almost like taking a second degree at university. When I say philosophy, I mean living or eco philosophy, as against the academic subject studied in universities. A living philosophy is just that – a philosophy that you can live by, that gives you guidance about how to conduct your life, as in Socrates' famous question – "What is the right way to live?"

In writing these books I have learned a great deal not only about the subjects I studied, but also about myself. Spiritual texts should do that. You go to them for understanding, and that understanding is your own question about how to live. The time needed for research and writing a book is a concentrated and lonely business as you struggle for weeks trying to tease meaning from a sometimes difficult subject. I soon realized that I would have to trust that this work was what I was meant to do at this time, and that questions of money would have to be put aside. If the universe wanted these books to exist, then a way would be found for me to stay alive while writing them, and if the world didn't care about what I had to say, then they would quickly be dumped and forgotten. Besides, how could I worry about money or material things when the philosophy I was studying claimed:

The Law of Spirit says that to give is to increase, and what Krishna is saying to Arjuna is that everything only appears to be material, but all things are in their essence spiritual, and if we treat material things by the Law Of Matter, we misunderstand their true nature, and so make mistakes in life. We are once more in the land of avidya –ignorance, or misconception. As someone once wrote,

> *We are spiritual beings having a human experience, not human beings having a spiritual experience.*

Can we understand that this applies equally to all other objects, including money, which is just a material symbol created by us to mark a transaction, a temporary relationship between people. Krishna wants us to see that our possessions and money are just material forms of spirit, and that the Law Of Spirit, rather than the Law of Matter, applies to them.

If I write that, I expose myself. Readers will see whether this teaching was really part of my life, or just skin deep. Do I walk the walk or just talk the talk?

***

PART TWO: The Twat From Hero to Zero

Reunion with Terry Gilliam

In 1970 when I was watching Do Not Adjust Your Set I saw Terry Gilliam's name on the credits. I thought there couldn't be two cartoonists named Terry Gilliam so I rang the company and left a message for him to contact me, which he did. We had a reunion, and soon rekindled our friendship.

Through Terry I met Michael Palin and Terry Jones, and watched Terry in his flat cutting and colouring his artwork for the first series of Monty Python's Flying Circus. I followed their great success and the subsequent and problematic feature film – And Now For Something Completely Different.

Eric Idle had gotten in some TV advertising gigs, and through his contacts he brought in a sponsored short film for the group to make. Terry Jones was interested in film, and wanted to direct the short in order to get some experience. Terry Gilliam asked me if I would produce them and I introduced the two Terrys to Julian Doyle, since I assumed we would work together.

The film praising Close Up toothpaste was sponsored by Elida Gibbs, a pharmaceutical company. Julian photographed, I produced and recorded the sound and we both edited the film. Terry Jones directed. Elida Gibbs were happy with the film, and commissioned a second one for Harmony Hairspray - another product no one could live without. This was a more complicated shoot, so we brought on our friend Terry Bedford as lighting cameraman. Julian and I did everything else and Terry Jones again directed.

These little films were successful, the clients liked them, and the Pythons were happy with the result.

****

Monty Python and the Holy Grail

Ever since their experience on And Now For Something Completely Different, the Pythons had thought about making a second film themselves. Both Terrys were interested in directing, and they wanted to have greater artistic control over the new film. A first draft script was written, and their manager at the time - John Gledhill - tried to raise the money to make it. But the industry was conservative, and the project seemed to them like turning the asylum over to the inmates. Other than the two short corporate films, neither of the two Terrys had directed anything. Tony Stratton-Smith, who ran Charisma Records, the Pythons' record label, promised that he could find the money for the new film. Unfortunately for John Gledhill, Strat failed to deliver and this failure came at a time when the Pythons were increasingly unhappy with Gledhill's managerial efforts. According to Michael Palin's diaries, it seemed as if John was being shown the exit.

In the summer of 1973 Terry Gilliam gave me a copy of the first draft script and asked me if I wanted to produce it. Of course I said yes, since it would be great to work with a group I admired. As the Pythons were popular, the film could happen but I felt the script did not really work. It was set both in the present day and in medieval times, and featured two parallel stories, one about King Arthur and his Knights and another, a contemporary story, about a man (an accountant?) called Arthur King. The medieval story had much more potential for laughs and for cinematic pastiche.

Terry offered the project to me on behalf of himself, Terry Jones and Michael Palin since they were close friends and allies in the group. Eric was a loner who wrote on his own, while Graham Chapman partnered with John Cleese, but the latter three were less focussed it seems on the fate of Python.

The problem was one that was familiar to producers. There was nothing in the kitty. The Pythons asked me to collaborate initially with Jill Foster who was Michael and Terry's literary agent, to see if we could find some independent finance. We worked well together, and Palin acknowledged in his diary entry of 28 October

1973 that meetings took place, results started to happen, and the Pythons were kept informed of what we were doing. Palin notes that he respected my honesty and that I had claimed credit for bringing in both the NFFC deal as well as Michael White.

Michael and the two Terrys realised they had to let John Cleese, Graham and Eric know about my involvement. Michael Palin explained in his diary on Saturday September 22, 1973 how this came about. At the end of a Python meeting to review their new album material Terry Jones told them that I would be acting as the producer of the new film. John Cleese exploded, asking who I was and what I had done. He was not at all happy that no one he knew was being given the job, and Terry Jones had to sneak off to avoid responding in kind,

I had to go face-to-face with 'headmaster' Cleese to seek his approval. At the time Cleese was living with his wife Connie Booth in a modern house in Kensington's Addison Road furnished with contemporary Scandinavian furniture. We met in his study. After an awkward start we had some drinks and chatted about the film. I explained to them that the problem with their first film was that they did not control the copyright; that is, they didn't own the film but were working for someone else. To really have control of the second film, besides directing it, they would also have to own the copyright. The plan I put forward made that central. I would attempt to raise finance for the film on that basis. This plan, idealistic in that the people who created the film owned it, worked perfectly for them, so perfectly that they used it against me 30 years later.

Michael Palin's diary entry of Thursday November 1 1973 shows that he was surprised at how relaxed and constructive the meeting went. I suppose he expected Cleese to give me a rough ride, but all was cordial.

At this time the Pythons decided to look again at the script. Although they vehemently deny that I ever had any 'artistic' involvement, I recall a script meeting where I said that King Arthur was much funnier than Arthur King. I'm sure this must have been obvious to all of them, and no doubt without my two cents the script would have gone the way it did, but I did express an opinion and it was listened to.

While the script was being re-written, Jill and I were chasing the money. Almost all industry people were sceptical about the Pythons directing, but I went to see Sir John Terry at the National Film Finance Corporation, a government backed film fund (which no longer exists). Sir John thought the project of interest, was not afraid of the two Terrys directing, and asked me to send him the new script. After reading it, he expressed interest in funding 50% of the film, if I could find the other half.

Michael White was a theatre producer who had worked with Eric Idle and John Cleese. I went to his office in Duke St. in St. James to see him and his associate John Goldstone. Michael liked the Pythons and thought the idea amusing. Depending on the script and budget he might be able to raise 50% of the finance if I could find the other 50%.

It was then that John Gledhill, their manager, did a bizarre and foolhardy thing. On the same day that I had received Headmaster's Cleese's blessing, that night the Pythons were at a party to launch their latest book, the **Brand New Bok**. As Palin explains in his diary, Gledhill told them all that there was now a deal offered between the NFFC and Michael White to fund the film. He had a Heads of Agreement that he wanted them to sign, which they all did. Palin thought the document was to get hold of £ 6000 of development money to write the script.

Without telling me, John Gledhill had gone ahead and tried to conclude a deal with Michael White and John Goldstone to produce the film with their company. That deal depended on bringing in 50% of the budget from the NFFC. Since I had introduced the NFFC into the project, and had led the discussions with Michael White and John Goldstone, I did not appreciate these attempts. It was also not very clever to get the Pythons to sign an agreement at a drinks party. Palin's diary records the aftermath on the following Monday November 5, 1973. The Pythons, myself and John Gledhill met at Cleese's house, where the atmosphere resembled a morgue. Gledhill was clearly uncomfortable. We went to Tethers Restaurant for lunch and to talk over the document that the Pythons had signed. Terry Jones asked me to discuss the clauses, and as I did so, the Pythons understood that they were once again being asked to assign their copyright in the film to the investors, which would have lost them the key issues of control and copyright. At the end they asked me to draft a new agreement to present to John Goldstone.

Gledhill desperately wanted to be involved, but he could see that it was slipping away, which is why he acted so recklessly. This move backfired on him, since the Pythons were now committed to replacing him as manager.

After this incident, the Pythons decided to start using Palin's accountant Henshaw Catty and Co., to take over the Python's financial affairs and eventually management. Michael Henshaw, who had a reputation as a glamourous accountant to the stars was not actually a qualified bean counter, but the rarely seen Mr Catty was. (Cleese had a father sensible enough to change his surname from Cheese; Catty's parents could have learned from him). Henshaw's wife Anne was given the task of overseeing the Python activities as an 'acting manager' while they sorted out John Gledhill's departure. Anne was in her mid 30s, smart, very business-like, and quick on the uptake. I liked working with her, since she got me answers quickly, and had a very decisive mind.

We needed a lawyer to work with us on the film. I was introduced to Simon Olswang, a young up-and-coming lawyer at Brecher and Co. Simon agreed to act for the new Company that we set up to make the film- Python (Monty) Pictures Ltd.

The Heads of Agreement that Simon presented to Michael White and Goldstone was not to their liking. It called for the film to be made by a Python controlled company, and to be directed by the two Terrys. This was the plan that I had put to the Pythons at Cleese's house, and I was determined to deliver it for them. However, White and Goldstone wanted to make the film through their company, and this would have repeated the Python's experience with Victor Lownes. We did not want to give up copyright of the film, and since we still had the offer of 50% of the finance from the NFFC we could continue to look for the balance of 50%. The Pythons asked John Gledhill not to continue acting on the film, and at this point Tony Stratton-Smith stepped in again with a new idea- to try to find funding from record company and music group sources. Tony identified Island Records, Chrysalis Records, the Pink Floyd, Led Zeppelin, and Ian Anderson (Jethro Tull) as possible investors, and he and I started a campaign to gather in their contributions. In the end we raised the missing 50% from the music business to add to the NFFC's 50%.

At this point Michael White requested another meeting. He and Goldstone said they would be prepared to enter the film on the original basis that I had outlined – the Pythons would own the copyright and their company would control and make the film, with me acting as their producer. I agreed to use their 50% rather than the NFFC's money, since they would be able to move quickly and were less beaurocratic. I also felt that Michael, with his great creative reputation, could be useful in working with the Pythons. This proved to be correct. So we now had 100% of the finance from independent private sources and could proceed with production. I had now been working on the film for 9 unpaid months to achieve this result. John Cleese in his Witness Statement said that the Pythons employed me to work on the film. That is true, but John never bothered to add the clause chivalrous (since we are dealing with King Arthur) that my "employment" was 9 months of unpaid and speculative work. I didn't begrudge spending the time. The film was a big deal for me.

But I was taking a risk - and living off what? Air...

Back to the movie. My partner in Chippenham Films, Julian Doyle, had prepared a schedule and budget based on the new script, but he was unable to do any real work on the film until I raised the finance. It seemed to me that our partnership only worked well when people (like Stan Joseph and the Pythons) came to us with a fully budgeted project and said 'make this for us.' Here nothing could be done until the money was in the bank.

Julian's original budget for the film was £ 167,000 but it soon crept up to £ 186,000. This sounds like a ludicrously small sum to make a period film, and it was, even for those days. Early on we had told the Pythons that our budget wasn't going to run to horses and their wranglers, and this led to their writing in the coconuts gag that so enchanted audiences and is explained later. The film went over budget both during shooting and in post-production, and ended up costing £ 229,000.

On And Now For Something Completely Different, Victor Lownes objected to Michael Palin's wayward character Ken Shabby, and he forced the Pythons to remove him from the film. They had no power to stop him altering their script. With the structure that I devised and fought for, the power to make all decisions rested with the Pythons.

Normally, when a director goes over budget, the producer can decide to replace him or her. But in this case, the Pythons owned the Company and would never have wanted to sack one of their own. This is one of the advantages of owning the copyright.

*****

The Honeymoon Period

I call the period from early January through March 1974 my honeymoon period with the Pythons, for it was during this time that the financing for the film solidified, and the making of the film became a reality. My work had paid off and everyone was pleased that the film could be made. It was in this happy time that my contract, including the later disputed merchandising profit share, was signed off.

Over 30 years later, during the dispute, I was surprised and pleased to see a Python document that reflected this honeymoon period. It was a report of a meeting of the Pythons on the 24th of February 1974 and point 1. said "That any future films would also be made through Python (Monty) Pictures with the intention of working with Mark Forstater." It was gratifying to see this document. My memory hadn't been playing tricks. The document confirmed this was an extremely positive time in my relations with the Pythons. Unfortunately honeymoons don't last that long.

The deal that we offered the investors was a 50-50 deal; that is, the investors would receive 50% of the profits after the initial cost of the film was recouped, and the remaining 50% would be for the 'talent' - the writers, actors, directors and producers. We settled the 50% of the talent share in this way: Tony Stratton Smith asked 5% for having helped to raise the finance. I negotiated him down to 4.5%. John Goldstone also wanted a 12.5% share of the profits for his role as Executive Producer. We ended up giving him 5.6875% which left a total of 39.812.5 %. We divided this 39.812.5% into 7 equal shares for myself and the 6 Pythons so that each of us had 5.6875 %.

I signed my Producer's agreement in April 1974, along with all the Pythons' contracts. I had a fee of £ 5000 which was equivalent to each of the Pythons (although the two Terrys collected an additional £ 1000 for directing). I repeat as the case was so much about fractions , my profit share was 5.6875 % which was equal to the profit share of each of the Pythons. The Pythons and I also agreed to defer £ 2000 of our fee until completion of the film, in case the film went over budget and the deferments were needed to help finish the film. In all of these financial matters I was treated as a 7th Python alongside the other 6 - in fee, profit participation, and deferment. As they were rewarded, so was I rewarded; as they had to bear some of the risk, so I had to take some of the risk. This is why the film's lawyer Simon Olswang and my trial lawyers considered that I was acting at this time as a 7th Python. No one was asserting that I was involved creatively or that I was part of their group, merely that for this film I was being treated equally with them. And their intention was to make more films with me, typed in black and white.

Tony Stratton Smith suggested that Charisma Records put out a soundtrack album. The Pythons reluctantly agreed to do this, but made it a condition that they should share in the record's revenue as to 50% for them, with the other 50% going to the investors. This was to compensate them for the extra work involved in creating the album. As I recall, I wrote to Anne Henshaw (unfortunately for me the letter no longer exists) and requested that I get a 1/7th share of the Python's 50%, since as the Producer of the film, and someone who was significant in helping it come into existence, it would be unfair for me to miss out on this revenue. I believe that she took the matter up with the Pythons at one of their meetings (I'm not sure if I attended or not), and replied to me that they agreed to give me that share.

This is what led to the appendix to my agreement- the Third Schedule - which deals with merchandising and spin off income such as records, books (and later Spamalot). From 1974-2005 no one bothered to look at it because the spin-off monies would have bought you no more than a large pizza- but along came Spamalot. Once real money was involved, the Third Schedule became very interesting to everyone and was analysed and re-analysed as if it was a key verse in the Bible like those that specify who has to provide how many talents of silver to build the walls of Jerusalem.

Bar Charts - 1. profit shares of film 2. Merchandising profit shares

****

Monty Python and the Holy Grail
Ancillary or 'spin-off' profits (including Spamalot)
Showing Mark Forstater's agreed share as 1/7th of 50%

Profit Participants : 50 %
Python (Monty) Pictures : 42.857 %
Mark Forstater : 7.1429 %

Monty Python and the Holy Grail
Ancillary or 'spin-off' profits (including Spamalot)
Showing the disputed claim of a 1/14th share

Profit Participants : 50 %
Python (Monty) Pictures : 46.428 %
Mark Forstater : 3.5714 %

Monty Python and the Holy Grail
Profit Participants as at April 1974

Python (Monty) Pictures : 34.125 %
Michael White Ltd : 22.455 %
Led Zeppelin : 8.982 %
Island Records : 5.988 %
Pink Floyd : 5.988 %
Mark Forstater : 5.6875 %
Gladiole Films : 5.6875 %
Anthony Stratton Smith : 4.5 %
Charisma Records : 2.994 %
Chrysalis Records : 1.7965 %
Ian Anderson (Jethro Tull) : 1.7965 %

The Making of the Film:

Monty Python and the Holy Grail tells the story of King Arthur and his Knights of the Round Table- Sir Galahad, Sir Lancelot, Sir Robin and so on - in their quest to find the Holy Grail. The Grail is the cup, dish or plate that legend says Jesus drank from during the last supper, and in the film an animated God tells Arthur and his Knights to find it. The film tells of this quest, and intercuts the adventures of the Knights with a contemporary police story, which eventually halts the shooting of the film when the police arrest Arthur, the Knights and their army in the midst of battle.

The original idea for Monty Python and the Holy Grail was in fact a script called *Arthur King*. It had a contemporary character called Arthur King who was a kind of nebbish, a loser. But these contemporary comic scenes didn't seem to go anywhere; the period scenes seemed to have much more going for them. After I'd read the script, I met with the Pythons and talked about what was working and what wasn't, and they started a whole new script process.

Not enough cash can lead to creativity. Arthur and his Knights do not have horses, but canter through the countryside accompanied by the sound of coconut shells banged together. One summary of the film said 'King Arthur and his knights embark on a low-budget search for the Grail, encountering many very silly obstacles.' As the log line on the poster said, it makes Ben-Hur look like an epic.

We shot the film in Scotland over April/May 1974 on, as was usual then, 35mm film, which had to be sent to a lab for processing and printing. The sound was recorded on 1/4 inch magnetic tape, and this also had to be sent to a sound studio to be transferred to 35mm magnetic film, so that the picture and sound could be synchronised. This is what the clapperboard at the beginning of each take provides- a means of syncing picture and sound.

We had to ship the negative and tape down to London by train every day and wait for the return of the rushes. To show them we had brought a mobile projector with us so that we could view the rushes in the hotel.

We didn't have enough money for the luxuries of big budget films where the producer has three glamorous assistants, the stars get their own driver and, I don't exaggerate, their own special brand of toothpaste The hotels we stayed in were adequate but not grand. It was a struggle to make the film, partly because the two Terrys were meant to be directing the film together, and this is rarely workable. Both men had different ideas of what the film should look like, where the camera should go and so on. As a result, the camera team in particular were being asked to do different things by each of the Terrys. It was frustrating for them too. I was worried about the budget and schedule, and this was reflected in my attitude to both directors.

The fact is that we were all learning on the job, since this was really the first big film that any of us had undertaken. The crew that Julian and I had put together were largely people we knew from film school or people the two Terrys had worked with previously. We had too low a budget, too short a schedule, and it was always going to go over budget. The saving grace, of course, is that when you have a hit film all of that is forgotten. Well, almost all of it is forgotten, as you shall see.

Overtime soon pushed us into our contingency, and we never managed to shoot all of the scenes in Scotland. We retreated back to London and Julian went out with Terry Jones and Terry Gilliam to shoot the bits that had been left incomplete. The entire Black Knight scene, one of the most memorable in the film, was shot by Julian and a pick-up crew in Epping Forest. Bits of special effects and other linking scenes all had to be shot during the post-production period.

Script/Ideas

Much of the following is material from: Monty Python Speaks, by David Morgan. I have capitalised the speakers' names to show that the quote is from David's book:

TERRY JONES: Originally the script went between the Middle Ages and the twentieth century, and ended with him finding the Holy Grail in Harrods. I was very much into the Middle Ages with my Chaucer stuff, and I had not been very keen on the twentieth-century stuff. Mike had come up with this horse and coconut thing at one stage, and so I suppose in a group meeting I said, "Why don't we do it *all* Middle Ages?" And everybody seemed to agree.

MICHAEL PALIN: There was this Arthurian start about swallows and the people at the battlements which caught people's eye, and from then on, yes, the idea of the knights seemed
promising. I was more keen on keeping the narrative in the Arthurian world than making jokes about Harrods. I was interested in creating this world and making the convention, the background setting, so convincing that you don't have to defuse it, you don't have to apologize for it, you don't want to *leave* it! We were forced to invent things that could happen then and there, lovely things like Tim the Enchanter: that was fine, it didn't need Tim to be a modern character at all. So in the end maybe those of us who believed you could keep it consistent - do it with comedy but set it in medieval times-won the day.

I don't think anyone *else* but John and Graham could have written the "Black Knight" sequence, hacking legs off. That's very Graham-ish, because Graham's a doctor and loved all sorts of visceral ideas like the human body being ripped apart. And Terry and myself started off writing the peasants in the field- "I'm only thirty-seven" -and then John and Graham took it on and did all the stuff about "moistened bints lying in lakes lobbing swords is no basis for a system of government." That was theirs at their verbal best. They beefed an idea which we had, which was that people answered back to the king and it was terribly hard for him to be Arthurian!

TERRY BEDFORD (Cameraman): I don't think there was actually a kind of decision on the
[film's] style; they didn't come to me, and say, "We want this film to look medieval," or anything like that. I think we just fell in because I wanted to make it look moody and to conjure up the

atmosphere as much as possible, which is very different from anything
they'd ever done before, [which was] all very much TV and in-your-face. What we were really talking about here was bringing a
cinematic mood to it, but they were all very, very gung-ho for that; they loved it all, especially Terry Gilliam. I suppose one would have to say that the dark side of Gilliam was the one that was chaperoning that along. And of course Terry Jones is interested in medieval history
and stuff, so it all does fit really that they would want to create this sort of atmosphere.

MICHAEL PALIN: This wonderful idea of the anti-Hollywood medieval film was very important to us, where people didn't all have even teeth, blond hair, horses!

In addition to Morgan's book, I asked some of the crew to recall their memories.

Gerry Harrison, who was the First Assistant Director, shared his:

In a freelance career there comes a time when one decides one should move on and up. I had been working as Assistant Director for a number of years, from 3rd assistant to 2nd to 1st, upgrading myself when I felt ready. The description of assistant director, I have often felt, is a misnomer, because the job is essentially that of assistant to the producer. It is the AD's job to chase things along, get the picture shot on time and on budget. He is the eyes of the producer on the set. However, believing for some reason that I was a more creative person, and not a producer, my ambition was to become a director and so for me there was sometimes a conflict. For a smoother life, I therefore tried to work with more creative directors, who also might themselves have some control over the film. For this reason I found myself as an assistant director on films by Tony Richardson, Joe Losey and Ken Loach.

Through a music journalist I got to know Tony Stratton-Smith, the boss at Charisma Records, who took a chance on me – as a horse-racing man he was famous for backing outsiders – and asked whether I would like to make a film of his star band, Genesis, in performance. My job was to set the whole thing up, shooting it with four cameras and recording it on 8 or 16 track. At short notice I was very lucky to put together a good crew.

I don't think my efforts really worked. But the genial, eccentric and brave producer, loved by all as "Strat", was delighted. As my first real shot as director, forty years later I am quite proud of it.

Soon afterwards, the phone rang and, unbelievably, there was "Strat" asking if I was interested in working on a film the Pythons were making. "Strat" was one of their first investors. Their previous director was not re-hired, and the two Terrys – Gilliam and Jones – would co-direct this one.

For "Strat", these were untested directors. He had phoned me to ask whether I would like to be their 1st Assistant during the shoot, and give advice when necessary. With only an hour or so of Genesis footage behind me I thought that as a director, I was also pretty untested myself, but I remember that my response indicated that I now was looking for work as a director. "Strat" said, frankly, that he expected me to contribute to the film, to be called *Monty Python and the Holy Grail*, in a more creative way – not just to shout "Quiet" or "Turn Over" - and to help patch things up if the two Terrys were ever in dispute.

Although I had watched *Monty Python* on television, I would not say that I was an obsessive. Terry Jones was an old school friend. He had been head Prefect, a star of the Sixth Form and immensely witty, quoting and mimicking the Goons. I was now worried about the role I might have on *Holy Grail*, answerable to "Strat", not the producer but the man who gave me my first break.

I agreed to meet the team. The film was already in pre-production, and based at an historic location, a house in the Mall Studios in Belsize Park which had some heritage. This small terrace had been something of an artists' colony, beginning with Walter Sickert, who was followed by Ben Nicholson, Barbara Hepworth and her husband John Skeaping. When I arrived, the production office was buzzing with activity, particularly in the Art Department which was interpreting the designs of Terry Gilliam.

In this office I noticed a friendly, almost family atmosphere, which flourished among its untidy surroundings.

Very soon, however, I noticed that the pre-production process was not as smooth as it should have been, and there had been mishaps along the way. One of these was the loss of permission at a major location in Scotland, a castle at which they had hoped to shoot. This had been withdrawn by the Department of the Environment which had responsibility for all castles in state care, but I cannot remember the reason. It may have been that its perception of the irreverence of the Pythons was not in accord with the stuffed shirts behind their civil service desks. A looming problem was that the first day of shooting was only two weeks' away.

It was very clear that this film was under-budgeted. This was, in effect, a mini-epic, with a tiny budget more appropriate to the studio-based *Carry On* films. Hence, the use of coconut shells to replace horses. The under-budgeting that this symbolised and what I could see around me, soon convinced me that I did not wish to become involved. I thought it would be a disaster, and that as 1st AD I would be a part of the wreckage. I had also been informed that, for budget reasons, my 2nd, Paul, could not be afforded. We had to hire someone, with perhaps no experience in feature films, locally. Although I had no contract, I resigned.

I think it was a midnight telephone call from my old school chum, Terry J, that persuaded me to return. Within 24 hours he and I were on a night-sleeper, armed with library books on Scottish castles and a bottle of whisky. Once in Edinburgh, we rented a car and, listening to Billy Connolly cassettes, set off on a quest for our particular Holy Grail. As a result of the intransigence of the Department of the Environment, we now had to find castles which were privately owned. We were lucky, both Doune Castle in Stirlingshire and

Castle Stalker in Appin were perfect. Doune, where a number of scenes were shot, is now a tourist attraction to which people arrive with their souvenir coconut shells. Castle Stalker made a picturesque and fitting end to the film.

Once we started shooting, the crazy, tiny budget soon became apparent. Little allowance had been made for poor weather, with no alternative scenes scheduled that could be shot in dryer surroundings, so in the first few days our overtime budget had been spent. I could also see that many of the unit had brought with them a more relaxed BBC way of working. In fact I think that only four or five of us had made a feature film before.

Although his wife played an intrepid part as an actor in the film, I hardly saw Mark Forstater, the producer. This is not necessarily unusual: some producers need to be talking to the backers and constantly away from the set. He was not "hands on", and when I later did two more but extremely enjoyable children's films with him, I realised that this was his style. Once shooting had started on a film, Mark's great ability was to be thinking about his next. He was a deal-maker rather than a practical producer: he preferred to allow the team which he had hired to get on with it.

In Scotland things seemed increasingly threadbare: Mark and Julian had bought second-hand film stock which had worried the cameraman, Terry Bedford. One time the laboratory that was processing the rushes overnight reported some fault in the negative. The scenes had to be reshot, but were to be paid for by an insurance claim. Mark was immensely skilful in negotiating the best terms, so that when we reshot this scene it looked very much better. I heard that Gentle Ghost, a hippie outfit which advertised its services in "International Times", had been hired to drive all the costumes up to Scotland, and, predictably, one or two of the vans had crashed off the road because their drivers were stoned. There was little forward planning – a location for a battle scene had not been found, and no-one had thought about the 200 extras we required. It was a day or so before the scene was scheduled that I learned this, and I had to leave the camera, find the location at Sheriffmuir (I had no idea that it had been the location of a battle during the Jacobite Uprising of 1715) and then invite myself to Stirling University to recruit the extras. I remember that once make-up and costumes had been applied the fiercest warriors were the girls.

Julian had no experience as a Production Manager. We seemed to make it up as we went along. I hope it was only for reasons of cost, but I was particularly hurt that I was not hired as AD for the couple of days of the duel between the knights in Epping Forest or for the final scene that was shot on Hampstead Heath. I could continue, and in fact regretted that I had been recommended, but there was always a wee malt whisky waiting for me in the hotel bar in the evenings.

It was not all sweetness among the Pythons either: I soon learned that there were divisions among the personalities in the group, which were reflected in the writing partnerships. The only one who was always smiling was Terry G. Graham gave me a difficult time by offering his many boyfriends work on the film. John was often away in the evenings (he had taken note of my list of the Castle Anthrax girls and was, I think, in Glasgow some nights getting acquainted with it.)

I have mixed feelings about the experience. As the last film I had intended to do as an AD I will never forget it. The Pythons were generous: they knew that I had just moved house and was doing it up, and gave me a cheque with which I bought the bathroom furniture. I would rather have been hired for the additional days on the film. However, I have since heard that at festivals where Terry G has spoken about it, he has kindly put in a nice word about me.

After the edit at Twickenham Studios, Mark called me to ask me to join him for lunch. He said that he would like to hear what I had to say about the production of the film and how I thought it could have been improved. We met in Maxwell's hamburger place in Hampstead, but in advance I had thought what I was prepared to honestly say. However, before I could commence, Mark cut me short by telling me that the film had been sold for a surprisingly large amount of money. And that the timing of the Pythons at the Hollywood Bowl together with the purchase by PBS of the BBC TV series had usefully coincided to encourage the deal. There was nothing more I could add.... I do think that an unrecognised attribute of the film was that it looked very good indeed, probably the first British comedy film to do so, and for this I applaud the cameraman, Terry Bedford. For the Pythons it had been a highly lucrative search for a Holy Grail.

I am very pleased that my relationship with Mark was undamaged. He offered me work as a 1st AD on two more films, "The Battle of Billy's Pond" and "Glitterball". I had decided that the Python picture would not be my last but, actually, working with Mark Forstater again was fun.

ARTHUR

The role of Arthur was the lead, but he was also the 'straight man' among the characters. The other Pythons all wanted to play the more eccentric and lively characters in the film, which meant they could play a number of roles, so it was left to Graham Chapman to play Arthur, his sole role in the film. I think Graham surprised everyone with his performance, keeping a serious and slightly peeved lordly persona going throughout the film, never responding to the silly antics taking place around him. He took the most thankless role and made it his own.

Graham did have a problem during the filming with his drinking, which had been getting worse. Sometimes he didn't remember his lines, and whenever there was any kind of stunt required, he just fell apart. He couldn't face walking across the Bridge of Death which Gerry Harrison had to do, When he was perched on the side of a gorge for a shot his panic was real. His shaking and trembling were not just fear but from trying to give up booze.

THE TWO HEADED DIRECTOR

Having two directors turned out to be a major problem. Even though they were both named Terry, that is where their similarity ended. They were very different characters, and each had their own idea of where the camera should go, which meant that whenever one of them took over from the other during a set-up, the camera team had to move all the gear and start again. This was frustrating for them. Terry Gilliam was more concerned with the visual look of the film, while Terry Jones concentrated on the script and performances, so the actors were also treated to two different styles of direction when they were in front of the camera. This led to the actors also becoming quite annoyed.

In addition, Terry Gilliam was used to moving little pieces of paper around in making his animations, and his paper actors didn't complain when he kept them locked in one spot. However his fellow Pythons didn't appreciate finding themselves stuck in a particular position while Terry got his perfect camera angle. They let him know their feelings.

David Morgan recorded a telling interview with the two Terrys:

TERRY GILLIAM: So when it came, a chance-"Here's the money to make a
'Python film" -we just decided we wanted to do it. We were the ambitious directors, and others went along with it.

TERRY JONES: I'm not sure why it was I wanted to direct; it's just I didn't want *not* to, if you see what I mean. Everyone was saying, "Well, you do *it,* Terry," but I was feeling a bit nervous about the idea. It was I who suggested that Terry G. should codirect; I thought since Terry's got such a good eye that it would be very good to work together. So that's how it came about.

DAVID MORGAN: Did you actually think you could function as co-directors?

TERRY GILLIAM: Yeah, we did. Terry and I tended to agree on most things,
until we actually started working together and then we discovered we didn't agree *quite* as totally! The real difference came in that I've got a better eye than Terry, is what it's about. I'm better at those things, and he's better at other things. Ultimately that's how we ended up working it; I ended up being at the camera, and he worked

with the guys, because having been in my little garret all those years, my social skills were not as highly developed as they are *now!* The idea of going out there, slogging your guts out and trying to get *them* to do what was needed for the sake of [the shot]? Again, John and Graham didn't particularly like all this cumbersome stuff. Eric was all right. I mean, they just want to go out and do the funny lines; that's a *bit* extreme, but it was kind of like that.

One of the problems when you have two directors is that they must not confuse the crew as the Camera Operator explained to David Morgan:

HOWARD ATHERTON, CAMERA OPERATOR:
Terry Gilliam and
Terry Jones, both lovely guys, Terry Gilliam sometimes would tell me the
setup he wanted, and I would set it up and get things organized, and then
Terry Jones would come across and look through it and say, "No, this is
not what I want," and I'd have to move it. And Terry Gilliam might come
back and have it moved back again! There was never any animosity between
them, but they would go off and have a little, you know, "I wanted it this way" sort of thing, very gentlemanly. And they'd sort it out and they might do it one person's way one time and the other way another time.

TERRY JONES: The directing wasn't really regarded like someone taking
control, it was the director basically having to do a lot of leg work and a lot of graft that nobody else wanted to do, really. [The anger] was mainly focused on Terry G, because he was so focused on the look of the thing and on what he was shooting that he could sometimes
forget that people were being [made] uncomfortable.
There was a little bit of bad feeling that went on between Terry

and John and Graham. I think John didn't feel Terry was paying him enough [attention]. There had always been a little friction between
them in a way, because John is always making fun of Terry being American, and I think Terry wasn't tactful enough with John in asking him to do things, and John would find himself in very uncomfortable situations where Terry is getting the thing to look right. Whereas I had always been a bit more careful with the *artistes*, I suppose.

TERRY GILLIAM: When we actually got around to making *Holy Grail,* it
was like, "Oh, now we've got to do all the things we claimed we could do that Ian *couldn't* do," and I think we did. But I think it was the end of the first week of shooting, where everyone got pissed one night, Terry and I were just shattered because everybody was going, "Wrong!" A lot of shit had been dumped on us and a lot of things had happened and we were actually managing to survive and keep things going. And Graham got really pissed one night and said what a complete disaster we were making - this was a time we were feeling very, very vulnerable!-and how Ian should be in there, and what egomaniacs, megalomaniacs, useless pieces of shit we are. Oh, that's *great.* "Fuck you, Graham! Get your lines right!"
I just thought, "This is horrible," but the one sad thing is, deep down I think we both felt they may be *right - we* might *not* be able to do this.

A HIPPIE FILM

We went up to Scotland by car, van and train. My ex came up on the train to Edinburgh with our one year old daughter Maya and she (my ex) became one of the pages in the film, following after Arthur and his knights and banging coconuts. She was naïve about how things worked in front of the camera, so each time she was in a scene Terry Gilliam, who also played one of the pages, constantly manoeuvred himself in front of her to hog the camera.

TERRY BEDFORD, DIRECTOR OF PHOTOGRAPHY:
It was very hippie, in my recollection of it all. It was a family affair; everybody
seemed to have their children with them, if they had children.
It was all very entertaining. I didn't see a great deal of the friction between them other than it was a bunch of egos trying to make one project.

I wasn't long out of college, either, so as I said we were trying to do things differently
from everybody else. [And] the Pythons were fairly anti-Establishment. If you were
to say to Gilliam, "This is a professional way of doing something," it would really put
his back up.

Things weren't organized as well as they could have been, so it was a little ragged
around the edges, a little bit amateurish to me. It was more like a circus than a film!
But it all [came together] at the end of the day. It just seemed like fun, really. Even
some of those arguments to me felt like fun, because the sixties were a time about arguing and putting your point of view and getting cross and then forgetting about it the following day. That kind of creative energy is what was expected of one.

THE DISASTROUS FIRST DAY

Julian and I had purchased a sound blimped second-hand Arri camera to shoot the film, as well as a second one for back up. On the very first day of filming I helped the crew get the equipment up the side of Glen Coe and then went back to the hotel where I had a makeshift office. I soon got a phone call with the dreadful news that the camera had broken down on the first shot. Up a mountain! A replacement had to be brought up from London, and we carried on shooting with the second camera, which was too noisy for us to record sound. I wish I could say it was smooth sailing all the way after that, but we had our problems, although none as serious as that.

TERRY BEDFORD: The first day was a disaster. They wanted to go to the top of Glen Coe, which is a mountaineering trip. It was a dialogue sequence, and on the budget that we were shooting we had a very old Arriflex
camera, it was in like a cast-iron coffin to make it soundproof, and it was dragged up the hill along with other pieces of heavy equipment.
It took half a day to get all the equipment up there.
And I suppose in their mind they thought they'd be up there in half an hour and within a half an hour of that they would be filming.
But by lunchtime the camera is only just up there, half a day's gone. And then the devil got in the works because on slate one take one, the camera
broke down, quite seriously; it'd stripped its gears. It wasn't something
that could be fixed out on location. We had to shoot everything on the second camera, which was not a sync-dialogue camera,
it was to be used for picking up inserts. So the whole opening part of the film had to be post-sunc.

SAVED BY THE RUSHES

After the first day debacle. the shooting continued without any major problems. But the crew were a bit unsettled by the slightly ragged nature of the production, and the Pythons were unsure of what the two Terrys were concocting. This led to a certain loss of morale as the first week came to an end. We had finally received our synced up rushes from London, and everyone was eager to see them. Was this a disaster looming? must have been in many minds. We were going to screen a week's worth of rushes in a makeshift cinema in the hotel, and the local drinkers in the bar wandered over to have a look. I didn't see any harm in it so allowed them to stand in the back and watch. After the rushes there was a definite buzz among the cast and crew. The film was going to be OK, maybe better than OK.

HOWARD ATHERTON: Coming from a film background, I can remember the rushes have always been a secret. I worked as a loader for a particular cameraman for a couple of years, and he was very protective of his rushes in that he wouldn't let anyone else see them. And being brought up in that school, I thought the rushes should be a very private thing as well. But the Pythons had it set up in one of the main rooms of this local hotel, and of course all the locals heard about it so they always used to come along and watch the dailies as well. The first couple of days I tried to stop them. I protested to Mark Forstater: "We can't allow them in, people watching our dailies."

But as it turned out, it was a blessing in disguise because they used to sit in the back and laugh their heads off! It was good feedback to the Pythons as to whether they got their humour right. And it was a good cover for us if ever we made any mistakes. Because as everyone was laughing, no one was worried about looking for our technical errors. So having the local audience actually lightened the whole thing and made it quite a fun affair, something we all looked forward to.

TERRY JONES: I think once we'd started seeing the rushes we felt pretty good; we had good material in there, we liked the look of it because Terry Bedford's camerawork was just superb, so yeah, I think the rushes were the thing that kept us going, really, because, everybody laughed, everybody had a good time. You'd come out of rushes feeling a charge of adrenaline, thinking, "WOW" this is really good, this is really worth doing." Otherwise you might have given up!

Neil Innes, who did the songs for the film and acted as Sir Robin's page, told me about how he got involved,

Eric rang to ask if I fancied coming up to the TV Centre. Their warm-up man was ill. "I don't do warm ups," I said. "It pays £ 25."

"Oh - alright." In those days the average monthly mortgage payment was about £40 so £25 was not to be sneezed down the toilet. So we went on, sang a few songs and kept the audience happy.

The Pythons were about to do an album, so I said, "What sort of songs are you writing?" And Eric said "Michael's writing this song about Agrarian reform in the Middle Ages". Oh I thought - ' great, get in there before Motown.' And John Cleese said 'What kind of music do you see for that, Neil?" He's always to the point, so I said, "Well, I don't know? Reggae?" It was wonderfully mad.

I went on tour with them in Canada and in Drury Lane. I was handy, I was useful, since I could do a song while they were doing set changes. When I was sent the Holy Grail script, it was the only script I ever read that after 10 minutes had me on the floor crying and slapping the floor- from the script alone. Those lyrics- they are dreadful rhymes:

We dine well here in Camelot
We eat ham and jam and spam a lot

In war we're tough and able, quite indefatigable
Between our quests we sequin vests
And impersonate Clark Gable

I couldn't wait to write film music. I had run the film society at Goldsmiths College of Art so had a long-standing interest in film. I wrote great Arthurian themes for the film, but since I only had the budget for 12 musicians- a budget of £ 3000 - it could never sound epic enough. At least the fanfares and the choirs and medieval stuff survived.

The production sent me a script and I worked out and pre-recorded the songs and chants: 'He's going to tell', the Monk's Chant, the Camelot song. Sir Robin's song. John Halsy was the drummer on Camelot, and he brought all his kitchen utensils to do the Camelot drumming.

***

The Disastrous First Screening

It was one of those evenings when Python flopped. - Terry Jones

Back in London, we worked hard to produce a cut of the film that we could show to the other Pythons and the investors.

The preview took place on October 1 1974 at the Hanover Grand Preview Theatre in central London. We had invited about 200 people, including most of the investors. This screening was one of the worst film experiences of my life.

Every screening has a certain mood that you can feel in the theatre, and the mood at the end of that screening was certainly pretty grim. People weren't responding, they weren't laughing the way they should have been. There was laughter at individual scenes, but no sustained build-up. The main problem was that the sound effects were too prominent. Because the comedy is quite slight, the jokes need to have a context in which they work, and if you overwhelm them with sound, they will just get drowned, which I think is what happened.

This was the first time that either of the two Terrys had ever done this kind of film sound mixing, so it's very easy to try something which doesn't work, and at that point it can all be thrown away, can all be redone. But someone who doesn't know the technical side, might think looking at it, "God, this is it, and we've got to live with what we're currently seeing," which of course is not the case. A certain amount of inexperience may have led people to think it was a disaster which couldn't be repaired.

Afterwards, there was a feeling of "This is a mess, what have we let ourselves in for?" I think there were people who probably felt the film was a lost cause. And it's
very easy, when you're in a position like this, to panic.

Eric Idle walked out halfway through the film; everyone else stayed to the bitter end. There was polite applause at the end. White and Goldstone didn't speak to the Pythons.

Here is how everyone remembered the event, in David Morgan's book, Monty Python Speaks:

TERRY JONES: Terry G. had done the dub, and you know what it's like when you're making a film: you've got two or three sound editors working away for months and months building up wonderful, incredibly thick soundtracks. It started off everybody laughing at the beginning and then after a while just *nothing;* the whole film went through [with]
no laughter at all. And it was awful, I was sitting there saying, "It just can't be *unfunny."*

JOHN GOLDSTONE: We'd already spent all the money by then and couldn't quite go back to them and say, "Can you put up some *more* because we'd like to refinish it?" So we had to go to a bank and borrow money against personal guarantees to make up the difference.

TERRY JONES: So we went and redubbed it and as soon as anybody started talking I just took all the sound effects out, all the atmosphere, everything. I went through the entire film doing that, and that seemed to help, it was something about the soundtrack filling in all the pauses.

TERRY JONES: Neil Innes' music sounded quaint, it didn't have an epic
feel to it. And we'd run out of money by that time, so I went along to De Wolfe Music Library in London and just took out piles and piles of disks and just sat here at home trying out music to it, trying to get something to work. So it felt like what you needed was really corny, heroic music.

NEIL INNES: The Arthurian themes were too thin with the instruments we had available- two French horns, two violins. Terry rang to say we can't use the music because it's just not strong enough. The 12 piece orchestra couldn't cope with the 120 piece orchestral sound that the film required. Artistically it was a better solution to go to a library to get epic music. We would never have had the money to record that size score. I wasn't that disappointed. I understood it. If it was my film I would have made the same choice.

*

We had some very heavy meetings over the next few days, a post mortem to see if we could bring this dead film back to life. Michael White was very supportive; he didn't panic and I was glad that I had kept him involved in the production. In the end we remixed the film, bringing down the level of the sound effects to let the dialogue punch through, and added the mock heroic library music score. We knew there was a good film buried there, and if we went back and remixed it, we'd have a funny film. The next screening was very positive. Now we knew the film was very good, it was very funny, it was working well. I think everyone was very happy with it. So it was really night and day.

If the Pythons had not owned the film, the director (or directors) would probably have been replaced at that point, or at least told to stay out of the cutting room. But the structure I set up meant that even through a disaster, the two directors had the time (and we had to find the extra money) to let them correct their initial work.

Everyone benefited from the great success of the film, and thirty years is plenty of time for memories to blister and fade so that some of the Pythons seem to have had a bout of amnesia concerning who raised the money – and much else. The two Terrys, Graham and Michael all knew what my role had been, but Cleese and Idle had no involvement with the setting up of the film, so had no idea as to what I had done for them. This became a real problem when the management changed, and Anne Henshaw was no longer there to keep alive that memory.

***

The 'Royal' Premiere

John Goldstone, the Executive Producer, had a relationship with EMI, one of the two major UK distributors, and he brought them in. EMI paid no advance to acquire the film, but had to pay for the prints and advertising to promote it. It was their decision on how much to spend on the film, and which cinemas to book it in. They could be a powerful ally for the film if handled correctly.

Unfortunately there were soon clashes over publicity. EMI asked us to write a synopsis of the film for marketing and press purposes, and Eric obliged. Michael Palin's diary of February 6, 1975 explained that the synopsis had nothing to do with the story of the film. Eric's synopsis (which I can't remember) was probably very funny, but it was a literary device. A synopsis for a film distributor is a marketing tool, and to mislead the audience about the content of the film is a risky thing to do. Even clever advertising that seeks to make fun of its own product always leaves you knowing what the product is. The Python fans who knew about the film might get the joke, but everyone else would be bamboozled. EMI was concerned because there were 'film critics' in parts of the country who sometimes reviewed films from the synopsis alone. I agreed with EMI and suggested that we offer a straight synopsis as well since we needed the film to cross over beyond the core Python audience. The Pythons were annoyed, but worse was to come.

EMI Films was run by Nat Cohen, a butcher's son from the East End who through hard graft had raised himself to a position of wealth and power. His family came from Poland, like mine, so I knew what Nat Cohen was like - he was a richer version of my Uncle Sam Nameroff. The contrast between the supremely British we love Chaucer and cricket, pass the Yorkshire pudding Ethel would you, middle-class Pythons and someone like Cohen, an old-fashioned conservative mogul, was vast. Had any Python eaten gefilte fish in his public school? Not likely.

Clashes soon erupted.

The Pythons had made a dummy of Princess Margaret for their TV series, and had propped 'her' in a box at the Drury Lane theatre during their stage show. Now they suggested staging a 'Dummy Premiere' with a limo bringing the dummy Princess to the cinema with the Pythons lined up to shake her hand. It was a very funny idea, but I knew this would be a hard sell to EMI. They already had real Royal Premieres for their bigger films, and they would not want to jeopardise their relationship with Buckingham Palace. Palin writes on February 19th that Terry Jones said, "Mark, if you don't feel that you can fight EMI for the things we want, then someone else ought to be doing the job." So I carried on with the fight.

EMI had given us the Casino Cinema (now the Prince Edward Theatre) for our opening. This was a big cinema so we were pleased. But on February 24th they had downgraded us to 4 smaller screens. We were not happy, so the next day we went to see John Hogarth, Head of Distribution, to try to win him round. By the 27th we had been given the Casino again, as well as two of the small cinemas.

This change was no accident. The film had earlier been shown to magazine critics, and would soon be shown to the daily papers. No doubt Hogarth had shown the film to his cinema managers, and I suspect the results were good, good enough to make EMI change their mind.

The film opened on April 3rd and was an immediate smash. The press loved the film, and EMI even understood that we were going to bring along our dummy Princess. We had a very good party at the Marquee Club, dancing, drinking, and congratulating each other. I felt that I had really achieved something that night. I felt like a hero.

The Pythons and I did have differences over publicity, but I knew that their approach would never be accepted by EMI, and it was my job to finesse the situation so that we got what we wanted. In the end, we had the right cinema, the dummy Princess in all her finery, and the film was a huge success. (In fact some wag at the Palace (I like to think it was Prince Charles who is a good mimic) rang me up to see if we would rent them the dummy Princess because some of the royals found all that hand shaking so tedious.) In court it suited the Pythons to only cite the problems we encountered.

***

Triumph - The UK Premiere of Monty Python and the Holy Grail

On April 3, 1975, the Casino Cinema hosted the UK premiere of Monty Python and the Holy Grail. The house was full; paying customers were in the stalls and invited guests in the circle. There was an air of expectation. Would the Monty Python team disappoint in their second film, as they had in their first, or would they deliver the kind of comic genius that their fans were used to? The lights dimmed and the credits began to roll. As the clever, original and unexpected opening credits started and then unexpectedly stopped, began again and then stopped, and finally changed style altogether, the audience whooped with delight. As one newspaper critic wrote, "The opening credits had more laughs than most comedy films in their entirety."

When I watched the first animated sequence in the film- the one where the angels bring the long trumpets up to their bums and blow out a stirring fanfare - I realised we had created something remarkably funny and original. It was a delight.

The audience roared its appreciation of the film. Buoyed by their laughter, I floated up Wardour St.to the after party at the Marquee Club. Wearing a natty blue corduroy suit, and probably glowing with satisfaction and success, I was greeted inside the entrance by a beautiful young woman who planted a kiss of beatitude on my face.

All the agony, all the work, the arguments and discussions, all the months of fund-raising, problems during shooting the film, disasters during the post-production, had all ended, and we were left with a marvellous, astonishing rule-breaking comic film that was capable of amusing audiences for a very long time. My feelings of relief and joy were overwhelming. In that state of euphoria, I felt I could float away to Heaven.

Those were the days my friend

I thought they'd never end. But they did, all too quickly.

*****

How I lost The Holy Grail

I now come to the part of the story that is most difficult to write and I have been dreading it. I have left it for almost last because I knew that emotionally it would be the most challenging section to write. The feelings associated with this time are still tender, but for many years they were painful, too painful to examine.

This section deals with how the Pythons and I parted company. When the actual parting took place, in 1975, I wasn't even aware of it. The rupture was never communicated to me, and I had to learn through a letter from their manager Anne Henshaw two years later that I wasn't going to be working on their next film. I should have known it by then; in fact emotionally I did know it, but was not admitting it to myself. Perhaps I thought that there was a way that we would continue working together (a bit like a bad marriage). At that time, and for many years later, I would have said to myself (and to no one else) that I screwed this up, but the need to review the past in order to prepare for the trial meant that I had to look again at what had happened, and in doing so I realised that it was not my fault that I had lost this opportunity. It was a jumble of all of my and the Pythons' reactions and feelings so that I understood that the years of blaming myself and of regret were really wasted emotion and wasted time.

The schism between myself and the Pythons started when my relationship with the two Terrys broke down. This began during the shooting of the film in Scotland, when the effect of having two directors brought up a number of problems, including the film beginning to go over budget. Almost all films have only one director, and you can understand the problems that can ensue when there are two people at the helm who have very different approaches to the film and to life. This is the situation that Terry Gilliam and Terry Jones had to face in co-directing the film.

Carol Cleveland summed it up from an actor's perspective ((from David Morgan's book, Monty Python Speaks),

*In the scene I was involved in, "Castle Anthrax," what would happen is they would sort of designate different scenes to each other and that particular one was quite a long sequence. I can't remember which came first but I think Terry G. was going to do the first part of it anyway, he was there in the morning setting it all up, the. lights, camera, da da da, and got everything going, and then later on Terry Jones came along to take over, and didn't like at all what Terry G. had set up and so changed it all: the whole setup,
the lighting, everything was changed. Now this apparently was happening all the time, because they just couldn't agree on what they were doing. And so, the crew were tearing their hair out, literally; they were apparently often near rebellion, by the time I arrived to do that scene because to them it all seemed so unprofessional, so disorganized.*

Every time one or the other Terry came on and said, "Well, no, we won't have that," you can see them all throw their eyes up to the heavens going, "Oh, God!"

But it wasn't just the differences between the two Terrys that were causing problems. The other Pythons were also on their backs, as Michael Palin recalls,

MICHAEL PALIN: What was most difficult was the combination of the two directors. And there was a sort of merciless divided room attitude of John's - if he didn't like something that Terry Jones was doing, he'd praise Gilliam extravagantly and say, "I wish he .were here"; if he didn't like something Terry Gilliam would make him do, he'd say, "Well, Jones is the only one who *really* understands how to
do comedy!" So I think that was pretty intolerable, and never repeated. It was
very hard for the two of them to co-direct like that. You had to have *one* person who was responsible.

Eric Idle saw it in this way,

You must understand that the rest of us have a healthy contempt

for directors. This was the least-wanted job; obviously the two who wanted it got it. Since they are both control freaks (as are all directors),
it drove them both mad. But Terry G. won; he drove Terry J. more mad! Terry J. would be cutting by day and Terry G. would undo it and be re-cutting by night.

Given the fractious atmosphere on set and in the cutting room, the fact that the film was going badly over budget and later the disastrous preview for the investors, it's hardly surprising that the two Terrys were taking so much flak. However, by 2003, Terry Jones seems to have forgotten all the other sources of aggravation and decided that all the hassle coming their way was down to me, as a kind of scapegoat, as he reflected in the Python's Autobiography:

The worst thing was that our producer, Mark Forstater, tended to go around saying, 'Oh, it's a disaster, and what can you expect when you've got two directors.' So the main tension was with our producer.

Normally in the film business, if you make a successful film, there is a tendency to keep working with the same people, since success is rather hard to come by, and should be rewarded. Of course, if you can't stand each other or find your fellow filmmaker to be a monster then there is less likelihood that you would want to continue to work with them. But that was not the case with the Pythons and myself. We had differences, and did not see eye-to-eye on a number of matters, but on most films there is a tension between producer and director, and this is often a creative tension which makes the final result better. Our film was not just successful, but phenomenally so, and has become a classic, so I felt aggrieved that they did not want to continue working with me

Of course I was concerned that there were two directors who were helping the film to go over budget and who were the focus of so much concern from the other departments. Perhaps if I had more experience I would have been able to deal better with the situation, but we were all making our first film, and were learning on the job. I had to cope with a great mass of problems.

The Pythons realised the tension between me and the two Terrys, especially Michael Palin, who was Terry Jones' writing partner. I now know that our relationship came to a head not over any disagreements about the making of the film but over a profit share for Julian Doyle. Or perhaps the profit share for Doyle became a convenient way to engineer my exit from future involvement with the Pythons.

At some point in early 1975, Julian Doyle asked me whether he was to get a profit share. I have to admit that this embarrassed me, since I had not considered that Julian was entitled to a profit share. I explained to him that my profit share related to my producing activities, and that all the available profit shares had been allocated. However I told him that I would raise the question with the Pythons. Here is the letter I wrote them, which the Pythons found in their archives, dated February 1975:

February 17, 19 ENTIRE

Dear Terry, Terry, Eric, Michael, Graham, and John,

I hope you don't mind me writing you a joint letter, but to do individual ones would be tedious. I find myself with two problems on my hands that I would like to put to you, for possible help and advice. Both of the problems are financial and I shall have to go back to the early days of the film to fill in the background.

You will recall that I started looking for finance for this project in June 1973 first with John Gledhill and then on my own. From about September when Michael White showed interest I was involved in negotiations with John Goldstone to attempt to get a better deal from White than he was offering. In order to get this better deal, I had to raise (with Tony Stratton-Smith's help) enough alternate finance to force White to give us either better terms or to get out of the production. These negotiations were not easy and spread over 6 months. The end result of these negotiations was to add over 6 profit percentage points to your share.

When we finally had the best terms we could get from White, and a good final script, we had our package together. I asked for a fee of only £5000 for raising the finance and producing the film, which is a very low figure for this type of job. Normally a producer will expect 5-7½% of the budget, in this case £ 9000-13000. I asked so little because there was not much in the budget for any of the above-the-lines, and we all wanted the maximum amount to go on the screen. I also wanted to limit my fee to peg it with the two Terrys.

Because the film has gone so far over schedule I find that my fee has been reduced to a very low figure, considering that I have now been involved solely with this production for over 18 months. The period from Oct.-Dec. 1974, when I had to raise the further £30,000 to complete the film, was totally unpaid work for me. It was also extremely difficult work, since getting money from people who had lost their initial faith in the project was not very pleasant. Most people involved in the production, including yourselves and Goldstone, have all been able to fit in another production or series during the post-production period. I have not been able to do this, having to stay on and complete the work on the film. To do this involves me taking the film through UK release by working with EMI on distribution, and in selling the film, along with Goldstone, to the US and Canada.

I feel that a further fee of £1000 would help to cover my additional time on the film, and I would like you to consider this at your next meeting. Where this money would come from I am not certain, but I really want you to be aware of the situation and to canvass your opinions.

My second problem also links up with this, in that it involves my profit participation. At the moment 5.6875% is in my name, equal to the percentage of each one of you. However, it was my intention, and it was also the desire of the two Terrys, to give Julian Doyle a percentage of profits, taken from my share. However, given the work I have expended on this film, and the time, I do not feel that I can fall behind the two Terrys in terms of eventual profits. I feel that I must at least keep up with you in that.

I was originally planning to give Julian 1% from my share, but I would like to suggest to you that it would be possible to give Julian his 1% by taking only .1428% from each of our shares. This would reduce each of our profit shares to 5.5447, not a considerable drop.

You will perhaps think it was very foolish of me not to have taken a greater fee to begin with, and asking for more profit early on in the negotiations. I want you to be aware that I did not do so because I wanted to be as fair as possible, and not let you feel that you were being ripped off in any way. In the end, of course, I may well have ripped myself off. I hope you will discuss these proposals and let me know what you think of them.

As Ever,

As you can see, I was asking for an additional £1000 fee for myself due to the fact that I had already been working on the project for over 18 months and was expecting to put in a few more months to help oversee distribution. Everyone else on the film had gone on to do other fee paying work, which I had been unable to do. I was also asking the Pythons to put up a small share of their profit percentage to allow Julian Doyle to have a 1% share of profits.

I didn't hear from them for quite a while, and asked Anne to remind them. In disclosure of documents I discovered that Anne had written an internal memo to them in June setting out what they needed to decide. She asked them to write to her with their thoughts. I can't reproduce this memo as it is her copyright, but it set out a number of questions for the Pythons to consider and asked them to write to her. The questions related to whether they thought my fee and profit share were fair or unfair in relation to other profit participants, and whether they were prepared to give up any of their fees or profits in order to comply with my request.

I don't know if any of the other Pythons wrote to Anne, but the archives disclosed a letter from Michael Palin where he told her what he thought. Again I can't reproduce this letter as it is Michael's copyright, but I can paraphrase it. Basically, he was against giving me any increase in fee or profits and felt that that I had done well out of my involvement with the group in terms of getting a good credit, experience and contacts. He went on to say that he thought that our relationship should come to an end, and that we should not work together on future productions. Anne either wrote or told me that there was to be no further money or share, but she did not reveal that our collaboration had ended. This I had to discover by myself through a process of elimination. Unfortunately it was me who was being eliminated.

Years later, when we were in the midst of the dispute, I met Terry Gilliam at a dinner and he told me that the Pythons at that time were 'naive'. I think he meant by naive that they did not understand the ways of the film business, which I accept is true. I also think that they responded as 'artistes', as writers and performers, and not as film people, and so made decisions based on an emotional response when others might have made a different kind of decision. However, my experience of being in dispute with them 30 years later would lead me to say that the Pythons' behaviour now was certainly not characteristic of naiveté. Anything but.

I decided to give not 1% of profits to Julian Doyle but transferred to him 2.5% of the 5.875 % of profits from my share. I felt at the time that I was being overly generous, and I still think I was. Perhaps I gave him this high share as a reaction to the Pythons' unwillingness to make any contribution. Julian did a great deal to help make the film a success, and I valued his efforts.

To date the film has made nearly £ 30,000,000 profit from the production cost of
£ 229,000, meaning the investment has been returned over 130 times. This must be one of the best profit ratios of any film ever made.

I kept 3.2% of the profits and from that share received about £ 700,000 over the next 30 years. The share I gave to Doyle earned him £ 670,000 and each of the Pythons' 5.6875% share produced over £ 1.5m.

I also had my 1/7th share of the merchandising profits and these brought in about £ 6000 from the spin-off record and book in the years before Spamalot. However Spamalot changed everything in relation to that 1/7th, and my share became the subject of a needless dispute which lasted for 7 years.

The Grail's Worldwide Progress

With the UK release being organised, we decided to send the film to Filmex, which was the Los Angeles Film Festival, held in February 1975. John Goldstone and the Pythons were there to see that the film, which had no publicity of any kind other than a brochure listing, had queues stretching around the block.

John Goldstone took a print to New York and arranged for Don Rugoff of Cinema 5 to see it. Goldstone was not optimistic when he

realised near the end of the film that Rugoff was snoring. But at the end Rugoff came to life, stood up, turned
to everybody and said, "What do *you* think? What do *you* think?" They all loved it. He said, "Okay, I'll buy it."

In May we went to Cannes to launch the film internationally and to find a film sales company. We were introduced to Irvin Shapiro of Films Around The World, a veteran who had been in the film business for so long that he had been involved in the US distribution of Eisenstein's Potemkin in the 1920s. He had also worked with Sam Spiegel and was effectively the inventor of the way the international film business worked once the studio system lost its stranglehold. He sold films to distributors in individual countries, and we signed with him.

The film had opened big in the US through Rugoff's two theatres in New York - Cinema 1 and Cinema 2 - and this made selling the film internationally even easier. The film did well in Canada, Australia and France. It has sold well in most other countries.

When VHS came along, the film had a healthy new life on home video, and an even greater impact when DVD came along.

******

My Glorious Career

1943 Born in Philadelphia, USA
1961 Temple University, Philadelphia
1962 NYC. Attended CCNY Film School
1963 Temple University
1964 Married, Came to Manchester U. to study
1965 Return to Philadelphia - Temple University
1966 Return to Manchester University
1968 London School of Film Technique
1969 Assistant Editor Survival
1970 Producer - The Great Wall of China
1971 Producer - Six Reels of a Film to be Projected in any Order
1972 3 short advertising films for the Pythons
1973 Fund-raising for Monty Python and the Holy Grail
1974 Shooting and post-production of Holy Grail
1975 UK and US releases If Holy Grail
1975 Producer –The Battle of Billy's Pond
1976 Producer – The Glitterball
1977 Producer - The Peregrine Hunters
1977 Producer - Wish You Were Here (Pink Floyd)
1978 Producer- The Odd Job
1979 Co-Producer - Marigolds in August
1980 Producer- The Grass is Singing
1982 Producer- XTRO
1983 Co-Producer - The Cold Room
1983 Exec Producer -Not For Publication
1984 Co-Producer- Number One
1984 Producer - Forbidden
1985 Producer- The Fantasist
1986 Co- Producer - War Zone
1986 Exec Producer - A Sense of Wonder (TV)
1987 Exec Producer - Wherever You Are
1988 Producer- The Wolves of Willoughby Chase
1988 Producer - Paint It Black
1988 Producer - Streets of Yesterday
1989 Producer - Shalom Joan Collins (TV)
1990 Producer- Separation (TV)
1991 Producer - Paper Marriage

1991	Producer - The Touch
1993	Exec Producer - Grushko (TV)
1994	Co-Producer - Between The Devil and The Deep Blue Sea
1994	Co-Producer - Provocateur
1995	Producer - Doing Rude Things TV)
1996	Producer - Citizens Arrest (TV)
1997	Producer - The Investigators (TV)
1997	Producer - Tao Te Ching (audio)
1998	Producer - The Lolita Story (TV)
2000	Author- The Spiritual Teachings of Marcus Aurelius
2001	Co-Author- The Spiritual Teachings of Seneca
2002	Author - The Spiritual Teachings of the Tao
2003	Co-Author- The Spiritual Teachings of Yoga
2004	Author - The Living Wisdom of Socrates
2009	Producer - The Age Of Anxiety (audio)
2011	Co-producer - The Power
2014	Author- I Survived a Secret Nazi Extermination Camp
2015	Author- The 7th Python - A Twat's Tale

Since making the Holy Grail, I have gone on to make 30 other feature films, a few documentaries, and a television drama series. I have also become the author of six books, and created audio versions of them. But nothing I have done in the forty years since has been as successful as the Holy Grail. This isn't surprising, since it is not often that a producer can make a film that becomes a classic. How can you top that? With difficulty.

Way back in the 90s I looked at the range of films that I had made at that time, and I characterised them under three headings: good, Ok, and lousy. I realised that if I had not made the lousy ones my track record would have been much better, and I resolved in future (if I were to make more films) that they would have to be at least good if not OK.

The productions of mine that I value (besides the Holy Grail) include two films I made for the Childrens Film Foundation - The Battle of Billy's Pond and The Glitterball (a precursor to ET); two films I made for HBO: The Cold Room and Forbidden (winner of a German film prize); a sci-fi horror film called XTRO, which was very successful but whose distributor cheated the director and I of our share; The Wolves of Willoughby Chase, The Devil and The Deep Blue Sea (Cannes Film Festival), and a couple of Polish films. I also did an animation film for Pink Floyd's Wish You Were Here tour, with Gerald Scarfe.

I also thought that a successful film career is marked by having a success at the beginning, another in the middle and a final one at the end. Arguably I am still waiting for that final success, and am still working in films (as well as writing books) to try to find that ultimate successful project. Watch this space.

****

My Journals

I first started keeping a journal in 2001 noting what is on my mind - positive and pleasant thoughts or negative and vexatious ones; many deal with the dispute. I have selected those for inclusion in this book.

As the dispute developed, I had to relive the past, and therefore expose my deep feelings, not always comfortable.

****

PART THREE: Caught in the tentacles of the law

He who in his life has never made a fool of himself has also never been wise.
Heinrich Heine

2005 Spamalot.

Eric Idle had long wanted to turn the film of the Holy Grail into a musical, but not all the Pythons wanted to see this done. In 2001 however, he got the others to agree that he and John Du Prez could work on a spec book and songs of a show based on the film to be called Spamalot, which they would present to the Pythons for approval. The Pythons all liked the CD Eric sent them, and gave him the right to try to mount a theatre production.

With the aid of his LA lawyer, Eric found a Broadway producer - Bill Haber- and Haber proposed the late Mike Nichols as director. The show opened at The Shubert Theatre, Chicago, in December 2014, and moved to the Shubert Theatre in New York, for the opening night in March 2005.

I had been following the progress of Spamalot with interest. Since it was based on the Holy Grail it was a spin-off from the film which counted as merchandising, so I was entitled to a share of it.

March 9, 2005

Tomorrow Spamalot opens, with $ 14m of advanced ticket sales. Obviously a hit, so this is a positive advance of yang. I feel very disconnected to this show, even though it's made from a film of mine. Somehow the man/boy who produced that film 30 years ago seems very distant from me, not that I know all that much about who I am now anyway.

May 21, 2005

Spamalot a huge ($25m advance tickets) hit with 14 Tony nominations. Word is that some of the Pythons (Terry J. ? Terry G.? - who knows) feel that they gave the rights too cheaply to Eric, but isn't this just sour grapes ? They had no idea it would be this big a hit, and Eric did all the work for it, so good for him. Unfortunately I would have been better off if they had done a better deal with him, since in the past I have gotten 1/7th of their merchandising deals. Let's see if they pay up!

June 8 2005

Spamalot won an Emmy this week, so hope that soon some dosh will come into the account from that source. Who knows what that could be worth for the next few years?

July 23 2005

Seeing bank manager Monday re: overdraft. Money from Spamalot should come in soon. I expect about 14k a year up to recoupment and more (twice more?) after - this would cover a lot of my costs, which would make life easier.

****

The Dispute - Year 1: A Demand For Reduction

In trickery, evasion, procrastination, spoliation, botheration, under false pretenses of all sorts, there are influences that can never come to good. Bleak House

In Spring 2005 I was going to New York for business, and decided to see Spamalot. I contacted Roger Saunders, the new manager of the Pythons (whom I had never met) and asked if he could arrange a couple of tickets for me, which he did. I was underwhelmed by the show, and agreed with Terry Gilliam's assessment that it was 'Python-lite.'

In early September I wrote an email to Saunders, asking him what was happening with the show. He explained in an email that the July 31 statement from the NFTC showed some income from Spamalot and the August statement would show still more. He explained that the show was doing huge business on Broadway.

From 1976 to 2005 I had sent invoices to Python (Monty) Pictures for my share of the record and book royalties that the NFTC 's monthly statements recorded. This was for the 1/7th share of the merchandising profits (50%) that the Python Company retained for itself. My invoices had always been paid. There had never been any dispute about them. However the royalties from 1976-2005 had only been £ 6000 in total (about £ 200 a year) but now with Spamalot making huge money on Broadway this share was about to become more substantial.

I had two choices; I could either send an invoice to Python (Monty) Pictures Ltd. for my 1/7th share of their income from Spamalot as per normal or I could reply to Roger's email with an explanation about my entitlement to this income. Since I had never met him I thought it best to do the latter. If I had sent an invoice he might come back to me and say, 'What is this?' I would then have to explain about my share. Instead, I decided to get the explanation in first. Did

I do the right thing? I thought I did during the trial, but I'm not sure now. Would it in fact have made any difference?

I explained to him that 'My deal with Python (Monty) Pictures is that I invoice a 1/7th share of all merchandising and spin-offs that are earned by Python (Monty) Pictures, such as the book and record revenues, and have been doing this since 1976. The deal is that Python (Monty) retains 50% of this merchandising income and I invoice for 1/7th share of it.' So there it is. I set out the deal that existed, and if he had taken the trouble to examine the invoices I had sent from 1976-2005 (30 years!) he would have said, fine, send your invoice. But that is not what he did.

I didn't hear back from Roger until the 28th of September, when he emailed to say that he did not know that I was entitled to a share of spin-off income, and so decided to review the original agreements relating to the film. He said that he had read my Agreement and also the Third Schedule to it, and concluded that my share of the spin-off income should be only 7.1429% - in other words a fourteenth and not a seventh.

In a later witness statement, Saunders changes his position from not knowing that I had this share to being 'vaguely aware' that I had it. This is not surprising, since his fellow manager, Ian Miles, who looked after the accounts, must have been fully aware of my shareholding, as he sent me the cheques since 1985. His initials - IM- are signed on every invoice that I submitted from 1997-2005. So why didn't Saunders just ask Miles instead of going back to the original documents?

Here is a sample invoice from 2002. There were a total of 188 invoices during these 30 years which had been paid like clockwork.

Accounts Dept
MontyPython Pictures Ltd
Chamberlaynes, High St
Flohvenden
Cranbrook, Kent
TN17 4LW

Date: 20 November 2002
Invoice no: 853
Your Ref:

INVOICE

MONTY PYTHON AND THE HOLY GRAIL			
VAT due on Royalty payments received for the periods ending			
31 Aug 2002	107.08	VAT	18.74
31 Oct 2002	11955.57	VAT	2092.22
1/7 of Record Album Revenues to Python (Monty) Pictures Ltd due for the period ending			
31 Oct 2002	211.85		30.26
		Record Album VAT	5.30
		INVOICE TOTAL	**£2,146.52**

TERMS: Payment due upon receipt.   VAT REG NO 386 3966 94

Mark Forstater Productions Ltd. 27 Lonsdae Road London NW6 6RA Tel 0171 624 1123 Fax 0171 624 1124
Mobile 0777 166 5382 email mforstater@email.msn.com
Reg No 1226955 Reg Office 27 Lonsdae Road London NW6 6RA

When I got Saunders' email I panicked, since he was claiming that my share was only half of what I had been invoicing for 30 years and had been expecting to continue to receive. I looked in my files for my agreement but could not find a single Holy Grail document other than some invoices. I must have lost them during one of my many office moves. So I couldn't even look at this 'third schedule' and the strange sounding percentage of 7.149%. I had been invoicing for 1/7th of 50% for 30 years and the fraction 1/7th was the only figure that I knew.

Still in a state of shock and without the agreement to consult, I decided to respond as best I could. I busked it, anxiously and hastily dredging up ancient memories, to try to convince him about my deal. I was terrified that he would slash my income in half; I couldn't afford to have that happen. So I wrote an email back to him on September 28th, 'Python Pictures and I agreed that as the producer of the film (i.e. a co-creator of the material) I should be entitled to a share of the 50% of the income that Python (Monty) Pictures was going to retain from ancillary sales. I put this point (and it was accepted) that I should be alongside the Pythons as a 7th Python and therefore should be entitled to 1/7th of the ancillary and merchandising income.' I speculated (since I had no idea what the Agreement that he was looking at actually said) that perhaps this arrangement was dealt with in side letters, and Saunders asked if I had copies of them. Of course I had no documentation at all- my files were gone.

I wrote back to him on September 30 "I have had a look and have no papers relating to this (side) agreement. Since you have no side letters regarding this agreement, it's very possible that this was done purely verbally. In any case, I would not have been sending invoices without agreement, and I am certain that Python Pictures would not have made payments without an understanding." I was clutching at straws although I knew that this was true- they would not have been paying me for 30 years without an agreement, and I knew we had made one. I didn't make it up.

There was a pause and then on October 6th Saunders came up with a rather strange reason why I received 1/7th of the book and record revenues. It was because the Pythons took a hefty chunk of the revenue off the top - in the case of the book 60% and for the record 40%. What was left was divided 50% to the investors via the NFTC and the other 50% retained by the Pythons. He claimed that I was paid a1/7th of the Pythons' 50% to compensate for so much of the revenue being taken off the top.

He then claimed that since there was nothing being taken off the top in relation to Spamalot they would only have to pay what the Agreement stated, which was 7.1429% of the Python 50%.

So he still wanted to pay me only half of what I was due. The 'reason' put forward about the record and book deal I had never heard before; it was news to me. Where did this come from, and where was it documented? Later, when I asked my lawyer Bob Storer to intervene, Saunders explained that this calculation about the amounts taken off the top came from Anne James (formerly Anne Henshaw). If this is what she really believed (and I knew this was wrong) then where could I turn to corroborate the truth?

In fact the percentages that the Pythons took off the top - 43% for the album, and 60% for the book, were merely ways to take more income from the investors and from me, since the 50-50 deal that had initially been put in place had been intended to compensate the Pythons for the effort they had to put in to make the record and book. But when they finally did these deals they took a large slice of additional percentage off the top. So for the album revenue, they took 43% off the top and then applied their contractual 50% of the remaining balance of 57%, giving them a total of 71.5%, and leaving only 28.5% for the investors. For the book, they took 60% off the top and 50% of the remaining balance of 40% giving them 80% and the investors only 20%. I was aware at the time that they were doing this, but had my own reasons for not making a protest. I still thought that we might work together on a second film.

Roger Saunders was intransigent, relying totally on his reading of the Agreement, and I didn't know how I was going to assert the truth. I decided that I needed legal help, so I asked my lawyer Bob Storer to have a look at the correspondence with Saunders. He asked Saunders to send us a copy of the Producer's Agreement, and finally we were able to see the Third Schedule that Saunders was referring to. This is it:

> THE THIRD SCHEDULE hereinbefore referred to
> ("Profits of the Film")
>
> "Profits of the Film" shall mean the balance remaining of the gross proceeds of distribution and exploitation of the Film and any part or parts thereof and any and all so called "merchandising" and other "spin off" rights arising therefrom throughout the world after deduction of distribution fees or commissions distribution expenses and the certified cost of production with interest thereon as agreed between the Company and persons investing in the Film PROVIDED ALWAYS that in respect of the exploitation of the said "merchandising" and "spin off" rights and in the event and to the extent that under the terms of the Companies agreements with persons investing in the Film it is entitled to receive 50% (fifty per centum) of the proceeds of exploitation of such rights (hereinafter called "merchandising profits") prior to the division of such proceeds amongst the persons entitled to participate in the profits of the Film the Executive shall be entitled to receive 7.1429 per centum of such merchandising profits in addition to his said shares of the profits of the Film.

Reading this document makes your head hurt, and many lawyers have given different interpretations of what it means. This is what the Schedule says,

"Profits of the film shall mean the balance remaining of the gross proceeds of distribution and exploitation of the film and any part or parts thereof and any and all so-called "merchandising" and other "spin off" rights arising therefrom throughout the world *less the merchandising rights herewith defined and* after deduction of distribution fees or commissions distribution expenses and the certified cost of production with interest thereon as agreed between the company and persons investing in the film PROVIDED ALWAYS that in respect of the exploitation of the said 'merchandising' and 'spin off' rights and in the event and to the extent that under the terms of the Companies agreements with persons investing in the film it is entitled to receive 50% (fifty per centum) of the proceeds of exploitation of such rights (*such share being hereinafter called* "Merchandising profits") prior to the division of such proceeds amongst the persons entitled to participate in the profits of the Film the Executive shall be entitled to receive 7.1429 per centum of such merchandising profits in addition to his said shares of the profits of the film."

The italicised words above are the handwritten amendments to the Schedule, and these have been initialled by me and by Michael Palin. The original Agreement was signed by Terry Jones. No one knows when or why these amendments were added, although I have a vague recollection of them. I seem to recall that when the first album royalties were reported in a statement by the NFTC, I issued an invoice for 1/7th of the entire 100% of merchandising profits, and not the 50% that the Pythons kept. Anne sent the invoice back to me, explaining my error and asking me to amend the invoice, which I did. Because of my misinterpretation of the Third Schedule, I believe she asked Simon Olswang to clarify it, which is why these handwritten amendments were added. They unfortunately didn't really clarify what it all meant, but if anything made it more confusing.

The dispute with the Pythons centres around whether you read the Third Schedule as saying that the Executive (i.e. me) is entitled to 7.249 % of 100% or only 7.249 % of 50% of the merchandising profits. The Python's manager and lawyers read it as 7.249 % of 50% (which is only 1/14th of 50 %), while my lawyers argued that Schedule Three was intended to reflect the fact that I was entitled to 1/7th of 50%, which in decimal terms is 7.249 % of 100%. You may need a PH.D. in maths and logic to follow these convolutions. The problem arose, as my barrister Tom Weisselberg remarked, due to the production lawyer "Simon Olswang's love of decimals over fractions." If he had written the Schedule in fraction terms - the 1/7th of 50% that had been agreed - there would have been no confusion. However he didn't, and we had to live with it.

The problem for me was that if Saunders held to his view, it was just his interpretation against mine - his word against mine. What evidence could I bring to bear to convince him of the truth? The only thing I had was the 30 year history of invoicing. I knew that Anne Henshaw was still alive and was a colleague of Michael Palin's. Could she shed light on this?

***

My Journals 2005

It's not that it's so good with money, but it's so bad without it. Jewish saying.

I was starting to get worried about the effect of my income being reduced by 50%. By 1989 my first marriage had ended, and I had married a second time, to Jo Manuel, who was a yoga teacher and therapist, and we had two children: Cleo, aged 12 and Lily aged 4. I was still close to my daughters from my first marriage- Maya, now aged 32 and with two sons of her own, and Asha, 29. I had a financial responsibility to provide for my new family, as well as to contribute to my first wife.

The journal entries around this time show my state of mind.

October 5 2005.

Money woes. The Pythons may not want to pay my invoices for ancillary sales, so I'm financially adrift. To get this money I'll probably have to take them to court. In doing this, will I lose my equilibrium, get angry, annoyed, lose my cool? I hope not. Maybe this is an important test, how to keep going smoothly even with the loss of so much money. Can I do it?

October 9 2005

I seem to be dominated by money questions. I am owed money that I can't get and must fight for, and this is upsetting me, unbalancing me, disturbing me. This appears as an obstacle, and it is becoming clear that this is a learning device for me. That is, this has arrived to test me and to teach me. How should I deal with it? It's obvious that the way I am dealing with it now is completely wrong, since it is only upsetting me and causing me to overthink about my problems - they dominate my mind.

October 29 2005

Today I read an article about I Ching and Synchronicity, which talked about how synchronicity was a resonance between the physical world - external events and happenings - and the psychic world - internal events and especially the meaning that one takes from the things that happen to you or appear to you.

This got me thinking about my Python problem, and which is providing me with some meaning - ie a lesson or advice about how to deal with life now and in the future. Jung's archetypes and the I Ching hexagrams both provide symbolic images and ideas that reflect on the inner-outer resonance that is occurring between the mind and the world and provides a depth of spiritual meaning for interpreting the situation that exists. Tonight I will consult the I Ching about this situation and see what it says, but perhaps I need to reflect on the meaning of this problem and why it has happened now. What does it mean for me and what lesson does it hold?

It involves money, and would provide security of income for at least 5 years which will give me confidence to pursue my activities - either film or otherwise. It represents a pot of gold - worldly wealth that can provide benefits - security, confidence, reduction of debt etc. If I do not get this money, then what - am I insecure, lacking confidence etc? Or will I manage to get along, to keep going, find a way. Is my internal self or essence able to carry on as per normal (natural being) even if this money does not get paid to me. What is more important - your money or your life? When I consider the physical and mental state of my being, the quality of my relationships with others, and my relationship with the external environment, then surely this money is not really the important thing. Your life is good and solid, and means so much more than this cash.

Perhaps the lesson to be learned here is about values. What is more valuable and what is it important? Is it money or something else, something more valuable than money, something which has no cash value. If this problem makes you understand about what is truly valuable in your life, and to really appreciate these things in your life, and to give the value and importance far above the cash that you are owed, then you really would learn a valuable, perhaps even priceless lesson.

Money has long been a kind of God for me, even a kind of nemesis, because money was very important to my mother and was the ultimate value system when I grew up. Dealing with money, having the right attitude to it has taken me years of inward therapy and it's no surprise that it is a hefty money problem that I am forced to now face and to deal with in ways that leave me unhurt, still balanced and stable, not angry, not bitter, not full of regrets.

I have to learn the right perspective, how to live without getting what I am owed and not letting it damage my mind and heart. This is the lesson I must learn now for all time.

****

My I CHING Reading

When I am uncertain about how to respond to an important event, I consult the I Ching. Below is the reading I got when I asked the oracle 'Can I win my dispute with the Pythons?' Looking back the form of the question is interesting. It's not the blunt, direct 'Will I win', but 'Can I win'? Can I win implies a great deal more about the questioner, ie me. There is a doubt expressed here not about the outcome but about whether I am willing to take this on, to see if I have 'the right stuff', knowing the odds that are against me. I am outnumbered, outgunned, and am the underdog. I am wondering if I have the guts to take this on.

The I Ching (the Classic of Changes) is an ancient Chinese book of divination. Its roots go back 3000 years and it is one of the oldest books in the world. Confucius studied it diligently and wrote many commentaries on it. My late teacher Ming Liu translated a version of the book, and in his introduction he says,

The book has a central wisdom. This wisdom is that all beings and things share a common capacity to adapt. Our capacity to adapt is also change itself. Life is simply a dialog between a capacity to adapt and the opportunities that naturally arise.

There are a number of ways to consult the oracle. One way is to use three coins, a second is to use 50 dried stalks of the Yarrow plant, and a third is just to ask a question and open the book at random. I use the yarrow stalk method which takes about 20 minutes. Keeping my question in mind –'Can I win my dispute with the Pythons?' I manipulated the stalks and got the following Hexagram:

45: Gathering (or Asssmbly or Bringing Together)

There are 64 hexagrams in total. Each hexagram is made up of two trigrams. For example, The symbol seen above- Gathering - has three yin (broken) lines at the bottom, making the trigram Kun (earth) and one yin line over two yang (unbroken) lines at the top, making the trigram Dui (lake). So Hexagram 45 as a whole is made up of a large body of water resting on the earth. Now what does this have to do with my question? Directly this has little to do with my question, but Lake is water and water is life. If we have water then we can live and be content, even joyous. Earth is accepting, supporting, it helps things grow. With water and earth crops can grow and animals and people can survive. This is a good omen.

There is also a commentary on the Symbol, which says:

Lake over Earth.
An image of Bringing Together.
In correspondence with this.
The superior person repairs his weapons
To guard against unexpected happenings.

I read in a commentary that the weapons to use are the tools of wisdom.

Each hexagram also has a Decision, a short saying that illuminates the meaning. The Decision for Gathering is:

Bringing Together,
Prosperous and Smooth.
The king arrives at the ancestral temple.
Favourable to see a great person.
Prosperous and smooth,
Favourable to be steadfast and upright.
Use big animals: good fortune.
Favourable to have somewhere to go.

Gathering's message to me is not at all clear or obvious. It is a hidden or guarded message which requires a degree of interpretation However, within the Decision there are three favourable forecasts:

favourable to see a great person, favourable to be steadfast and upright and favourable to have somewhere to go. A decent spread of positive omens. My ancestral temple might be a court, partly because the word gathering refers to a group of people, and a court is probably one of the first places people gather. In addition, my Jewish name is Moshe (Moses) so I was named after the law-giver of the Jews. I don't presume to be the king who arrives there. Using big animals probably refers to a sacrificial ritual. What do I have to sacrifice?

Joseph Campbell, in his The Masks Of God: Occidental Mythology, says there are two types of sacrifice. The first, which he called 'Do Ut Des' says 'I give so you should give.' And is made to a benevolent God or spirit; it's a kind of contract or exchange. The second - 'Do ut abeas' says 'I give so you should depart.' The second kind of sacrifice is also a kind of contract, but one made to a more malevolent God or spirit: I give so that you will go away or not harm me. If I have to make a sacrifice or offering, which kind am I making?

The Decision says it is favourable to be steadfast and upright, which means to be consistent, correct and truthful. To go somewhere means to undertake something, to act. Maybe Gathering has something to do with a court full of people gathered together, seeing the great person- a Judge.

There is also a commentary on each of the 6 lines, but you only read the commentary for moving or active lines. In this hexagram, the moving line is the 5th one from the bottom, and so I read it for further guidance:

Line 5.

Bringing together.
There is a position. No fault.
No confidence.
Sublimely persevering, steadfast and upright,
Regret vanishes.

In truth, the I Ching has picked up very subtly on my question, I asked 'Can I win' and part of the answer comes back No Confidence. Yes, it's true that I don't have confidence that I can win. So the I Ching gives the remedy: if you persevere, remain straightforward and correct, then regret vanishes. Regret, if you haven't already clocked it, is something I carry with me, as my journals will confirm. To lose those regrets would lift a great burden from me. It says there is a position – true enough, but there are actually two positions- mine and the Pythons. The I Ching says no fault, so I have to assume that my position is right and will succeed.

This was enough to convince me that I could win the dispute. I consult several versions of the I Ching. There is one called The Fortune Teller's I Ching, a popular and simplified version. Here they called Hexagram 45 Collect, so I thought this must be the right decision.

***

Back to The Plot

I became concerned that Saunders, who was not around in 1974, was perhaps not consulting the Pythons and explaining what was happening. So (perhaps influenced by the I Ching reading) I decided to write to Michael Palin and Terry Jones to put them in the picture. I liked Michael, and trusted him; I thought he could be an honest broker in helping to resolve the situation. Perhaps **he** was the 'great person' referred to in the reading. I wrote to them:

October 31, 2005

Dear Michael and Terry,

I'm sorry to get you involved with this, but I wanted to bring to your attention a problem I am having with Python (Monty) Pictures, which I hope you can help me to resolve. The problem relates to my share of merchandising revenues on the Holy Grail. I don't want to take up a great deal of your time, so I'll try to make my explanation as brief as possible.

Do you remember that the merchandising and spin off revenue in the film was split 50-50 between the investors and Python (Monty) Pictures? I made the point at the time that as the producer of the film, I should share in Python Pictures' share of this revenue as if I were a Python, ie a 7th member of the team, and should therefore be entitled to a $1/7^{th}$ share of the Python (Monty) revenue. This was accepted and was enshrined in an Appendix to my agreement.

From that time on I have been invoicing Python (Monty) Pictures for $1/7^{th}$ of the merchandising revenue and these invoices have been paid regularly. However, now that there is a new and larger amount of merchandising income (ie Spamalot), Python (Monty) Pictures has questioned my $1/7^{th}$ share and has suggested it should actually be half of what I have traditionally been invoicing.

It seems that there was a handwritten amendment added to the Appendix which appears (according to my lawyer) to reduce my $1/7^{th}$ share to a 1/14th share. Now I don't recall why this rewritten change was made, or the circumstances around it, (it was after all over 30 years ago), but I certainly did not believe that it reduced my share by half. The proof of this is that I have been sending invoices for a $1/7^{th}$ share for the past 30 years, and these have never been questioned.

Roger Saunders and Anne James now claim that there was an allowance made that I could invoice for $1/7^{th}$ because other Python companies (KGB music etc) were taking so much of the merchandising revenue off the top before my share was applied. Their current argument is that since the Spamalot revenue does not have any monies coming off the top to other Python Companies, that I need to reduce my share to what is written in the Appendix. In response I have to say that this is the first time I have ever heard of this allowance argument and was certainly not aware of it at the time.

I don't know if your memory bank goes back this far, but I believe the true nature of our agreement at the time was that I should be treated as a 7th Python for this revenue which I did help to create. I feel it is fair and just that I should retain the share that I have had for the past 30 years, and see no reason why this should now be altered. Since the Holy Grail now represents quite a large chunk of my overall income, it would be a real hardship for my family if this reduction were to take place.

I'm sorry to have to ask you to intercede on this, but I really don't know what else to do. In the end my agreement is with you and the remaining Pythons, and so I believe that it's best that you collectively make the decision.

I'm very happy to review any of this with you at any time.

Kind Regards

Mark

I got a brief note back from Michael saying he passed my letter to Roger Saunders to deal with.

After reviewing the papers, my lawyer Bob Storer repeated to Saunders on November 18th that I had always invoiced for 1/7th of the Python's 50% share and had been paid. Storer added:

"You say that 1/7 has been paid on music and book publishing to compensate Mark for monies taken by Python off the top but Mark has no recollection of this agreement being reached, and it does not work exactly from a mathematical point of view. There have also been certain revenues such as PRS income where Mark has received his 1/7 share without a Python amount being taken off the top.

It occurs to me that your files may have evidence of the agreement reached at the time that Mark would be treated as a seventh Python and clearly when the third schedule was drafted, it was on the basis that such would be the case. The amendment five lines from the end of the third schedule has the effect of confusing the clause which goes on to say that Mark's percentage should be taken prior to the division of proceeds, i.e, from 100%. It is our case that the clause even with the amendment still entitles Mark to 7.1429% of 100%. In all the circumstances I believe Mark has a strong case to be paid on the 1/7 basis based firstly on the interpretation of the third schedule, secondly on the custom and practise of the parties over the years, and thirdly, if necessary, on the basis of a case of rectification of the agreement based on the above and the conduct of the parties and that it was always the intention of the parties that he be paid as a seventh member of the Pythons."

I thought this was a really clear letter, and would get a positive response from Saunders. The last paragraph, where Bob says that I have a good case for rectification, is in fact what we had to go to court to determine. Rectification means that the Judge has to decide to rectify the Agreement to make it clear that it reflects the intention of the parties before the agreement was committed to paper.

This was the first point where we could have settled this dispute. Saunders could have taken the view that the wording on the Third Schedule was not very clear, but the fact that 30 years of my invoices had been paid on the basis of $1/7^{th}$ was rather powerful evidence for my case. I thought this letter would get a positive response from the other side, but I was wrong.

On December 16th Paul Lambeth of Ent Law wrote to say that he was instructed by Python (Monty) Pictures Ltd. to deal with the issues raised. He had asked Saunders to search the Python's papers (largely in storage) for any relevant documents.

On January 16th, 2006, having heard nothing from Lambeth, Storer wrote asking for a response.

On February 1st he wrote another chasing letter.

On March 13th another chasing letter.

On March 22 Lambeth wrote that they had found no documents relating to the issue but stated that they did not agree with our interpretation of the 1974 Agreement. They were instructing counsel (i.e a barrister) to 'advise upon the proper construction of the Agreement'

On May 12th we had still heard nothing further. Bob wrote, "I am afraid our patience is running out. What is happening please? "

On June 5th we still had heard nothing.

On June 26th we were still chasing.

On July 18th we still were chasing.

We were entering the territory familiar to Shakespeare "The law's delay."

My Journals 2006

I continued to add my thoughts in my journal:

February 12 2006

Spamalot won a Grammy for musical album, will open in London in October, and I think there is a touring company, all of which will bring money. If enough came in there for 5 years I could really be semi-retired, which would give me enough time to spend meditating, exercising etc.

April 22, 2006

Yesterday money from Spamalot came in- £ 154k, and my share depending on my ultimate deal with the Pythons is either 22k (1/7th) or 11k (14th). Amazing that so much money is flowing. If this much comes in 4 times a year for the next 5 years it's really like a pension for me. It's such a windfall that I was amazed, staggered when I saw how much was there. Without doing anything my income is arriving, backing up my current activities, giving me running around money, security, and letting me continue with my semi-retired, Horace-like lifestyle, which is perfect for my health and well-being. How wonderful life is when things work out like this! Now all I have to do is win the court case and get on with making a film or three.

When I visited (my friend) Carl's dad's house- Dr Harry Frank - and saw a life of books and records, I said that's all I really need- enough money for books and records, and now it seems to have miraculously come about - enough money for I assume 4-5 years of living, enough to erase worry, to provide the books etc and to give me operating capital, to carry on making movies, but without the need to make money from them. How weird that things have worked out this way! How odd and how silently and secretively it has happened. The weirdness of life and destiny. That a film made 30 years ago can provide income to a semi-retired existence of a 62 year old!

April 24 2006

Thinking what to do with my 'windfall' which isn't a windfall at all.

In these years 2006-2010/11, enough money will come in from this source to enable me to work in the way that I want to, that in fact I have already started to. What I don't want to do is to use the money to either bunk off completely (ie retirement rather than a form of semi-retirement) or to spend the money frivolously on clothes trips or project development that is unnecessary.

July 8th 2006

Remembering a time in Rose and Mike's kitchen when I got a phone call- was it 1975? - when I got some good news about the Holy Grail. - distribution? theatres?- it was news of success- big success-and when I hung up the phone I remember saying to Rose- "Now I can take over the British Film Industry." Ridiculous idea, but potentially true. At the time, if my relationship with the Pythons had held, I could have achieved that position - films by Gilliam, more Pythons etc. would have given me the possibility of doing what I said. So this was a peak moment, but at the same time it was the beginning of the end, in a way, the start of a slide because my gig with the Pythons came to an end with Holy Grail.

It was good that what happened did happen, because otherwise my ego/power complex and all the rest of the dysfunctional parts of my psyche would have been inflated when actually it was best that all that finally got deflated, although it took 20 years for it to finally happen- by the mid 90s I had come to the end of my run, and it took 10 years of thinking, reading, writing, therapy to come back by 2004 to a good place, a place to start again, without dreams of empire-building, but only the ordinary desire to get a pension, to work on projects and with people that could achieve that end.

So now I am at a new beginning, and my body luckily doesn't reflect my age, I have the energy to keep going for a number of years, and my spirit is high enough for me to still have enthusiasm and a bit of hunger to get things moving, to be productive again, and not to take over the British Film Industry. Today I am much more modest, and I just want make a few films before giving up and going to the beach.

*****

The Plot Sickens

When things don't get better, don't worry- they may get worse.
Jewish saying.

Finally, after eight months, on 20th July 2006 we heard from Lambeth.

Litigation lawyers, when they are acting for the defendant, try to stretch out the case for as long as possible, hoping that one or more of the following events will occur:

1. The claimant runs out of money

2. The claimant runs out of enthusiasm for the case

3. The claimant runs out of energy

4. The claimant becomes ill

5. The claimant dies

Unfortunately for the Pythons I was not going away.

Please now put on those special glasses reserved for reading the small print since what follows is a good example of how lawyers argue.

In his letter Lambeth repeated the third schedule, and commented:

"This is obviously not the cleverest piece of drafting and the handwritten amendments are difficult to read. " Nonetheless, their position remained unchanged. And good lawyers will seek to turn a lack of clarity to their client's advantage. Lambeth added that it now looks like I was invoicing for all those years for 1/7th when I should have been invoicing for only 7.1429% , and the Pythons had been paying those invoices in error.

Good lawyers often hope that the other side will get worried. So it wasn't just that I was not going to get my fair share but I might have to pay the Pythons back. Lambeth claimed the ill- advised Pythons had only just discovered that I have been invoicing them **in error** for 30 years and they have been **erroneously** paying me for 30 years. It seems that we have now entered a comedy of errors, and we are all just idiots.

Lambeth employed lawyer's logic rather than the classical Aristotelian one. He makes the point that the dispute only arose once the Spamalot income arrived, since before that the merchandising profits had been very small. The point that the merchandising profits were small up to Spamalot is irrelevant. If my share was 1/7th of a small amount in the past, that does not mean it should be less than 1/7th in the future. A percentage share, large or small, is a percentage share. Now that there may be real money involved, it's worth bothering about. Before the monies wouldn't buy you a glass of Rumpole's favourite claret but now.... truly money obsessed millionaires will scrap for the least scrap of money.

Lambeth went on to add that the Pythons reserved the right to recoup the overpayments made during the past 6 years. What cheek! They were claiming that I had been cheating them for thirty years by sending in fraudulent invoices, which they had paid in error.

Their search of the archives did bring up some important correspondence between myself and Anne James (formerly Henshaw). Now this was interesting, as it was real evidence from the past. These letters were an exchange between myself and Anne Henshaw relating to the book of the film that the Pythons wanted to produce. Anne was asking me to approve the arrangements that were being proposed. The proposal was that the book would be produced by another Python company- Python Productions- which would receive a 60% share of royalties, leaving only the 40% remaining to be split under the 50-50 arrangement. I accepted the arrangement, even though I knew that it was intended to reduce the amount that the investors (and I) would get out of the deal. I still thought that I might be involved with future Python films, and so decided not to make waves.

And I made that clear when I wrote to Anne on 23 June 1977; " this new deal does affect me directly, since in the original deal negotiated I was allocated 1/7th of the Python's share of any spin-offs. Under this proposed deal I lose that share. Would the Python's be willing to bring me in on the Python Productions side so that this 1/7th share remains the same? "

Anne wrote me on the 28th July 1977, turning this request down, but she states very clearly and unambiguously that 'You will still after all be receiving your investor's share plus 1/7th of 50% of the amount paid to the NFTC which will be Python (Monty) Pictures' share'.

Surely this was the evidence that would convince Saunders of the truth. But I was to be disappointed as their lawyer did a splendid legal pirouette to claim that although Anne does refer to me receiving a 1/7th share, he assumes that she was simply parroting the language found in my letter and did not bother to consult the original agreement. He claims she is confused "in that she refers to Mr Forstater receiving 1/7th of 50% of the amount paid to the NFTC."

But Anne was competent and she was the person who did the original deal with me, and this correspondence is only three years after that deal was done. She was a sharp lady and had no need to go back to the original documentation to know what she and the Pythons had agreed with me.

Below is one of the letters I wrote. I can't reproduce any of Anne's since they are her copyright.

Mark Forstater Productions Ltd
9 Cliff Road, Camden Square, London NW1
Telephone: 01-267 6178
Cables: Markfilm London NW1
Telex: 22861 ATT F150

Ann Henshaw
Python Productions Ltd
20 Fitzroy Square
London W1

23 June 1977

Dear Ann

MONTY PYTHON AND THE HOLY GRAIL (Book)

I have received the letters from Python Productions and the NFTC regarding the proposed book deal.

It seems to me that the deal being offerred by Python Productions is a fair one for the investors and has been justly managed by the Pythons.

However, this new deal does affect me directly, Since in the original deal negotiated I was allocated 1/7th of the Python's share of any spin-offs. Under this proposed deal I lose that share. Would the Pythons be willing to bring me in on the Python Productions side so that this 1/7th share remains the same?

If you can find a way to accommodate me I would be more than happy to approve the deal and to recommend it to any investors who seek my advice.

Yours sincerely,

MARK FORSTATER

Mark Forstater Productions Ltd
Reg. No. 1206986 (England)
Reg. Office: 7 Fitzroy Square, London W1P 6BB
Directors: MI Forstater (USA), MP Forstater (USA)
GC Wheatley, RJ Harris, M Hatton

The National Film Finance Corporation (The NFFC) had a sister company called the National Film Trustee Company which acted as a collection agency for film companies; this is a body that collects revenue from film distributors and TV stations around the world, and then disburses them to the financiers who invested in the film. We did a deal with the NFTC to act as a Trustee for the Holy Grail film, and they collected revenue from film companies around the world who had distributed the Holy Grail, and then disbursed the income to investors and other profit participants.

When I later looked at the NFTC statement I realised that Anne was correct about my payment coming from the NFTC as the NFTC collected all the record (and later book) revenues, and then distributed them as to 50% to the investors and 50% to the Pythons. I then invoiced the Pythons for my 1/7th share of this 50%. She was correct in how the money flowed, and Lambeth was wrong. It was Lambeth who was the one who was confused.

As the dispute was about money here is one of the invoices:

```
                NATIONAL FILM TRUSTEE COMPANY LIMITED
                  "MONTY PYTHON AND THE HOLY GRAIL"
          Allocation of Revenues from Record Album to 31st March 1976

                                    £              £              £

Record Album - US initial advance
               £20,000           9,758.24

Less: Reserved for commission
      Nancy Lewis 10%              975.82
      Charisma Records Limited 33⅓%           2,927.47
                                                              5,854.95
Record Album - rest of world                                  9,000.00
                                                             14,854.95

Deductions
   National Film Trustee Co. Ltd 1% remu-
               neration                       187.98
   Charisma Records Limited - recording
               cost                         5,917.78
   Kay Gee Bee Music Limited
       Music Publishers royalties
       De Wolfe Limited             400.00
       Singers for sound transfer
       Fred Tomlinson               225.00    625.00
   Reserved for Legal Costs - USA           1,300.00
   Reserved for Legal Costs - UK            2,500.00
                                                             10,530.36
                                                              4,324.59
   Kay Gee Bee Music Limited   43%                            1,859.57
                                                              2,465.02
   Python (Monty) Pictures Ltd  50%                           1,232.51
   Transfer to film revenue statement                         1,232.51
```

117

n.b. The 50% going to the Pythons is the next to the last line, in this case £ 1,232.61. The last line represents the other 50% that is being transferred to the investors. When I received a statement I could see how much the Pythons retained, and so could invoice for 1/7th, in this case 1/7th of
£ 1232.51= £ 176.07. Here is the invoice I sent:

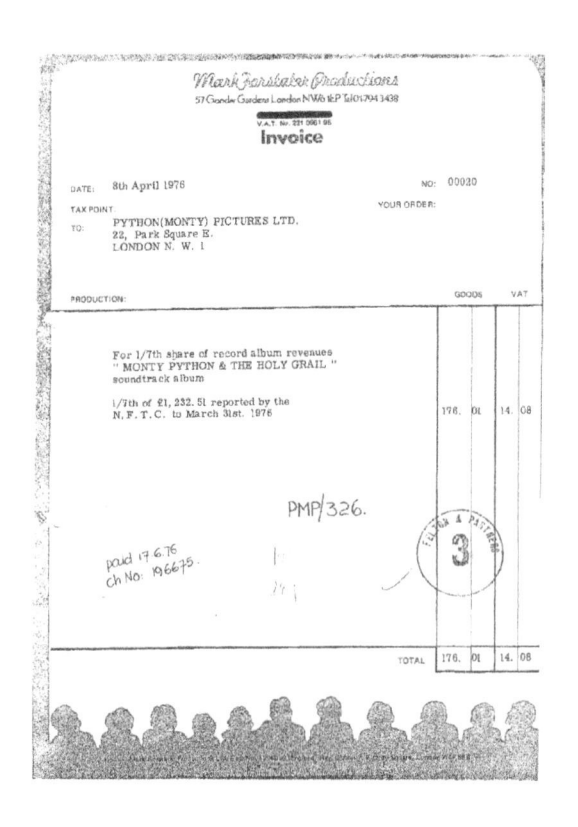

Mark Forstater Productions
57 Granda Gardens London NW6 1EP Tel 01 794 3438
V.A.T. No. 221 0901 95

Invoice

DATE: 8th April 1976
NO: 00020
TAX POINT
YOUR ORDER:
TO: PYTHON (MONTY) PICTURES LTD.
22, Park Square E.
LONDON N. W. 1

PRODUCTION: | GOODS | VAT

For 1/7th share of record album revenues
" MONTY PYTHON & THE HOLY GRAIL "
soundtrack album

1/7th of £1, 232. 51 reported by the
N. F. T. C. to March 31st. 1976 | 176. 01 | 14. 08

PMP/326.

paid 17.6.76
Ch No: 196675

TOTAL | 176. 01 | 14. 08

I invoiced like this for the next 30 years until in 2005 Roger Saunders decided to question the invoices, and accused me of overcharging them. Or as Richard Spearman QC put it in court,

'He woke up finally to the fact that he had been, in simple terms, overcharging for a long period of time but no-one had spotted it.'

Lambeth said that none of the Pythons remember agreeing to my being treated as a 7th Python and to my receiving a 1/7th share of the spinoff income. Lambeth calculated that until Spamalot came along my 1/7th share of the book and records totalled £ 6292.38, which was about £ 200 a year. Divide that by 6 Pythons, and you get £ 34 per Python per year. Basically a decent meal. Why would they remember this after 30 years?

This was the second point at which a settlement could have occurred. Here was the evidence that Saunders had asked me early on to provide. His own files had a black and white declaration from Anne Henshaw stating my position. This is exactly what he was asking for, but once it arrived it did not affect his position - he was not going to be moved.

My lawyer Bob Storer wrote back to Lambeth on the 4th August, explaining that the profit shares of the film were not calculated "arbitrarily, but were the result of quite detailed and well thought out profit divisions." He claimed no one would ever conclude a negotiation at a figure of 7.1429 of 100% of anything unless there was a good reason. "The intention at all times was for our client to receive an equal share of merchandising revenue to the members of Monty Python. The figure of 7.1429% can only have come from dividing 50 by 7."

Bob's letter made absolute sense. In most negotiations people deal with round numbers like 5% or 10% or a 20% share. Who would ever ask for 7.129% of something? (Not even in the Old Testament do you find an obligation to sacrifice 7.129% of a goat at the Feast of Percentages). Bob concluded by saying that if the Pythons did not restore my position to the 1/7th share that we would be forced to issue proceedings against them." We would have to take them to court.

There was no moving Saunders and it was clear that they were not going to be moved. Bob Storer wrote to Lambeth on September 7 2006, "having regard to the tone of the letter (of 25 August) that it is best that I pass this matter up to our litigation group." Bob thought it was time to turn the case over to one of the litigation lawyers- Lawrence Abramson.

***

My Journals - 2006

I managed to go on holiday to Devon with my family that summer and continued to ruminate in my journal about the case:

July 26 2006

Instead of being angry at Roger Saunders and the Pythons, I need to find compassion for them. They are being driven by greed.

I thought back to all the things that affected my heart, gave it pain and sadness and professionally all that started with the Pythons bypassing me as producer of the films after Holy Grail The deception over the revenue from merchandising just added to that. All of these acts hurt me by striking at my ego, my sense of self-esteem and struck blows at the core of my feelings of self- my foundations.

These pains lodged in my heart and I now have the chance to free them and let them go. This case has forced me to look again, to confront the pains of the past, and to try to integrate and transform them, This is actually a great opportunity for me.

July 28 2006

Meeting today with Bob Storer and Lawrence Abramson. Good lawyers who want to help and feel my cause is just. Today I wrote to Mike Palin (although they said not to yet) asking him why they are doing this? Trying to put the moral side of things rather than the legal. Will it work? I don't know but it's good that the Pythons see this in human terms they can relate to.

This whole episode has been very good for me, whether I win or lose. It has brought back old (and mainly sad) memories which I have had to deal with. and enabled me to put my career in perspective, to see clearly what I felt at the time, that some betrayals hurt my career at a vulnerable time. And I could see now how I have overcome these difficulties, that in fact these difficulties enabled me to grow, so much so that dealing today with a case that is blocking my income, something that normally would disturb me emotionally, has this time not bothered me so much. I have been trying, and so far mainly succeeding, in putting it all in perspective, not letting it make me depressed. I've not let the events disrupt my work (which at the moment is minimal) or my regime, of 2 hour meditation sessions daily, and which are having a very positive effect on body and mind.

July 30 2006

If the Python case has done me a favour in that it gave me the chance to re-examine my past, then I should be grateful to Roger Saunders for initiating this, rather than be angry at him and the Pythons. This is what makes an imperfect specimen into a more perfect one, the ability to be compassionate towards those who mean you harm. So if I get invited to the October opening of Spamalot and Roger comes up to introduce himself to me, I should embrace him, because he has been a teacher to me, even though he doesn't know it.

August 15 2006 - Devon- family holiday

On TV today, a news programme about the cost of a University education - £ 33,000. In the past I always worried about how we would pay for Cleo (and now Lily's) uni education, but now with the Python money to come in, this appears less daunting. Win the case and I'd be able to cover their education without a problem. What a dream. I really feel like I've won the lottery and it is dreamlike, although you could argue that it's just collecting my just rewards. This is both the prosaic and the poetic interpretation of this income, but I must say my main feeling is one of disbelief and a kind of floating dream-like reality surrounding this money. It's a nice feeling and I hope it continues.

August 20 2006 - Devon- family holiday

Palin responded to my letter by saying the Pythons want to leave it to the lawyers to decide about the merchandising. Of course I'm disappointed, but if the lawyers don't agree I will have to take them to court. Why ? Because I have right on my side and they are trying to cheat me. If I lose I will have to pay my costs and theirs, which will probably eat up two years of the revenue, but if I win I will have 80k a year, enough to cover all my costs and leave me free to do what I want to, which has to be to get a few films made in order to have some future royalties once the Holy Grail money washes away which it will do eventually. If I knew the money was endless then I could do anything- write a book, do volunteer work, try to raise money for the yoga centre etc. But if it is only a 5 year thing, then I need to resurrect my career so that I can continue to make films for another 10-15 years or so. This money gives me a cushion, which I need to use well. No sense at this moment of thinking of buying a holiday home or even another car. Keep your spending to a minimum until you hear what the lawyers say.

As the Robert DeNiro character says to Dustin Hoffman in Wag The Dog, " You've got decades left in you."- and isn't that the case with me. At 62 I have the health of a 40-45 year old, maybe better than that, enough energy to do whatever I want, and now enough cash to travel, dress, pursue projects, feel free etc. This is such a privileged position that most people would find it ideal, and would think you were a spoiled and silly man who couldn't see the blessing and benefits that life had given him before and continues to give him. Be thankful.

August 21, 2006 - Devon- family holiday

The idea of 120k per year coming into the company infected me with materialism, with ideas of buying a holiday home, changing your car etc. First of all I may not get the 120k because of the dispute, it may only be 60k, and secondly I must use this money- whether 60k or 120k- firstly to give myself <u>freedom</u> - the freedom to choose my projects without any pressure, the ability to travel when I need, the ability to pay for projects when necessary etc. If there is money left over from giving me an amazing amount of freedom from anxiety and from money worries, then I can use it for other purposes, whether that is reducing our mortgage or buying a 2nd home. First of all, reduce desires, and that means desire for a holiday home, or for a new car or for anything else. If I can lose those desires then I can see the subtleties, see the beginnings and ends of affairs and things, and not get lost in the illusion of materialism.

August 22 2006 - Devon - family holiday

If I had continued with the Pythons in 1975 and reaped all the rewards of that, what would I have become- how would I have used that fame, power and money? I don't think I would have used it to become free, as I am now. I think I would have locked myself into a path of seeking more- I would probably have tried to do on a bigger scale what I was forced to achieve on a small scale- putting together productions in order to what ?: make myself rich or more powerful, famous etc. Eventually I would have come to the same conclusion and position if I had followed a 'higher' path: probably failure of a production or two, some flops just like I did with the smaller films - as Roger Watkins of Variety said of you - 'flop Forstater'. And even if I had success, like Bob Shaye, would I have given myself a heart attack or an ulcer, as the price of success?

***

The Dispute - Year Two

The heart goes hard quicker in riches than an egg in boiling water.
Ludwig Borne

When I met with Lawrence Abramson he did not think the letters from Anne Henshaw would do the trick. "I doubt if this will make them change their mind," he warned.

I could only think of six things that would make them persist:

1. There was some kind of macho element in Roger Saunders' character that didn't let him back down or lose face. Maybe embracing him was not such a good idea.
2. Saunders wanted to show how great a manager he was, in saving the Pythons money by screwing me.
3. He didn't get a commission from my income, and if he brought it into the Python purse he could take a 10% share of it.
4. He thought I was easy picking. How could I stand up to the might of Python?
5. Who was I anyway? To him, a nobody.
6. One of the Pythons wanted the dispute to continue. But which one?

I decided to write again to Palin to try to get him to intervene. On July 28th 2006 I wrote him this letter:

Dear Michael,

You took the trouble to write on March 23rd to say that Roger would get back to me in a week or two, after looking into the royalty question. Four months later there is finally a response from your lawyer which I enclose for you.

I find this response very dispiriting. Over 30 years ago I agreed with Anne (approved by the group) that I should receive equal shares of the merchandising revenue with the six Pythons (1/7th of Python (Monty) Pictures share). On this basis for the past 30 years I have been invoicing and the Python company has been paying my invoices. Now with Spamalot money coming in. these invoices and the whole arrangement are called into question.

I realise Roger's job is to maximise your income, but should this be at my expense? Are you guys so short of cash that you need to try to take half of my share away? I'm really sorry it has come to this.

Kind Regards

Mark

He wrote back to me on the 16th of August, saying that the Pythons had asked their lawyers to analyse the situation and come to a conclusion. Their conclusion was that I was only entitled to the 7.1429% and not the 1/7th , so "we feel this to be the end of the matter."

The end of the matter! So that's it. Their lawyers decide unilaterally what is the truth? This felt like shutting the door in my face, but I didn't want to give up. Perhaps Michael forgot the first law of film producers: Perseverance. I wrote back on the 21st, "I realise it's now down to the lawyers, but I'm not certain they'll find the objective truth. Often they find what they are asked to look for, and fit the facts to a preconceived notion. It's easy for Roger to try to re-write history because he wasn't around 30 years ago.

However Anne was, and she knows where the bodies are buried. Have you ever asked her frankly to tell you the truth in this matter? "

I felt certain that if he asked her to be frank with him, she would tell him the truth, and he could go back to his fellow Pythons and say, we've got it wrong here. She was his friend, and I counted on him asking her the question.

It had taken a year to establish the position of the two parties. I had hit a brick wall, and it looked like going to court would be the only way to resolve the situation. However this is an expensive option. There are five of them against me, and their pockets are deeper than mine. It was far better for me to continue to try to get a negotiated settlement rather than go to court. I also believed that the Pythons would never actually come to court. I thought it would be poor PR on their behalf to try to defend their manager's actions. But I was wrong. They had two previous bouts of litigation, when larger companies were trying to rip them off, and they took them to court and won. Perhaps this gave them a sense of confidence that they had a knack for litigation, and it would work out for them. Or maybe it was just arrogance. However in this case it wasn't a large corporation trying to rip them off. It felt to me like the opposite - a large, famous and powerful entity versus a minnow.

****

My Journals 2006

September 2 2006

Back home. Feeling a little anxious and off kilter today. Not sure what I should be doing. Not relaxed and feeling a bit angry. Is this all due to being home again after 28 days away? An unsettled feeling, perhaps aggravated by the fact that the Pythons are still disputing my case. Jo says of course they will, they will go as far as they have to, and so I have to have the will to continue fighting for my right.

September 5 2006

Palin's last letter (which arrived while I was in Devon) makes it clear that the Pythons are happy with their lawyers contention. They only want the lawyers to get them the best deal they can. This saddens me but shouldn't surprise me. What a fool I have been in my dealings with them going back to 1974. But that doesn't mean I should change the way I act or want to act now. I need to now lose all those negative feelings and just deal with it on an objective basis, acting with my lawyers.

September 6 2006

The euphoria that I felt when I realised that Spamalot was able to give me a windfall was an obvious reaction, but not a good one. Too emotional, too willing to allow an external matter to buoy up my security and sense of hope/activity for the future. I allowed money once again to determine meaning and value, and this is something I have been suffering from all my life, and trying to de-condition over the past 15 years, and there I go falling into it again.

The Pythons' behaviour has brought up all the old feelings of betrayal and loss that I had 30 years ago, and rather than relive them and keep those embers alive, it's better for me to transcend them, and move on, and to look for the positive not the negative.

The fact is that I will fight for my share, no matter what it costs, and whether I win or lose, I know that even the 1/2 share will yield about 40k per year, enough to give me a cushion to continue with my films and my life, This is a great benefit and privilege and if I don't acknowledge the great blessings I have been given, then I am spiritually shrivelled and near dead.

I've squandered more than most people ever get. I've had more chances to shine and excel than most people, more opportunities to express myself than 99% of the world's population, and if I don't stop feeling a victim (a false one at that) and realise the great benefits that have been given to me, then there is little hope for me to grow and succeed.

Betrayal is such a strong emotion- no wonder that Judas is the biggest villain in the gospels. Betrayed for money, that's the worst. And that's what I have been feeling, and remembering - betrayals of the past- and no doubt these feelings- anger, mainly bottled up, - parked in my body, in my belly, legs and back gave me the mental and psychological state that I was in from 1976 to when? - maybe now in a way.

Lily asked me to pick a card and I picked <u>Forgiveness.</u> Forgive those who betrayed you, and those who betray you now, and most of all forgive yourself for whatever transgressions you made on other people - those you hurt, including yourself. We need to love each other, we need to love ourselves unconditionally. As Rabbi Hillel says, " If I am not for myself, then who is for me? And if I am for myself alone, then who am I for? - and if not now- when? Of course the Rabbi never had to deal with the British legal system.

September 25, 2006

I realised how the Python case has come to dominate my thinking. I must find a way to let this go, no matter how important it is to me in terms of money.

The Python case is so tied up with emotional stuff from the past - lost career ops, money, feelings of self-worth, betrayal, envy etc that it is no wonder the physical work of clearing the stomach/solar plexus area and the emotional baggage it brings with it go together. The two are tied in, so dealing with one means that I must deal with the other. And if I don't deal with both, then I will never clear away the emotions, memories and physical blockages that are holding me back.

October 1 2006

Without a production going, how would I have survived without the Python money? I would have used up my overdraft, taken out loans and who knows whether that would be enough or indeed if my mental state in that kind of financial situation would have allowed me to maintain the calm steadiness that I will need to get this first production going.

October 8, 2006

Last night Python night on BBC 2. Doc on Michael Palin and two on the Pythons, as well as Brazil, which now seems visionary, with its view of London terrorised by bombs and stifled by bureaucrats, with a huge gap between rich and poor.

The night brought back reminders of how much I missed out on - Life Of Brian won a Jury Prize at Cannes but I would have had a problem with Brian because of its anti-semitic bits. Would I have said nothing about this and let it pass for a peaceful life or raised the question.

It was good to watch the programmes with pleasure instead of sour responses. I hope that this dispute with the Pythons has enabled me to now deal with all that old history and the hurt associated with it. I can't live with this old anger and frustration, and need to cut it out and free myself to start again. I do feel like it's a new beginning, and beginnings can be slow and difficult. I need to cultivate patience and wait until the right moment arrives.

In the programmes they complained that Holy Grail was made for so little money that the hotels were not first class and the schedule was very short. They went on to say that Life Of Brian was easier because they had more money to spend. Why did they have more money? Because Holy Grail was such a big success. Without Holy Grail, and the work that I put into it, there would not have been Life Of Brian.

Still, one can go back from Holy Grail to the TV series, and back to Adam to find the cause of something. Best to just say that I helped to make the film, and its success has been good for me. Without it, I would not have been able to do what I have done till now. Be grateful for that, and include it as one of the blessings that I have been given, a blessing that will continue to sustain me in the future.

October 10, 2006

Hard to believe these guys are trying to take the food out of my kids' mouths.

I missed the glitz by not carrying on with the Pythons, ligging about with George Harrison, and dealing with the majors. But it may be that missing that life was right for me, otherwise I might have become a monster too.

Instead I have reversed, and gone for the ordinary, and need to stay in ordinary and simple in order to stay genuine, and to fulfil this particular destiny that I am currently playing out.

Whatever happens is going to happen. Things will play out as they are going to, and nothing I can do will alter that. The more I try to fight or alter the way it is going, the more frustrated I will be, and the more energy I will lose trying to fight against the flow of things. And the flow of things is the Tao. Relax, lay back, play the cards I am dealt in the best way I can, but don't get too worked up or embittered. Better to laugh at it all, smile, take it easy and enjoy the ride.

This is real philosophy, if only I could live it like this, rather than just writing about it - that's the test, walking the walk, not just talking the talk.

****

A Visit To Simon Olswang

We knew that Simon Olswang would be a key witness if we had to go to court. The question was, would he be a witness for the Pythons or for us? Lawrence Abramson made contact with Simon, and this is his account of that meeting:

I had first come across Simon as a very junior solicitor with what was then called Denton Hall Burgin & Warrens. Based in Chancery Lane just outside of the City, Denton Hall was by quite some way the biggest and longest established entertainment law firm in the country. Simon Olswang had just started his own firm, Simon Olswang & Co, and was viewed as something of a young upstart. We were on opposite sides of a case involving a television production company whose chief executive had drunk far too much of the company's money at places like Annabels. We exchanged much correspondence, and spoke on the telephone once or twice, but I never met him.

By now, Simon Olswang &Co had grown into the largest entertainment firm outside of the USA. It had shortened its name to Olswang and had impressive offices on Holborn and a client list that boasted the likes of BBC, ITV, Chrysalis and News International.

Simon in fact no longer worked at Olswang. Although he remained a consultant to the firm in name, it soon transpired that he spent very little time there. In fact, by this point he was spending more than half of his time in Israel. Arrangements were made through his secretary for me to go and visit him at his London home in Highgate. The meeting took place on October 6, 2006.

I got out of a taxi somewhat nervously and rang the doorbell. His wife answered the door and showed me into a sitting room. Although the house was clean, tidy and tastefully decorated and furnished, I was struck by how unassuming everything was. I had been expecting to find the house more ornate, with plenty of trappings of the wealth I imagined Simon had built up over his many years at the helm of such a successful practice, but there was none of this. The flash brash man I was expecting turned out to be a quiet, polite and very respectful gentleman.

Simon told me how he had trained at Brecher & Co from 1966 until 1968. Upon qualification, he became an assistant solicitor and then after one year he was a partner there until 1981 (how things had changed; it now took at an absolute minimum six years to become a partner anywhere in London). In March 1981 he left Brecher & Co to set up his own firm. In June 2002 he retired from the firm and from legal practice entirely.

He remembered Mark very well. He recalled that he had drafted and negotiated a number of agreements at around this time in connection with the film. This was a memorable piece of work for him, because it was the first time he had acted as the production lawyer for an entire independent production. He was technically instructed on behalf of the Company, but as Mark was to be the film's producer, he took his day to day instructions on matters concerning the film from him. He did recall having some direct contact with Anne Henshaw, who had been his point of contact with the Company when discussing corporate matters (as opposed to matters relating to the production of the Film), and how the money was going to flow.

He recalled an amusing story when some of the Pythons attended a meeting in the boardroom at Brecher & Co, bored out of their minds and not taking him or any of the other lawyers there all that seriously.

Although not surprisingly he could not recall the detailed wording of any agreement, it was his clear understanding that Mark was to be treated in the same way as the other Pythons, as for instance in the matter of his deferred fee. Likewise Mark's share of the profits was to be the same as that of each of the Pythons. When I showed him the Third Schedule of the Agreement he immediately confirmed that the handwritten amendments were his. Although these were the days before word processors, it would not have taken very long to retype the Third Schedule to the Agreement and so he could only assume that the handwritten comments were points that were raised very late in the day, probably at a completion meeting.

The Agreement provided that the profits of the Film were to be paid back to a series of people who had invested in the Film. Profits for these purposes were to include all of the proceeds from any merchandising or spin off activities from the Film e.g. the sale of records, books, articles of clothing and the like. However, the agreement between the Company and the investors provided that when one or more of the members of Monty Python carried out further work on a product, the profits from that product were to be split so that 50% went to the Company off the top (which was owned by the members of Monty Python in equal shares) and the remaining 50% to the investors. Simon's very clear understanding was that it was the intention of the parties that Mark would be treated the same as all of the other members of Monty Python such that where they were to be entitled to deduct their 50% off the top, he was entitled to receive $1/7^{th}$ of this. In effect, he was to be treated as the "7th Python", a phrase he said he recalled being used at the time. This statement was to cause a huge emotional reaction by the Pythons when they subsequently saw it in Simon's witness statement. .

Looking at the Third Schedule to the Agreement now, he said that he could see that it was capable of being read so as to suggest that where the Company deducts 50% of the merchandising income off the top ("the Top Half"), Mark was entitled to a 7.1429% share of the Top Half. That seemed to be something of an understatement but in any event he was clear that that was not his understanding of what the parties had agreed. 7.1429% is $1/7^{th}$ of 50% and $1/14^{th}$ of 100%. The intention of the parties was that Mark would receive $1/7^{th}$ of the Top Half, (or alternatively 7.1429% (i.e. $1/14^{th}$) of 100% of the merchandising income before deduction of the Top Half).

In all, I was with Simon for just over an hour. When we were finished, he kindly agreed to drive me to Highgate Station and agreed that he would sign a witness statement for Mark. So I now had not only 30 years of practice of the Pythons paying Mark $1/7^{th}$ of the Top Half, plus Mark's very clear recollection of the fact that this is what had been agreed, but also the equally clear recollection of the lawyer who had drafted the agreement. I felt we now had all we need to bring an end to this case with a very favourable settlement for Mark. How wrong I turned out to be.

The Dispute- Litigation - Year 2

A quarrel is like an itch: the more you scratch, the more it itches. Jewish saying.

In April 2005, one of the investors in the film wrote to the NFTC asking what was happening with Spamalot. Louisa Bewley of the NFTC wrote back saying that the show was starting to bring in some revenue, but there was a legal bill to offset against the revenue. I saw an email between Ian Miles (of the Python management team) and Ms Bewley dated June 14, 2005 which showed that the legal bill was $ 65,000 which was paid by all the profit participants in The Holy Grail.

This sounded like a lot of money to me, so I asked a lawyer friend in New York how this appeared to him. He told me the legal fees to license a film to be made into a theatre production (which this was) could cost as little as $10,000 and as much as $ 25,000. For it to be $ 65,000 meant it was extremely complex or complicated. Why was it so complicated? It should have been a straightforward licensing of the right to make a theatrical show out of the film of the Holy Grail. We discovered later why the bill was so high.

Once Lawrence Abramson took over the case, we started to look at other issues surrounding Spamalot. There had been press reports that Eric Idle was making large sums of money from Spamalot at the expense of the other members of the team. An article in the Independent said "Idle took two-thirds of the profit, the last third to be divided equally between the remaining members." In another report, Roger Saunders said the Pythons were earning each year between £ 300,000 - 500,000 from Spamalot.

I wondered why they were being so mingy about disputing my income when they were making so much themselves. It just didn't make sense. Why bother? In any case, the money coming to me was from the Spamalot box office - it wasn't coming out of their pockets. We also wondered why Eric was giving money to the other Pythons. According to the deal that applied to all spin-offs, the Pythons were meant to retain 50% of the income and 50% was to go to the investors/profit participants. The company that controlled the rights- Python (Monty) Pictures Ltd. - was owned by the 6 Pythons, and that included Eric Idle.

So he was meant to get a share of the 50% of the top half with all the other Pythons. Why was he paying them? And where was he paying them from? Was there another company that had been put into the income stream (as had been done with the music and book deals) to give the Pythons money off the top before the investors (and I) had their share? Had the Python team done a deal outside of the 50-50 arrangement? This is something we wanted to know.

******

It was October 16, 2006 and Spamalot was about to have its London premiere. Michael White rang to ask if I was going, and I had to admit that I was not invited. I thought this was very petty.
This is how I recorded it in my journal:

Today spoke to Michael White who asked if I was going to the Spamalot Premiere and party. I told him I wasn't invited and he couldn't believe it. I explained I was in dispute with them, which is why I was not invited. He said without me it would never have happened and he said that without wanting to flatter. He meant it, and of course it's true, but as I said to him, they don't want to believe it.

It would have been good to go, but it would also be awkward, which is why they didn't invite me. No matter. What I am interested in is getting the money owed me, and I need no credit or time in the spotlight. It's yet another missed opportunity, but then you've gotten over all the others, why won't you get over this one?

In hindsight (oh how easy is hindsight) I should have stopped wondering about how the Spamalot deal had been constructed, and should have just made my Rectification claim against the Pythons for my 1/7th share. I would have won the case and could have saved myself years of continuing dispute with the Pythons. But their managers were being so cagey that I thought they must be hiding something. I thought that there was more income being hidden which by right I should have had a share in.

On December 20, 2006 Lambeth responded to Lawrence Abramson. He made it clear that Python (Monty) Pictures was not the producer of Spamalot, but Ostar Enterprises of New York was, and they had licensed the rights from Python (Monty) Pictures.

On 25 January 2007, Abramson wrote to Lambeth, saying that if Idle was the only Python to 'materially' contribute to the making of Spamalot, and his remuneration for doing so was being paid outside of Python (Monty) Pictures Ltd, then Abramson was querying on what basis were the Pythons taking their 50% share. They can't take it because of Idle's contribution, since he is being paid outside of the Python company. This is an interesting point, and of course it's actually one that would not work in my favour, since if the Pythons had no basis for charging the 50% of Spamalot income, then I would not be able to invoice for my 1/7th of it.

Lambeth responded on February 13 2007 saying that Python (Monty) Pictures Ltd. did in fact contribute to the making of Spamalot. Although not involved in the actual production it was "actively involved in all stages of script and musical development."

Not according to Eric Idle it didn't. In his online history The Tale of Spamalot he makes it very clear that the book, music and lyrics were written totally by himself and John Du Prez on spec. He notes that they began writing the first draft in late 2001 and it was finished by the end of January 2002. They then recorded the book and songs on CD and sent the speculative work to the Pythons for approval. The Pythons all responded well to the script and lyrics and gave it their seal of approval.

The two Terrys, Michael and John all agreed that Eric should go ahead and try to mount a production. They agreed that it was his project but they could be useful in providing some feedback. Eric and John then produced a second draft incorporating the Pythons' comments and criticism. Again this was well received, and Terry Gilliam expressed initial interest in helping with the design, but decided he should stick to movies.

It's pretty clear to me that the only Python to do any writing or make any material contribution to Spamalot was Idle alone, and none of the other Pythons were "actively involved in all stages of script and musical development."

In his letter of January 25, Abramson pointed out that I had the right under Clause 11c to hire accountants to examine the books for the purpose of checking the accuracy of the Python accounting. He also asked to see copies of all Agreements in place between the Pythons and any other party (be it Eric Idle, Ostar Enterprises or anybody else) in respect of Spamalot. "Will your client produce copies of these to me, or does my client have to engage a chartered accountant to get copies for him?"

This request was greeted with a comment from Lambeth (in his letter of February 13, 2007), that in his view we were not challenging the 'accuracy' of the accounting but only the 'basis' of the accounting. We couldn't audit because we were questioning the basis of the accounting rather than the accuracy? At this point it was clear we were facing yet another blank wall, and gave up corresponding with them. Lawrence Abramson wrote to Lambeth on March 20 2007 saying, "My client will be pursuing this matter through the courts."

****

My Journals 2006-2007

My journals record my not always consistent thinking:

October 17, 2006

Today I remembered when I first saw the credits for the Holy Grail film, and I was shocked and taken aback (read upset) about how my credit was treated, and I believe deliberately belittled. I never mentioned this to anyone, then or later, but I remembered it now, when I have not been invited to the Spamalot premiere. Two small petty acts, but somehow they capture the Pythons' attitude to me. For years now I have blamed my arrogance, my youthful stupidity in publicly discussing the competence of the two Terrys as directors as being the reason why they didn't continue working with me. And I think the above is true - I didn't know how to handle 'creative' people then as I do now. But I also realise now that they were too sensitive and also arrogant too, in the sense that they weren't big enough to realise that the film would not have happened without me, and that the success of the film had something to do with my involvement. Perhaps they knew that I was not a yes man, was not going to agree to everything they wanted to do, as if the sun shone out of their asses. So they were happier working with an easier going, more compliant producer.

Seeing that my non-involvement was a two-way street, involving not just my arrogance but also theirs helps me to not put all the blame on myself. The fact is I was the producer of a very successful film, but I didn't have the experience or the nous to know how to capitalise on it. In that sense I had no one to 'blame' but myself.

Today I feel good, very strong, very determined. Funny but when I first realised there would be money in Spamalot I worried about whether they would pay my invoices. When they questioned them, my fears were realised. Then Bob Storer read the contract and thought my case was bad. At this point had they offered me my 1/7th if I didn't pursue any other claims I would have jumped at it. Now I am pursuing them whole-heartedly, without fear, and with a strong sense of righteousness. How my attitude has changed. And I'm happy charging them with my courage than cowering in my fear. I think the past few months have given me many chances to move out of the fear of old into a different future.

October 18, 2006

Yesterday an article in The Times about how much the Pythons are making from Spamalot-
$ 10,000 a week. It annoyed me that they are taking so much and disputing my small portion. It's going to go on for a long time with its many ups and downs and I've got to find a way to deal with it without getting on an emotional rollercoaster or letting myself become obsessive about it and let it take over my life. Find the right perspective on it, otherwise all my practises will be ruined. Find constancy, serenity, tranquillity and detachment in it. Don't let emotions like anger and envy take me over. Stay in the sage's posture and attitude. Whatever will work out will work out, relax and let it go.

October 21. 2006

I hear that Terry Jones has bowel cancer. I knew he had two hip replacements, but I didn't realise he was this ill. I feel sorry for him. Perhaps this is what Eric Idle was referring to when he said they will only get together in future for their funerals.

October 29, 2006 - Philadelphia

My mother's funeral. It's good that I have the money to make this trip like this- air fare, car hire, hotel- A few years ago it would have been harder to spend that kind of money, when things were tighter, but now I can splash out- great privilege. I always worried about whether I would find it difficult to pay for the trip when my mom dies, and now I see how useless that anxiety was. The need arises, the money appears. Isn't that always the way it has worked, even though for years I never trusted that it worked like that.

January 20 2007

Response from the Pythons. I need to decide how to proceed: by myself or with the other investors? Via court or asking for documents through the NFTC? I'll talk to the lawyers on Monday and decide. Perhaps consult the I Ching.

I'm worried about the cost of my court case but I suppose if I can collect a production fee this year I can afford to pay for it. Hope so. Am I just wasting my money or will it pay off?

January 26 2007

Looking back I can see that I was very naive, and also fearful and insecure. I was acting from a fractured sense of self, but now I am feeling much more whole, much more integrated, and so I feel that I can now act with them in a better way than I did in 1975. Maybe they think I'm still the same person, but I know I've changed, and maybe that will make the difference. I want to see this through. I want to be paid what I'm due. And I suppose I want to prove to myself that I have changed - I am my own master, and whether I win or lose this case doesn't matter. It's important for me to see this through.

January 27, 2007

The person suing the Pythons is not the person who made the film with them in 1974. I have transformed since then, and the old fears and insecurities I once held that I associated with my relationship to them are now all gone or should be.

February 11, 2007

I read an article by Melanie McFadyean about her grandfather Herbert Guttman from Berlin whose father started the Dresdner Bank. Guttman went from an 80 room villa in Berlin to homelessness in London in 1939, but his attitude was that "Money lost, nothing lost. Sense of humour lost, everything lost". This is the right attitude to have in my current situation, where I am starting to worry about how I can fund everything. But this will all work out. Have faith.

My Python case is from the past, so it is in some sense karmic, and has come to teach me something, and also to be perhaps the last remnant of the old way of living and being. I can't say that no other karmic residues from the past will not come up; after all, the past was long and I did many things with many people. I may still have some comeback from things I did then.

February 27, 2007

Funny how things work out. Now I feel that whatever I missed from that time, which led to a feeling of loss, has now been made good by standing up for myself in this case. I say to myself I have my own position, I have my own rights and no one can take them from me. This standing up for myself gives me strength, or perhaps it has only come about through inner strength (cart before the horse?) and so I am now the person I am, and that person is able to stand up for himself.

March 31, 2007

Spoke to Bob Storer. On the Python front, he thinks they will not want to go to court, and that they will settle beforehand if I take them to court. I agree with this.

April 12, 2007

I'm worried about money- how much will come in from Spamalot, and will it be enough to not just pay for life but also all the legal fees that are projected.

June 22, 2007

Having the Spamalot money has given me the cushion that lets me have positive thoughts rather than negative ones. Or is it the other way round, that it is the positive thoughts that has attracted the money. Chicken or egg, which came first? They all arise at the same time.

December 5, 2007

How would I have coped without the Spamalot money? My life for the past 2 years would have been completely different. I think we would have had to sell the house to pay off the mortgage and I would have had to get some kind of job - who knows what? Lecturing? At £ 120 per day.

Spamalot is keeping me alive. Should I just let it carry on without making a fuss? Or should I try to get what is owing to me?

****

The Claims - Year 3

God loves the poor and helps the rich.
Jewish saying.

On July 4 2008 Lawrence Abramson sent a Letter of Claim to Lambeth setting out the three claims we were making. The first and most important was the Claim for Rectification of the written agreement. In simple terms, rectification means that if the agreement can be read as to give me only $1/14^{th}$ of the Spamalot and other merchandising income then the true intention of the parties has not been executed in the Agreement. The true intention of the parties, we claimed, was to give me a 1/7th share of the merchandising and spin off income. The Pythons were arguing that the Agreement, as they read it, was correct as it stood and did not need to be rectified.

Our main arguments were that I had issued invoices for a $1/7^{th}$ share for 30 years and that these had all been paid, and that the correspondence with Anne Henshaw from 1977 showed that the Pythons understood the true nature of the agreement. To pursue this claim we asked that the Pythons disclose to us all the invoices that I had sent them (I didn't have a complete record) and that we have a chance to look at the unpublished sections of Michael Palin's diaries to see if further evidence could be found there.

The second Claim was specifically about Spamalot. We were unhappy that we were being denied the right to look at the Agreement between the Pythons and Ostar Enterprises, the theatre company, as well as any other agreements with Eric Idle's company. Without sight of these, we could not ascertain how the income was flowing from Spamalot to Python (Monty) Pictures Ltd. The only way we could force them to disclose these agreements was by making a claim, We were also concerned about the $ 65,000 legal bill and wanted to find out why that was so high.

The third claim did not involve the Pythons (only their management company) so I won't go into any detail on that. For those of you struggling with all this legal stuff that is probably a great relief.

On August 28 2008 Paul Lambeth responded. Firstly, he complained that he hadn't heard from us since March 2007 and so assumed that the matter was closed, Regarding our claim for Rectification, he saw no logic in my receiving an equal share of any merchandising or spinoff income if I made no contribution to it. He's right that I made no contribution to Spamalot, but it's also evident in Eric Idle's account of the making of Spamalot that none of the other Pythons contributed anything either.

Lambeth added that he was not going to ask his clients to waste time and expense locating the invoices I requested and said that the personal diaries of Michael Palin did not belong to his clients but that anyway they did not accept I had a right to see them because Palin was a company director of his client and added no one agreed that I should be paid 1/7th of the merchandising profits. So -get lost!

So basically- get lost!

****

My Journals 2008

January 10, 2008

Three days ago I thought that someone would make a film about the Holy Grail, for TV, and the next day I got a call from someone at the BBC saying they want to do it, amazing.

January 20, 2008

Last night in the bath I realised that this TV show- Movie Connections- about the Holy Grail, will give me a chance to look again at the events of 74-75, mainly by reading Michael Palin's Diaries.

Come to think of it, I haven't heard from the BBC for a while and I wonder if the Pythons are suggesting to them that perhaps I shouldn't take part. Is this me being paranoid, or would they be petty enough to do something like this? Given that they failed to invite me to the Spamalot premiere, I wouldn't put it past them.

If this is the price I have to pay for pursuing my rights than I just have to live with it. It would be good for me to have the exposure, but if I don't get it it's not the end of the world.

January 21, 2008

No word from the BBC re: Movie Connections. I think the Pythons may have said to them, include Forstater and we don't take part. Just a hunch, maybe I'm wrong.

I'll have to make my way on my own, can't rely on the old successes to help me, especially when I have such a petty enemy trying to hurt me- no invite to Spamalot, this. They have become like the people they used to despise and mock. Sad.

January 24, 2008

What I am missing is compassion for my enemies. Difficult to feel compassion for the Pythons when they are trying to take away my income. But that is the mark of a truly great person, like the Dalai Lama, to have love and compassion for those who want to do you harm. Can I really feel like this? I know that it's necessary if I really want my heart to grow, and my spirit to evolve.

February 6, 2008

How to pay for the case? I guess I need to increase my overdraft if they want to take this all the way to the High Court.

February 7 2008

No further news from the BBC re: Holy Grail TV show. I suspect the Pythons have put pressure on the Beeb not to invite me to take part. The show was to record Feb-March so it must be in planning now. I think I've been cut out. So petty of them. Amazing, well let's hope I can get back something from them in court.

March 9, 2008

I thought that I understood the Taoist hermits who would not give up one hair from their head to save or serve the empire. They had found tranquillity and life was giving them everything they needed. Why give that up to take on the troubles of running the empire? So it is with me. Every day is fine, every hour and minute the same, I feel no ambition, no desire for things to be different, or better, and yet here I am actively trying to get some films made, to give myself a lot of work and activity. Film production is no way to achieve tranquillity.

And I'm suing the Pythons, to endure another year of anxiety and worry - for what? Money.

March 12, 2008

Reading Palin's Diaries, I saw how things developed in the early days of the Python film. How John Gledhill, their then manager, wanted to produce the film but I got to do it.

Reading it I felt proud of how well I handled myself and what a good job I did for them. I felt my competence, my power, and I realised how well I did things then. It filled my heart with gladness.

I almost feel like writing to Palin again, but it's gone too far for that.

All of the weakness, all of the failure I felt after being dropped, all that I can now see was a response to, in a way, my hurt. I needed their approval to feel good about myself, and when that wasn't there I collapsed in a way. Now I think I'm somewhat different - I don't need anyone's approval, and I can feel good about myself without having it reflected from someone else's opinions.

It's taken me a long time to get here, it's really been the journey of a lifetime, but here I am, and they won't be able to budge me or knock me over or roll over me so easily. They have the name, the power, the money and I have only the right, and a thirst for justice.

It's just for a while I forgot how strong I was; maybe that strength lost something that made it effective, that made it work. What was that, what happened to me? For a number of years I certainly did not feel strong, I had a feeling of loss, of inability, of weakness. Maybe I lost my strength.

I didn't want to read Palin's Diaries because I thought they would make me sad, would remind me of times I would rather forget, but so far I'm pleased to be reminded of who I was at 30 years old - 34 years ago - a young, dynamic, ambitious but fair guy who was able to work hard and achieve something. Success, however, teaches you nothing, but failure- ah, that's the great teacher - and loss - embrace loss, as Cheng Man Ching said.

Auden's poem - Alonso to Ferdinand - says it all. Incredible that it has taken me 33 years to get over that slight. Had I died young, I would never have known this moment. What I would have missed. That is true loss.

March 14, 2008

Reading Palin's Diaries. Remembering how difficult it was to make the Holy Grail. These Diaries pinpoint dates of Python meetings, say when Anne Henshaw takes over running of Python, and I'm sure the later ones deal with Spamalot, so there will be ample corroborating evidence in these original diary pages if we can call them.

March 16, 2008

In the Python Big Book Terry Jones really slams me about complaining about having 2 directors. This reminds me of my credit on the film which was really buried and which I felt shocked by when I first saw it. Perhaps this case of mine will make up for it.

Idle remarks how litigious the Pythons are "when someone takes advantage of them". But now the shoe is on the other foot- they are taking advantage of me. I don't want this case to be one of revenge, I don't want to feel resentment at all these old slights. Keep my feelings and resentments to myself and try to transform them, transform anger into compassion, see them as flawed people not malicious ones. Better to feel sorry for them than to be angry at them.

March 17 2008

I got angry at Terry Jones because of what he wrote in the Python Autobiography book. That came out in 2003, and he still is angry about how I acted in 1974, 30 years later. The fact is that the Holy Grail film gave the Pythons the chance to make Brian, gave the 2 Terrys directing careers, and made them all millionaires. Yet all I have ever heard from them for 30 years is complaints!

King Lear says ingratitude is sharper than a serpent's tooth. He must have been thinking of the Pythons. Anger towards them is wrong however. I need to be compassionate towards their ignorance.

The fact that all these qualities - of competition, greed, self-obsession - has now given me an opportunity to get at them (for money genuinely owed to me) is again another benefit and blessing for me.

Not inviting me to the Spamalot opening, bad-mouthing me 30 years after the event- this is really low behaviour. It's now my time to get back at this. I'm in a fighting mood.

March 21, 2008

Good Friday. Finished Roth's I Married a Communist, which dealt with betrayal, and Roth said that Burton's Anatomy of Melancholy dealt with everything except what caused you to be melancholic. Roth thought that betrayal was one of the reasons people became melancholic or depressed.

This got me thinking about my own betrayals - by the Pythons and others. Roth argues that betrayal is an act of revenge, a hitting out against someone who they could make vulnerable to begin with, who was perhaps even strong.

The Pythons, in not asking me to continue with them, did betray me in the sense that they showed little appreciation for what I had done for them, and wanted to belittle my contribution. They hurt both my career and income prospects, but I did not understand till now that it was not my weakness or vulnerability that brought on the betrayal, but my strength, which is now not only intact but also greater than ever.

I did make mistakes in handling the Grail situation, - inexperience, my own inadequacy of character. I blamed myself for this failure. I was right to blame myself, but this was only half the story. The other half I now see, was their inexperience, their inadequacy, their pettiness and 'artistic' reaction, their bruised egos- that was the other side of my 'betrayal'. Now having all this in proper perspective I want to put it all behind me. and just carry on as if it did not happen.

Woke this morning wanting to read again about Cheng Man Ching's idea of accepting loss and accepting pain, since this is what I have to do, in fact what I feel I have now done.

Also reminded of Richard Sennett's 'corrosion of character', about dealing with failure. He says there are many books about achieving success but few about coping with failure. We have to buy into our failure in the same way that Cheng says we must buy into our pain and loss - they are all the same thing, Accept your failure, incorporate it into your body and mind, let it become part of you, but do not let it distort you. To make loss pain and failure streams that flow into the ocean of your strength and therefore can't harm it or alter it but only add to it.

That which does not destroy you makes you stronger.

March 24, 2008

Yesterday I told Lawrence to go ahead with the Python case. I'm convinced that I am owed lots of dosh and I'm going to have to fight for it if I want it. I have lots of plans, things I could do with it. I have to assume that as long as I pursue this case I will be better off than accepting the status quo. The difficulty is if they decide to fight the case and I need to pay for the court. Can I do that?

April 20, 2008

The Python case has enabled me to take a new view of those events and has given me the chance to sweep away that negativity, which must be one of the main obstructions to my image of myself, and my feelings as a producer. Not only that, but Spamalot has been a windfall, giving me the finance to not just develop movies, but also to reprint yoga and Tao Te Ching books and audios both of which are important to keep alive.

May 26 2008- Juan-Les-Pins (attending the Cannes Film Festival)

Re: The Python case: "Better to live like a lion for one day than like a lamb for 100". But if you are a 'sheep' like me, maybe it's better to live like a sheep for 100 days than like a lion for one. Lion or sheep, I don't want to lie down and let someone cheat me without doing something about it. Is this just my ego acting, or is it a response from my essence, a part of me that was injured and is now feeling intact and so powerful again. There is always the possibility of loss; my lawyers are certainly not confident. But I believe that much is hidden, and if the hidden is revealed I believe it will vindicate my position. And I'm willing to fight, which is really indicative of a younger me. I also trust the I Ching which gave a positive reading to the case. I have to trust my gut response, which from early on, the first bit of information that seeped out, that I was being taken for a ride. If I'm wrong, I've misread this situation badly. But can my belly be so wrong? Don't think so.

When I produced the Holy Grail I had a very idealistic view of what I was doing, and about looking after myself, not trying to get as much from the film, in profit percentage terms, as I probably should have.

When Julian asked for his share of the profits there was nowhere to give them but out of mine. It has made him a lot of money and made me less.

Now I find it incredible that the Spamalot situation has brought me to a point where all of these old slights and betrayals can get paid for, a karmic revolution has come about, in which I have been able not only to see that my 'fault' was really very small indeed and that their pettiness and ingratitude that were the other side of the coin. This rebalancing and recasting of memory and of the past had been so good for me psychologically and I also hope it will make up for what I had to give away.

This karmic revolution or retribution also leads me to believe that it is right to pursue this case since it is an opportunity to put right something which has affected me for a very long time.

There is some revenge here, but it is totally unsought. It's been delivered to me by time, circumstance, their continued behaviour, in fact it has arisen "of itself". I have not tried to create it, it landed right on my plate.

I suppose to win back what I lost all those years ago will be satisfying, in financial terms, but haven't I already gained back what I lost in character terms?

June 8 2008

On my return to London I read the first Claim letter to the Pythons and was heartened by the contents. I think my cases (three of them) are all good, and I am hopeful that they will negotiate rather than defend.

June 11, 2008

Dinner last night with Uri, Ahmed and Terry Gilliam. Realised later that I have known Terry since 1962- 46 years! It's a shame our friendship died with the Holy Grail, Last night he said they were all 'naive'. I suppose that also includes me, but it sounded like this was his excuse for the way I was treated. It made me realise that it was not just opportunities and dosh etc that I missed by not staying in that gravy train but also friendships and companionship. I had to make new contacts and friends but there is no doubt that I became isolated. This was the loss that I didn't acknowledge before, but that I understand now. Ironic that this link with Terry is being made just at the point when I am about to sue them. As Jo says, lawsuits and friendships don't go together. This Python thing will very likely end whatever relationship I had with Palin, Terry J and now Terry G, but how much is their friendship worth when they are happy for their manager to try to screw me out of half of my profits, which are a small portion of what they are getting.

June 15th: Jo and I decided to separate. We both felt that our love had eroded over the years, and we were travelling on different tracks. We didn't want to stay together for the sake of the children, so we told them what was happening and I moved temporarily into the spare bedroom, a box room. The breakup was amicable. Cleo, 15, was pleased at the idea of eventually having a 2nd home to visit, and Lily, 7, was concerned that I would take all the furniture with me. We assured her that I wouldn't.

July 3, 2008

Tomorrow the claim letter goes to the Pythons and they have 30 days to answer- August 4th. There are two possibilities- either they want to talk or they disclose the evidence. The third possibility is that they fail to disclose, waiting to see if we go to court to get disclosure, but it seems to me that this is a serious letter and they would have to assume that going to court is the next step. I have always thought they would not want to disclose these agreements and I also think Palin will not want to disclose his diaries, so my hunch is that we will be in talks. I certainly hope so, as I don't want to go through a year of court, I can't really afford it.

August 7, 2008

No response from the Pythons, so now we prepare a court order. Meeting tomorrow. Are they just waiting to see if I will go that next step or what? In a way it is a huge poker game- who will last- will it be my resolve or theirs?

September 2, 2008

Today the Python's response came in and I thought it was fairly weak. I will wait to see what Lawrence and George (Hayman - Barrister) make of it. I'm glad this is active again - it gives me a focus for my energy. Also I need to be feeling aggressive and offensive in relation to the Python claim.

***

The Dispute - Year 3

An Opportune Encounter

In which the Third Chance for a Settlement occurs

Only a few days after receiving yet another unhelpful letter from the Pythons' solicitor (five pages long in which they rejected all of my claims), I was walking away from Soho Square when I came face to face with Michael Palin. We both smiled at the incongruity of this encounter, and Palin jokingly pulled his arms and upper body away from me (as if expecting an attack). We had a laugh about meeting like this, and a quick discussion. He said that we should never go to court on this matter; friends should not have to let things go this far. I agreed, and I told him that as I was getting nowhere with his lawyers and manager that that we were inexorably heading for the courts. He asked what we could do to prevent it, and I volunteered to ask my lawyers to stop their preparation and to make a settlement offer.

So later that day, September 3, 2008 I wrote to Michael,

Dear Michael,

It was very good to see you (and your smile) in Soho today. I am pleased that you agree with me that our current problem should not become a public squabble, which will be messy, time-consuming and expensive.

However, leaving it to the lawyers was always going to lead to court.

The current situation is this: In July my lawyers sent your guys a letter of claim, and this week your lawyers responded by saying effectively, 'go away'. The next stage will be that my lawyers respond to your letter giving a final deadline for disclosure. If that deadline passes then we would have to go to court for disclosure of the documents.

To avoid this scenario what I would instead like to do is to ask my lawyers to respond to your lawyers' letter, but at the same time to suggest an offer of settlement, which if agreed would remove any need to go to court.

I hope this can make a sensible conclusion for all of us.

Kind Regards

Mark

So I consulted my lawyers and made an offer to settle. The letter read:

"Our client would far prefer that matters between him and the various former members of Monty Python do not end up in Court. With that in mind, he is prepared to compromise this dispute on the following basis:

Your client pays to our client such sums as are required so as to ensure that he receives the same share of income from Spamalot as all other former members of Monty Python with the exception of Eric Idle, together with interest on his underpayments at the rate of 2% over base from time to time.

Your client pays our client such sums as are necessary to ensure that he receives one-seventh of all other merchandising income received by your client together with interest thereon as provided for in paragraph 2 above.

Your client agrees to account to our client in this way going forward.

Your client reimburses our client his legal costs in this matter.

Our client in return will drop his remaining claims against your client."

Basically what I was asking for was to be treated equally to all the Pythons (excluding Eric Idle, who was receiving substantial income for writing the book, lyrics and music from Spamalot).

Given that the money being paid to me was coming from the Spamalot box-office and not from the Pythons' own pockets, I thought this would not be a difficult position for them to accept.

My legal fees were only about £ 5000 at this point, and theirs was possibly the same, so it was no hardship for them to have covered that. I thought this settlement offer could work if they really wanted a way out.

From my journal:

September 11 2008

Yesterday we sent the Pythons the Settlement offer and gave them 21 days to respond- October 1st deadline. Lawrence thinks they will not do a deal, so I must face going to court. If they did settle, wow, what a result.

September 27, 2008

I realise that making an offer to them is a very good thing, because it will force them off the fence. Either they say no to the offer completely (in which case court beckons) or they make me the 1/14th offer of all the income in which case they are admitting there is other income. This would lead me to A. make a fight about the 1/7th and if that failed to perhaps go to a mediator regarding the 1/7th. A Mediation is not a court - we wouldn't need to prove what the contract said, we would only need to convince that the Pythons knew the deal was 1/7th as evidenced by the letters and invoices. In this way we avoid costs of court and I think I would win with a mediator.

October 19 2008

I saw a news report that Spamalot's Broadway run is coming to an end in January. Suddenly the bottom fell out of all my plans. No more money through property development and making money through property, since I won't be collecting the levels of royalties I envisaged (assuming of course that I win my case against the Pythons). So I am back at square one, needing now to make a film or two that makes money so I can carry on.

I also may not be able to have the luxury of not making a salary on these films, , since I may now need to make money and will not have any excess to invest. Reality check. How this news will effect my plans to move out will also be a question? I'm more than ever dependent on resolving the Python case to give me any chance of starting a new life. Maybe I need to re-think the whole thing from scratch.

I've got a wobble in my being today that I didn't have before. Isn't it pathetic that it is income that gives me my security and once the thought appears of that income disappearing suddenly my insides turn into jelly and I become a hopeless case. Where is all the strength, confidence and stability that I said was mine before? Has all my philosophy and practice really just brought me to this state of helplessness and hopelessness? Do I really think this new situation will just drop me into a trough of despond from which I cannot emerge Am I really a lost cause? The spent force that I joke about? Do I see myself in a couple of years' time asking for my old age pension and just trying to live on that somewhere without having any extra cash to put into development, travel, clothes etc? Am I that sad a case, or can I, before it all runs out get myself established again so that I can restart my career and really have that second act? It's time to consider which way this will play out. Do I need to consult the I Ching or do I want to just read the signs and see how it all plays out over the next few months? As Bucky Fuller said, Treat your life like an experiment and see how it plays out and where it leads you. This is the way to keep it fresh, not to make concrete plans for the future based on false thoughts, but to respond to things as they happen and to keep it real by responding spontaneously to reality itself.

Nov 17 2008

The Python lawyer says they are now considering my offer. Being on the offensive against the Pythons feels good to me, like a pent-up dam is about to give way.

***

Lambeth responded on October 2 2008 asking for clarification, which we gave him on October 15 2008. I also conceded that if there was a settlement that I would not need to conduct an audit. Finally on December 02, 2008 we got a letter saying that the Pythons rejected my offer to settle.

There is no attempt to negotiate or try to find an acceptable compromise. It's very black and white, cut and dried. I make an offer and they reject it. No discussion, no haggling, no wriggle room.

Here is my journal entry reflecting on it:

Dec 3 2008

The Pythons do not want to negotiate and Lawrence feels I owe too much to start another case. I plan to write to Palin. My preference is to go to court and seek the documents so at least I will know what they have done. With those I can judge how likely a case would be to succeed. Difficult time. I plan to write to Palin, possibly tomorrow or Friday, and then wait and see what response I get. Do it little by little, stage by stage.

So ended the third (and I think best) possible chance for a settlement.

Never Give Up

I have looked well into the papers. I have been deep in them for months, and you may rely upon it that we shall come out triumphant. As to years of delay, there has been no want of them, heaven knows!
Bleak House

This is the letter I sent to Palin (edited version)

December 4, 2008

Dear Michael

I have just received a letter from your solicitors rejecting my proposal for an equal share of the merchandising/Spamalot revenue. As you know I put this proposal forward in an attempt to avoid going to court. However this response leaves me with no alternative.

Before I do that I wanted to explain to you directly about my proposal. I want to make sure you understand the nature of my claims. I hope you will take the time to read this letter to the end, and I will try to keep it as brief as I can. I've left out some details, but I think I have covered the main points. I have three claims. This is claim one:

1. The question of merchandising or spin-off revenues and profits arose in 1974 when Tony Stratton-Smith wanted to produce a record of the Holy Grail soundtrack. Anne Henshaw requested that for making this record the Pythons (as Python (Monty) Pictures Ltd.) should have a 50% share of the revenue/royalties/profits of this record and any other spin-offs in which a significant amount of Python work was required. The investors agreed with this proposal.

2. I raised with Anne the fact that under this arrangement as the producer of the film I would be missing out on a share of the spinoff revenue/profits that I would normally be expecting. I thought that in the circumstances I should be entitled to an equal share of what you were receiving– ie 1/7th of that 50% (based on 6 Pythons plus me =7). She thought my point was reasonable and suggested I come to a meeting of the Pythons to put my proposal.

3. I attended a meeting at the Henshaw's house on Regent's Park Road in March or April 1974 at which at least 3-4 of you were in attendance to make this proposal. My memory is that you, the two Terrys and Graham were there, but it was a long time ago and so I cannot be certain on that point.

4. You agreed that I should have this 1/7th share and Ann asked Simon Olswang, the lawyer dealing with the

film, to put the arrangement into a Third Schedule to my producer's agreement. I attach for you a copy of the wording of this Schedule. Even your lawyers admit that the drafting is very confusing and it can be interpreted in a number of ways. From that time on until 2005 I invoiced Python (Monty) Pictures for 1/7th of 50% of spin off royalties and these invoices were never questioned and always paid.

5. To back up my original claim I cite correspondence between Ann Henshaw and myself regarding the proposed publication of a book of the film. In that correspondence I wrote to Ann on June 23 1977 seeking to clarify how my merchandising share would work with the book. I wrote to her::' in the original deal negotiated I was allocated 1/7th of the Python's share of any spin-offs. Under this proposed deal I lose that share. Would the Pythons be willing to bring me in on the Python Productions side so that my 1/7th share remains the same?'

Ann wrote back to me on July 28th 1977 confirming,

'You will after all be receiving your investor's share plus 1/7th of 50% of the amount paid to the N.F.T.C. which will be Python (Monty) Pictures' share!

For clarification, let me explain that at that time the NFTC were collecting all the film and spin off revenues and distributing them to the investors and to your company. My invoices were based on the statements of revenue from the NFTC. In this letter Ann confirms my interpretation of the spin off share, which Roger Saunders later disputes. I attach the letters for you.

6. In 2005 when the Spamalot revenues started appearing I invoiced for 1/7th of the 50% that you had retained. This is as I had been doing since 1975 as per Ann's letter. However Roger Saunders claimed that the agreement does not refer to 1/7th of 50% but to only 7.1429% per cent and so he has only agreed to pay 50% of my invoiced amounts.

(The figure of 7.1429 % in the agreement can only have been arrived at by dividing 50 by 7). This interpretation is directly contrary to Ann Henshaw's letter and the practise of the past 30 years.

7. Effectively accusing me of false accounting since 1975, your company then clawed back 50% of the moneys that I had been paid under invoice for the 6 years leading up to 2005.

8. So my first claim is that the 50% of the invoiced amounts that have not been paid should be paid to me, including repaying the amounts clawed back, plus interest.

Claim number two:

1. It is clear from press interviews that Eric is paying the other Pythons a third of his royalties from Spamalot, bypassing Python (Monty) Pictures Ltd. Without seeing the agreements (due to confidentiality clauses) I can't tell how this has been done, but my surmise is that Python (Monty) Pictures Ltd. did not license the entire film to Ostar Enterprises Inc., but artificially limited the license to the screenplay of the film for a small royalty. This allowed the individual Pythons to license other production elements from the film (such as art work, lyrics, music, costumes, performances, brand etc) to Eric's company to pass on to Ostar Enterprises. In this way royalties that should have gone to Python (Monty) Pictures and been shared with me and the investors have gone to Eric's company and been transferred to you.

2. If this has been the mechanism, then I feel entitled to an equal share of those royalties, under my merchandising agreement. If I take the case to court, these agreements will be opened and I will see if my surmise is correct. I assume the other investors might also find these of interest.

(I omit my reference to Claim 3)

It's on the basis of these claims that I asked for an equal share of the Spamalot royalties with you, John, the Two Terries and Graham's estate. I think you know my character and reputation; I would not be making these claims as a try-on, but only seek to be paid moneys which I am entitled to as per our original agreement.

I still believe that going to court is not the right action, but you leave me no alternative. Stop hiding behind your lawyers and ask Ann. She was there at the time and knows the truth of the matter. What would she say in court regarding our agreement and correspondence?

If you need further clarification of any of these points or have any questions, do get in touch. I expect to hear either from you or your lawyers about these claims, failing which I will have to pursue court action.

Kind regards

Mark

Of course I didn't get a response to this letter and did not hear from their lawyers again. I had no alternative but to pursue the claims in court.

*****

The Dispute- Year 4

Since it appeared that we had no chance of a settlement, Lawrence Abramson wrote to Lambeth on March 30 2009 attaching a Draft Particulars of Claim setting out the three claims that we would be making. He wrote that we would issue this on April 9th unless the Pythons agreed to the claims. He also wrote about publicity, "Our client is mindful of the fact that any claim that he may issue against your client will inevitably attract publicity. Our client therefore intends to issue a press release to ensure that any coverage is accurately reported. Our client would prefer any press release to be issued to be a joint press release and we attach a draft for any comments that your client may have.'"

DRAFT PRESS RELEASE

Holy Grail Producer Sues Pythons over Spamalot Royalties

The film producer responsible for launching the feature film careers of iconic comedy group Monty Python is suing the Pythons for a fair share of the royalties resulting from the hit show *Spamalot*.

Mark Forstater, who produced *Monty Python and the Holy Grail*, the 1975 movie which became a comedy classic and on which *Spamalot* is based, is claiming royalties from the stage musical In accordance with a written agreement made 35 years ago with John Cleese, Eric Idle, Graham Chapman, Terry Gilliam, Michael Palin and Terry Jones. This agreement entitled Forstater to an equal share with the Pythons of royalties from the film and from any spin-offs from the film.

The agreement, signed in 1974, will be the centrepiece of his evidence at a hearing due to begin shortly at the High Court in London. Lawrence Abramson, partner at the leading entertainment law firm Harbottle & Lewis will represent Mark Forstater.

According to entertainment magazine Variety, *Spamalot* has made more than $162 million (£114 million) at the box office in five years, excluding touring productions.

"This is incredibly disappointing for me," said Mark Forstater, who is based in London. "I've known some of the Pythons since we were students and my contribution to *Monty Python and the Holy Grail* has never before been in question."

"In fact, I get royalty payments for other spin-offs there have been from the film over the years and I always have done. I just don't know why they think *Spamalot* is any different. It is an acknowledged spin-off from *Monty Python and the Holy Grail* and a very profitable one too."

Spamalot has been a phenomenal success since Python member Eric Idle had the idea of turning *Monty Python and the Holy Grail* into a stage production. It has played to packed houses on Broadway and in the West End and has spawned numerous touring productions worldwide.

Forstater, who has gone on to produce a number of films including *The Grass is Singing*, based on the book of the same name written by Nobel Prize winning author Doris Lessing, and *The Wolves of Willoughby Chase* and who has also forged a successful career as an author, is asking the High Court in London to enforce the 1974 contract and order an independent audit of revenue from *Spamalot* to assess his entitlement.

"I'm not asking for anything other than what we agreed back in 1974," said Mark Forstater.
----- ends -----

Note that this press release was never issued.

The threat to issue the Claims woke the Pythons up. Lambeth wrote back that the Python company was now prepared to locate the old invoices I asked for, and was also willing to allow me to audit their books. So something was moving, at last.

I had made contact with a Chartered Accountant named Philip DeNahlik, who was an expert in this kind of forensic auditing. He was the partner in charge of forensic accountancy at Begbies Traynor.

On the 28th April Abramson asked for "an open book audit, i.e. where our client's auditor is permitted to look not only at the invoices themselves but also to examine the underlying documents relating to the invoices including all statements rendered to our client and all relevant agreements. In particular, the audit will only be of any value if our client's auditor is also permitted to see:

1, Any and all agreements between your client and the producers of Spamalot
2. The legal costs bill relating to the Spamalot agreements

Lambeth responded on May 8th that the agreement with Ostar Enterprises (the producer of Spamalot) has a confidentiality clause but that they had obtained approval that this agreement would be made available to Philip DeNahlik.

He then made an unsubstantiated slur that I would be likely to discuss my claims with the press, and pointed out that the Ostar Agreement is confidential and should not be discussed. Earlier I had been talking to Richard Brooks of the Sunday Times about the case, and he was interested in the story. In the end the paper's lawyers decided they couldn't publish anything, other than a small diary item. Yet Eric Idle was not being reticent. For example, here is an article that appeared in the Times on October 17, 2006:

Royalty cheques buy Pythons' loyalty

By Jack Malvern, Arts Reporter

Idle's surviving former colleagues — Terry Jones, Michael Palin, Terry Gilliam and John Cleese — were initially reluctant to give their approval to *Spamalot*, but have been mollified after a stream of royalty cheques.

Three members have shown their support for the show by agreeing to appear at the gala opening on the London stage tonight. John Cleese is the only surviving member not to attend. He is filming in Australia.

The success of the musical in New York, where it has taken more than $1 million (£537,000) a week at the Shulman Theatre, has ensured weekly royalty cheques of more than $10,000 for the rights owners of *Monty Python and the Holy Grail*.

Each surviving Python and the estate of Graham Chapman, who died in 1989, takes approximately 10 per cent of that figure.

Jones, who co-directed the original film, voiced the group's unease about the project when the surviving members attended the show when it opened on Broadway.

"It is Eric's show," he said. "He will make more out of *Spamalot* than anybody has ever made out of Python. Good luck. But if we had known it was going to be such a success, we'd have gone for a better deal." He added that he liked the songs, but found Spamalot to be "utterly pointless and full of hot air".

Idle told *The Times*: "The hardest thing to do was to persuade them that this was something that would go well," he said.

He made a breakthrough when he played them one of the new songs. "We played them *The Song that Goes Like This* and they cracked up. That was the secret of it."

"It is a money-spinner for us. It will continue to be, because there is a touring version as well. It is a big opportunity," Idle added.

Lawrence Abramson responded on May 11 by asking when would be a convenient time to make the audit and added "It is our client's position that the auditor must be permitted to take copies of any documents he deems appropriate to take copies of, albeit that our client accepts that he will enter into a confidentiality agreement in respect of them.'"

Lambeth responded over five weeks later that my auditor couldn't take copies of any documents.

We wrote back a week later, a nanosecond in legal time, on June 26, "Auditors normally make copies of important documents in the course of their work, in order to write up a report and to refer to these documents. If Mr. DeNahlik is not permitted to make copies of documents then he must at the very least be able to make notes of what he considers relevant whilst he is working."

When I explained to DeNahlik the restrictions that the Pythons wanted to place on the audit, he wrote:

"In my opinion as a forensic accountant were this to go to Court all the relevant documents would become discloseable such that the Court could reach a balanced decision. Thus by seeking to restrict your access at this stage they are clearly and simply endeavouring to close down your contractual rights in obtaining information that is rightfully yours."

The Pythons were not making anything easy for us. Surprise, surprise. What I did not realise was how taking notes from the documents rather than making copies would eat into Philip's time, and would make this a protracted and expensive audit. This limited even more what we could achieve.

Ian Miles, the Python manager responsible for accounting, said that the audit couldn't happen before mid-April since he had to retrieve documents from storage. In April Miles said he was still not ready, and that the earliest date for the audit would be mid-July.

We first raised the question of the audit on January 25, 2007. Now the audit was finally about to happen, and it was only 3.5 years later! The negotiation over the terms of the audit alone took a year from May 2009 to May 2010. In his report Philip wrote, "I was not permitted to take any copies of documents whatsoever. This means I was expected to read, understand and make comprehensible notes on the spot. This methodology is in practical terms quite absurd. It is wholly unreasonable and impractical as well as being professionally discourteous to both me and those instructing me. It will of course add to the cost."

As the Agreements relating to Spamalot were confidential, and the Pythons would not permit me to see them, I had hoped that the audit would shed light on how Spamalot was structured and on the relationship between the three entities: Idle's company, the theatre producer (Ostar Enterprises), and the Python company (Python (Monty) Pictures Ltd).

I had other reasons for pursuing this second claim:

1. There were so many reports in the press of how much Idle and the Pythons were making from Spamalot that I wanted to know if there was more there than was being reported.

2. Idle complained that he had hired lawyers to do a deal with the other Pythons, and that aroused my curiosity - I wanted to know how that deal was structured.

3. Roger Saunders and his lawyer were so difficult in their dealings with me that I imagined they must be hiding something. They were never open and transparent about things that later proved perfectly innocuous.

Philip spent two days at the Python accountants' office, and he did manage to find out a good deal but his inquiries generated a slew of new questions.

The NY lawyer who I consulted also volunteered that if there was a third party (such as the investors in the film) involved as sleeping partners in a deal such as Spamalot, one way to reduce the amount paid to the sleeping partners would be to create a structure where a portion of rights and therefore royalty payments would be hived off to a different entity. In this kind of triangular structure, the third entity could then pay those royalties anywhere they liked. I wondered if the Agreement with Idle was the means to do this royalty sleight-of-hand. I needed to see these agreements to work out if this was the case. But the agreements were confidential and frankly I couldn't understand why?

Idle complained that he had given too much away to his fellow Pythons, and Terry Jones thought it was a lousy deal for them. In May 2005 he was reported as saying at the Rose d'Or TV festival in Switzerland,

PYTHON JONES SLAMS 'POINTLESS' SPAMALOT

British funnyman TERRY JONES has slammed MONTY PYTHON'S SPAMALOT, the Broadway musical based on his cult movie MONTY PYTHON AND THE HOLY GRAIL.

The 62-year-old co-directed and starred in the 1975 film, but is horrified by the sell-out stage adaptation by ERIC IDLE, his fellow member of legendary comedy troupe MONTY PYTHON'S FLYING CIRCUS.

And he's furious Idle is making more from the popular show than he or the other three surviving Pythons - JOHN CLEESE, TERRY GILLIAM, and MICHAEL PALIN - made from their TV shows and films made during the group's heyday.

He complains, "Spamalot is utterly pointless. It's full of air.

"We agreed a deal. If we'd known it was going to be such a success, we'd have asked for a better deal. Eric is making more from Spamalot than the rest of us ever made from Python.

"I like doing things I'm interested in. Regurgitating Python is not high on my list of priorities."

I eventually had to abandon this second claim because I could not find a 'smoking gun' and the Pythons gave me warranties that they had never had any separate payments from Eric Idle. So I accepted that the complexity of the deal was not sinister, just expensive.

I eventually had to give an undertaking to the Pythons that I would not disclose any terms or contents of the Ostar-Python agreement on Spamalot to anyone, so I cannot describe it in this book. What I can do is to outline the arguments about this agreement between the lawyers and comment on them.

****

My Journals 2009

BBC Scotland had interviewed me early in 2008 for a Movie Connections documentary that they were making on the Holy Grail. I was happy with the interview, but as the dispute with the Pythons deepened I wondered if they were trying to put pressure on the BBC to edit me out of the picture. This may sound a bit paranoid, but I later found that this is exactly what the Pythons did when they made their own documentary series - Almost The Truth. See the later chapter entitled Airbrushed Out of History for the shabby details.

Jan 7 2009

Tonight- Movie Connections- Holy Grail I think I looked OK - a little portly, distinguished, smooth, rich- softly spoken- will it do me any good? When should I write Palin again to chase?

Jan 9, 2009

Last night drinks with Gerry Harrison. Spoke about Pythons and Holy Grail. I explained how after I did not work with them again, that I felt I had not handled that situation well, but now having re-considered, I realised that it was their 'artistic sensitivity' that made them not continue with me. Gerry and I agreed that I did what I had to do to make the film, it was a hit, and it was wrong that I was not rewarded. They wanted a yes man like John, not someone like me.

Jan 10, 2009

Yes it's a difficult time, but the year of the ox is starting soon, and the ox energy must be one of perseverance, just ploughing on and on without regard to how much needs to be done or how stony the ground. I must keep on going at all costs to get my fair share.

Jan 23, 2009

No news from Palin.

Feb 10, 2009

No news from Palin. By the end of this week I should send it again. Palin is usually good at corresponding, so it might be that he is away or that they are considering. Who knows?

Feb 18, 2009

I decided last night or this a.m. to sue the Pythons, while I have some money remaining. They are jerking me around with the non-answer to the Palin letter and want to wait me out. So what I plan to do is ask them for mediation while we prepare the case and the draft press release. I've got to do it, no sense being scared. I really have nothing left to lose now personally or professionally. If I lose the house, so what, I have to leave it anyway. They are cheating me and I need to go for them now.

Feb 23, 2009

Watched King Lear on telly last night, with Ian McKellen. Seeing Lear and his daughters dead I wondered if my decision to go to court with the Pythons is reckless, like Lear, the actions of an old and foolish man. Will I bring disaster on myself and my family? I suppose the advice of the I Ching is good. Going halfway and stopping is ok - which means that if they show me the Spamalot agreements and it looks like there is no real case there, I could decide to drop claim 2, or to drop the whole thing if I thought they would defend it. This would cost me, but not cost me massively, and then we would have to make the decision about what to do with the house.

And there's a lack of self-esteem here, a feeling that I am not good enough or talented enough or valuable enough. I have spent the last year delaying with this, and now I really need to get rid of all the woe in my guts.

I think the defeatist attitude is karmic, it is left over in my mind and body from previous defeats and betrayals, and the fact that breathing has brought this up, shows that it is in the solar plexus and upper chest area that these old shocks, fears and defeats are stored. Clear them from my body clear them from my mind.

I do have a sense of fear, but it's not surprising, given the significant sums of money involved in the case. But I also have courage, the courage to persevere in what I know is right. I must increase courage decrease fear, lose this defeatist attitude and get myself feeling positive about things, that the films can happen, that I will get the Python money owed me, and I can succeed in what I want to do and achieve. So at 65 I am able to accept who I am and where I am, knowing that where I am headed cannot be quantified.

April 1, 2009

The Pythons have till next Wednesday the 8th April to respond to my claim. Otherwise we go to court and get the press involved. The big question is, will they fight or negotiate? My instinct has always been that for a number of reasons: their legal position is dodgy, they don't want publicity, they know my claim is real but don't want to pay unless forced to, etc. But what if I am wrong? I face an expensive legal battle and all battles are unpredictable.

April 24 2009

Deadline for Pythons. Nothing so far. Lawrence expects a stalling letter at 4:00, so it looks like going to court time.

April 26 2009

The Pythons wrote back suggesting I can audit them if I want. Need to decide how to handle this. They also sent the Fergus Spence Agreement, which before they refused to do, saying it was confidential. There may be some benefits in this change and the delay also. I shouldn't be in a hurry to rush ahead. Remember their 40th anniversary is coming up in October and that would be the perfect time to launch the case. Don't rush- think !

April 28 2009

Auditing the Pythons, it will cost quite a bit- 4k ? - and may not reveal much. So we will only do it if they agree to show us the agreement with Ostar and the legal bill, so we might learn from these. Expensive way to get access to documents.

June 19 2009

Pythons came back with very stringent conditions for an audit, so strict that I'm not sure it's worth doing it. I need to sit down and work out what I expect to get from an audit and see if this will be possible. Don't want to waste thousands needlessly.

August 25 2009

Tomorrow we meet to discuss the Python case. Do I have the will to go through with it? Do I have the guts to stand up for myself?

September 2 2009

I looked over the invoices I sent the Pythons from 1976-81. They are very clear and tie in perfectly with the letters to Anne Henshaw. There was also a short correspondence about VAT so there is no way they can claim ignorance about what I was invoicing them for. Good solid practical evidence for my case.

September 9th: I moved out of the family house today into a bedsit. I felt like a displaced person, uncomfortable, not knowing where I belonged. Knowing that no one was at home waiting for me or expecting me gave me a lonely, sad, desolate feeling.

September 14 2009

(Barrister) George Hayman says there is a problem if I don't do the audit. Need to clarify it with Lawrence. Don't want to do one but will do a short one if necessary.

Email to Anne

Since it looked like the Pythons were not going to rely on Anne Henshaw for evidence or support, I decided to email her and ask if she would be a witness for me,

> **Email for Anne James**
>
> From: **Mark Forstater** (mforstater@msn.com)
> Sent: 16 November 2010 17:24:19
> To: paul@maydaymgt.co.uk
>
> Email for Anne James:
>
> Hi Anne,
>
> I hope this email finds you well.
>
> I'm writing to you because of a current dispute I am having with Python (Monty) Pictures Ltd. regarding payment of my invoices. The dispute centres on the interpretation of my Producer's Agreement for Monty Python and The Holy Grail, and the 1/7th share of merchandising or spinoff income that I am entitled to. As you were involved with the management of the Pythons at the time of my agreement being made, and the allocation of the merchandising income, I wonder if you would be willing to provide a statement for me in regard to these matters.
>
> I'm sorry to bother you like this, but you are probably the only person who actually remembers anything of these distant events.
>
> I look forward to hearing from you.
>
> Kind Regards
>
> Mark

Unsurprisingly, I never got a reply. I wonder if she ever mentioned this to any of the Pythons or their management?

***

My Journals 2010

June 27 2010

I hope to make the Python claim by mid-July. To be free of this case and therefore free of money worries, would be an extraordinary fulfilment, it would be as the I Ching says, "To get out of danger is to become free", free of anxiety, free of fear, free to just express myself as I am. I've lived with this anxiety for so long that I can't imagine what life would be like without it, or what life would be like if I was free of financial concerns.

June 30, 2010: I moved into a rented one bedroom flat. Great to have more space and to have Lily stay over.

July 12, 2010

Today I got the first audit report from Philip on the Spamalot Agreement, and this looks promising. It seems that the Python Brand got a share of profits, plus there were other shares from Idle's profits that look promising. Also, I don't think the agreements are confidential. It also appears that we did get a percentage of the box office for the license, but then this got reduced to a flat fee. This is very poor for them, I think. They won't take this to court, I'm sure of it.

My life feels like it is on hold again as I battle.

August 23 2010

At the British Library I read in the Pau Pu Zi: "In pursuit of righteousness is no distress."

I took this to mean that if I pursue righteousness, then no matter what the outcome, I must not feel distress. Whether I win or lose, whether I gain or pay, if I have pursued righteousness then I must not feel bad at the outcome. Have no regrets for having done the right thing, no matter what the outcome.

Obviously this relates to my current situation, re the Pythons, but it gives me the right attitude to this case, so even if I end up in a mess, which I could see as 5 wasted years of effort, I should not look on the negative side, but only consider the positive, which has nourished the good seeds in myself.

We have within us tremendous potential to do many things. Whether we fulfil our potential depends on circumstances. If Einstein had lived in the Middle Ages would he have revolutionised physics? No - at best he'd have written a commentary on the Zohar.

Resolutions: if I do not allow regret, fear, and anxiety and all the other gutter emotions that might arise, if I do not let them arise, if I do not let them sabotage me, then these 5 years can be seen as training, as a time of rejuvenation, when my original too long buried strong qualities, blossomed once again.

August 30, 2010

Woke this morning with the thought that all my 'woes' are all there to make me discover in myself the strength or character or survival skills or philosophy to get through these events and emerge a different person. In that sense they are tests (or one giant test) of character.
If they are not tests, then what are they? Learning experiences? Karmic events?
Yesterday I understood that to think that it is through my ego (or will) that I accomplish things, is to assume that the toothpick that is the will can battle against the log that is the Tao. The Tao arranges all, and I fit into it in my small way. I don't create the situation I find myself in and I don't work out the ways to make those situations come out best for me. The Tao does it all, and I am more or less a bystander.
What have I had to do, which I would not have done otherwise, to cope with the impact of these events, and to continue to pursue them as I have chosen to do? And to dwell on what the money - money denied, money longed for, money lost - means to me.

September 5, 2010

I'm now starting to think that this case is happening in order for me to get enlightened once and for all, or to remain in ignorance and suffering (foolish pride and all). Unless I can use this situation to uproot longing and clinging, I will always be on the roller coaster ride of hope and fear, gain and loss, joy and anxiety. This is my best chance of doing away with this dual thinking. Tell myself "not two", unify my mind and body so that I no longer want or need the fruits of my actions and so can begin to live freely.

September 28, 2010

I may end up with very little from this case. Freud might diagnose in me a secret longing to fail, to be quashed. Hopefully I gain overall, but it might be small. The ideal now would be enough to buy a flat, if possible.

November 1 2010

Tomorrow we go to see the Judge. The two defendants have not delivered their disclosure bundle. We were ready. Will the Judge tick them off? We are going into mediation late November. Will we have full disclosure by then?

November 10 2010

The Judge on November 2nd said that they could not hold back confidential documents, so we await the subsidiary income document with interest. Also I have a list of docs for them to disclose which I want to press for.

November 25, 2010

At Lambeth's office. I discovered a memo from Anne Henshaw explaining to their accountant Anton (Felton) that I was to get 1/7th of the profits from spin-offs.

December 9 2010

Lawrence wants me to forgo asking for the missing Python dosh. Need to convince him to go on-

December 10 2010

Lawrence suggests not pursuing Claim 2 against the Pythons. I need to convince him to carry on, We need a smoking gun disclosure on that to push on.

December 23 2010

Email from Lawrence. He said that a young trainee in his office noted an article from the Daily Mail from last week. The article recounted a feud between Idle and Cleese, during it Cleese disclosed the amounts that Idle had paid Cleese and Palin.

Lawrence thinks we can seek disclosure of the statement that Cleese was referring to (I think.) In any case, it shows that the Pythons got money ($1.1m in Palin's case) from Idle.

This, coming a week after Lawrence had written to me that we should consider dropping this claim due to lack of evidence, was like a Xmas present from Cleese to me. It vindicates my position that I am owed up to $1m for my share of Spamalot. If we can only press this home now, it would be great. Of course, the world is going to sleep now for 2 weeks, so nothing can be done, but at least we have a smoking gun...,

December 26 2010

Julian Doyle told my ex I had little faith that Holy Grail would be successful. That's only partly true, I think. But I guess at the time I lost faith with the two Terrys and this helped seal my fate, I'm sure. Also my own selfishness, ego, and greed did the rest. What Julian is saying shows me that I was to blame for my own loss, that my earlier view was correct. All water under the bridge, past history. I'm a different person, I've learned from all of it.

****

The Dispute - Year 5: A Demand for Redaction

Following the audit revelations, we were concerned that the Spamalot legal arrangement was in breach of the NFFC Trust Deed, which required all payments to be made to the NFTC for onward distribution. In order to clarify whether I had a claim to make regarding this structure, we asked for sight of the author agreement as well as all the other agreements linked to it.

Paul Lambeth responded on October 11, 2010 by saying that they would ask Ostar if we could be provided with a copy of the Ostar Agreement, as long as we kept it confidential. Lambeth came back to us (November 16, 2010) with the news that Ostar Enterprises agreed that we could see a copy of the Spamalot agreement but with a bizarre proviso. My lawyer could see the document but no one else (including me) could see it.

Abramson responded to this ludicrous suggestion on November 24, 2010,

"It is just not workable for me to see the agreement and not share it with my client. If, having seen the agreement, I am of the view that my client needs to see it then I would have to take that decision myself without reference to my client. My client could not even be a party to my letter to you explaining why I believed the agreement would need to be disclosed to my client. If you refused to disclose it I would then have to take the decision of whether or not to apply to court for pre-action disclosure myself without reference to my client. My client would not even be able to see the application. This is notwithstanding the fact that the costs risk of the application failing would fall on my client and not myself."

Lawrence also pointed out that since Spamalot opened at the beginning of 2005 and one has only 6 years to make a claim, time was of the essence.

The audit had picked up the term Brand Recognition, and we had no idea what it meant.
Lambeth confirmed that there are "**NO** payments made in respect of "Brand Recognition". The agreement simply contains a formula by which part of the proceeds is attributed to "Brand Recognition" – this

is value added by my client in respect of the "Monty Python" brand." This was as clear as mud. Though it shows how the word brand, the kind of thing the comedians of the 60s and 70s would have satirized, had now infested show business.

Finally on December 8th we made application to the court requesting that we obtain from Python (Monty) Pictures an unredacted copy of the Ostar Agreement which I could read. Unredacted means no blacking out. The hearing took place on January 25th 2011 in front of Master Weingarten. There are in Britain grades of judges from Justices of the Supreme Court to High Court Judges down to what John Mortimer in his wonderful Rumpole called circus judges. These were in fact circuit judges who travelled to county courts outside London. A Master is a kind of assistant judge, an experienced lawyer who handles court matters like costs and preliminary hearings.

Master Weingarten decided that I could read the document, but that it would have to remain redacted. It would also have to remain Confidential. I was surprised when the Master gave costs to the Pythons. That is, he made me pay for the hearing.

****

The Dispute – Year 6

4th Settlement Possibility

In February 2011 after snippy exchanges, another master, Master Mark, suggested that we mediate in an attempt to come to a settlement rather than go to court. I was happy with that prospect.

Kafka would have appreciated the next move. We asked Python (Monty) Pictures Ltd. to give us 'disclosure' of all their documents which related to the dispute. The Pythons sent us some documents, but also a list of a second class of documents which they would only let me or Lawrence read at their offices. The python is known to be more paranoid than most reptiles.

On November 25, 2011 I drove to Paul Lambeth's office in the countryside near Southampton to look at the asterisked documents. There were two crates. Examining them took me almost all day. Two documents were of significant import. The first was a memo from Anne Henshaw written in 1979 to the auditor of the Python Company. On it, item number 1(c) was the one that caught my eye. It says, "I confirm that with regard to spin-off rights, Mark Forstater received, in addition to his share of the profits from the film pot, 1/7th of the 50% payable to Python (Monty) Pictures." In other words this document backs up the 1977 letters from Anne Henshaw in confirming that her knowledge was that I was entitled to my 1/7th share of the merchandising and spin-off income from the Holy Grail.

It was there that I also found the memo of the Python meeting held in February 1974 where the Pythons agreed that I would be the producer of any further movies they wanted to make. I thought this gave my '7th Python' status a bit of credibility.

By December the mediation date had been pushed back to February and we appointed Andrew Hildebrand as the mediator. Finally, after much delay, we met on May 28 2012. We met for a full day at my lawyer's offices. Since the mediation is also confidential I can't write about it in any detail. The Pythons were represented by their two managers- Roger Saunders and Ian Miles - as well as their legal team but none of the Pythons attended. They didn't make any offer even remotely capable of acceptance. Lawrence Abramson commented to me that it seemed like we were negotiating with ourselves, and so we decided to make no further offers. The whole day was a total loss. . .

As John Cleese said, after the expensive dust had settled, 'It's insane, why hadn't we settled 5 or 6 years ago?'

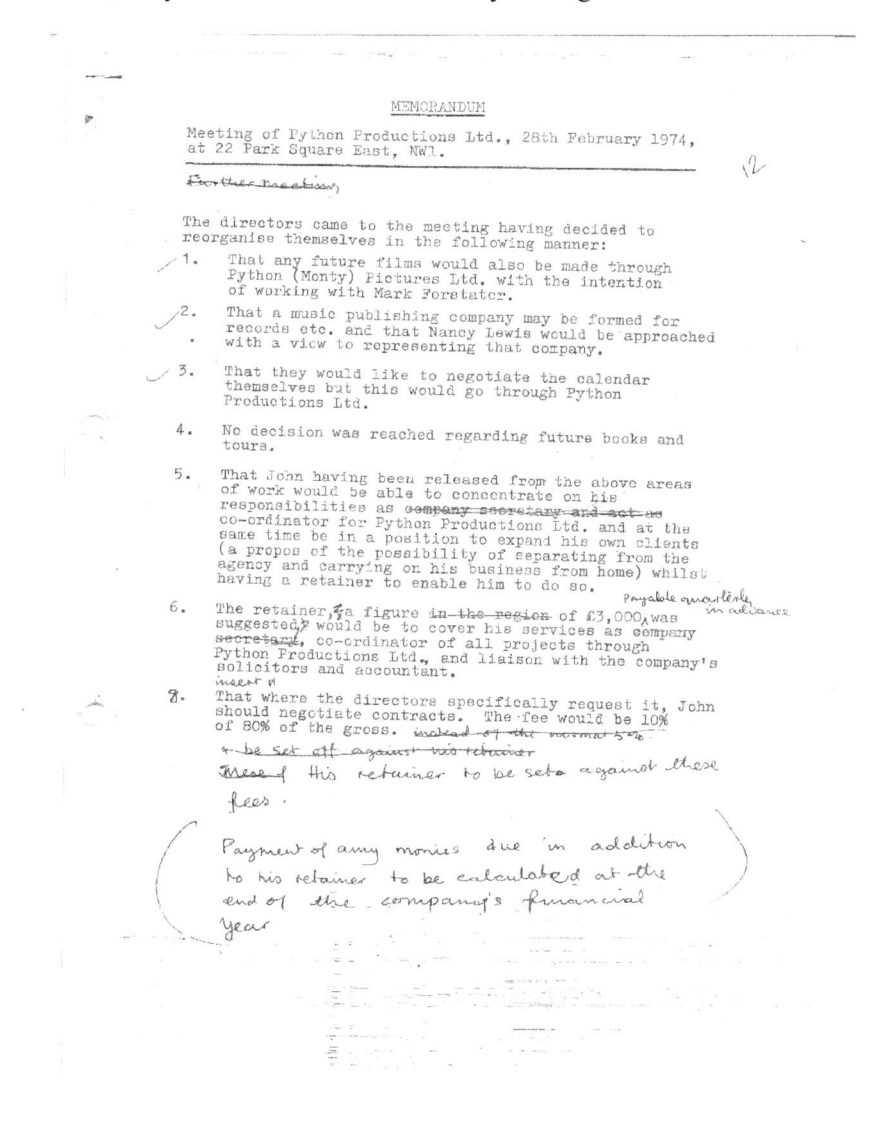

MEMORANDUM

Meeting of Python Productions Ltd., 28th February 1974, at 22 Park Square East, NW1.

The directors came to the meeting having decided to reorganise themselves in the following manner:

1. That any future films would also be made through Python (Monty) Pictures Ltd. with the intention of working with Mark Forstater.

2. That a music publishing company may be formed for records etc. and that Nancy Lewis would be approached with a view to representing that company.

3. That they would like to negotiate the calendar themselves but this would go through Python Productions Ltd.

4. No decision was reached regarding future books and tours.

5. That John having been released from the above areas of work would be able to concentrate on his responsibilities as co-ordinator for Python Productions Ltd. and at the same time be in a position to expand his own clients (a propos of the possibility of separating from the agency and carrying on his business from home) whilst having a retainer to enable him to do so.

6. The retainer, a figure of £3,000, was suggested, would be to cover his services as company secretary, co-ordinator of all projects through Python Productions Ltd., and liaison with the company's solicitors and accountant. *Payable quarterly in advance*

8. That where the directors specifically request it, John should negotiate contracts. The fee would be 10% of 80% of the gross. *His retainer to be set against these fees.*

Payment of any monies due in addition to his retainer to be calculated at the end of the company's financial year

---

After this failed mediation, we decided to drop the 2nd claim on Spamalot, and only proceed on the 1st claim regarding Rectification of my producer's contract to reinstate my 1/7th share.

*****

My Journals 2011

January 4 2011

The Python case now appears to revolve around the IP rights that the Pythons have given to the show and been paid for. I think this is where the Idle money has gone. But how do we prove it? Will the Judge grant us disclosure? We will need to ask him at the end of January.

January 13 2011

On Monday a long session with Lawrence and (Barrister) Mark Vinall. On Claim 1 and 3 they feel strong, whereas on Spamalot they see no evidence of a conspiracy or fraud and so perhaps I am wrong. There is no hidden $ 1m for each Python. We have to gradually drop the 2nd claim, which might make me liable for costs. The entire claim is only 260k plus interest, not a fortune. So I am feeling deflated about this now, as we try to move towards a mediation in February.

February 25 2011

On the Python front we have put in a revised claim adding my company as claimant. Waiting to hear if this goes ahead without a problem. We need to set a new mediation date, ideally in March.

I suppose if I get out of this case with nothing at all it will still be a gain. First of all, the relief of dropping the hassle, secondly the establishing of the 1/7th for future income, and thirdly the fact of winning, or more exactly putting yourself in a position in which you could express your character and create a winning situation.

March 10 2011

We have had to put a revised claim in for Holy Grail, adding my company to the claim. Waiting now for PMP to agree the format and to move on to a mediation date. This will probably be in April, but

I also have a hearing date with them in April over costs so I need to discuss with Lawrence how we should handle this,

I want this case to go away so I can get on with work. I have had three new projects given to me over the past few weeks. I could be busy in 2013!

March 23 2011

On the Python front can't get them to respond to the new claim so we can set the mediation. Have organised to meet the Judge April 23rd when we will try to sort it. Losing another month. I only have money till June.

May 1 2011

We have now set a mediation for the 28th May (not yet confirmed).

May 27 2011

Tomorrow is mediation day. Tonight I prepared all the papers. On Wednesday Andrew Hildebrand, the mediator, suggested I start the proceedings with a short intro which I prepared. Well, let's hope for the best. The I Ching said 'collect' for this case, but is it right?

May 28 2011

Life is so weird. I've just had one of the most frustrating and trying days trying to make a deal at the mediation. Normally the defendants make a claim first, but the Pythons wouldn't so we had to. So after much toing and froing we had to give up.

****

The Dispute Year 7

They are still up to it, sir, still taking stock, still examining papers, still going over the heaps and heaps of rubbish. At this rate they'll be at it there seven years.
Bleak House

Airbrushed Out Of History

I never thought I would share a destiny with Leon Trotsky, the creator of the Red Army and the man who Stalin toppled. Even though we are both Jewish (he was born Lev Davidovich Bronshtein) the main thing we have in common is that we have both been victims of an attempt to airbrush us out of history.

After Trotsky broke with Stalin, Stalin had the KGB airbrush him out of the photos that showed Trotsky's role in creating the Soviet Union, particularly that of leader of the Red Army. He became one of the disappeared.

In 2009 the Pythons made a six part documentary called Monty Python: Almost the Truth (The Lawyer's Cut). Watching Episode 4 which dealt with the Holy Grail I began to understand how Trotsky must have felt. They managed to discuss the production of the film without interviewing or even mentioning the Producer of said film – i.e. me. There is one photo in which I appear but am unidentified.

Interviews which said Mark helped get the film made but we're now haggling in front of judges would hardly suit the Pythons. So in a Stalinist move they just removed me from their history. 'Almost The Truth' says it all, and I now understand why it was called The Lawyer's Cut. Perhaps their lawyers advised them not to give me any credit for making the film, since one of the planks of their defence would be to suggest I really didn't do anything and anything that I did do was wrong. Stalin of course eventually had Trotsky killed and the Pythons do not yet seem to have gone so far.

The Pythons' Defence

I thought the Pythons' defence was very weak. It was totally a negative defence: we don't remember the meeting, we don't remember giving him this 1/7th share, we barely remember our own names. They tried to downplay my role and to claim that Chippenham Films, the company I had once owned with Julian Doyle, was the real producer of the film. So the thrust of their Witness Statements was:

My 1/7th share was a <u>mistake</u>.
They don't remember giving it to me.
None of them remember how it got into my Agreement.
I was not really the Producer of the film. Chippenham Films was.
They didn't like how I did things. They liked Julian Doyle.

We don't always like to see how others see us but going to court means you have to be ready for people to throw all kinds of insults at you and expose you warts and all. For students of abuse what follows should be sacred text. This is a summary of what the Pythons said in their Witness Statements:

Some Mistake Surely?

Terry Jones said paying even 7.1429% was a mistake.

Terry Gilliam said that if there was a mistake it was that 1/14th was included in the agreement.

John Cleese said he couldn't understand why the agreement gave me any share at all. Since they left me to deal with Simon Olswang it must have been a mistake or misunderstanding that a clause like this was inserted. It was certainly without their agreement.

Michael Palin was puzzled that my contract (which he initialled) let me share the spin-off income. He didn't think there was either discussion or agreement for me to have 1/7th or 1/14th. He suspected a mistake had been made and none of the Pythons were aware of it.

Eric Idle said that he couldn't remember any agreement for me to have a share (whether $1/14^{th}$ or $1/7^{th}$) of the spin-off revenue and he thought this was a lawyer's mistake.

The Pythons implied but never claimed that because I had been left to deal with the documentation for the film that I had somehow 'sneaked' this 1/7th share into my agreement. If I had, how stupid would it be to ask Michael Palin to then initial an alteration to this dishonest insertion, thereby drawing attention to it.

The fact is that the documentation of the film gave the Pythons everything that I said I would obtain for them, and that is why they have seen such an incredible financial return from the film.

Our Memories are Fading.

Idle couldn't remember the clause being negotiated. He had no recollection of the contract, nor any discussion about it.

Cleese had no memory of discussing or even agreeing that I should share in their spin-off income.

Gilliam didn't remember the clause being negotiated or any agreement for me to retain a share of their spin-off income.

Jones said he was certain that he would remember if they had discussed or agreed anything to which I was a party. But he admitted that he had signed my Agreement without now being able to remember where or when.

Palin said that he had no memory of either a discussion or an agreement that I partake in their spin-off income. He admitted that he had initialled the amendments to the third schedule but couldn't remember doing it, or being given any explanation about why they were necessary.

On my role as producer:

Cleese remembered being told that 'a Mark Forstater' was going to be a 'Producer' on the film. He was surprised that his fellow Pythons wanted an unknown and inexperienced person to take this job. He says that he did not like me after meeting me and told the Pythons about his feelings. He didn't think I could contribute anything. He claims that he finally dropped his objections when he thought I would only be booking hotels and dealing with the finances.

Let's shred his ego while we are at it:

Cleese says he recalled me coming to the set with a gloomy look on my face. He claims that he heard from the others that I was 'negative, critical and pessimistic' in my discussions with the two Terrys.

Cleese also remembers that they were all unhappy with my attitude to publicity and the premiere. I had a negative attitude about the film and to them and I seemed to assume the Film would not be a success. He had the impression that I was rather embarrassed about it.

Idle recalls that he only became aware of me when we were on location in Scotland. He describes me as 'a saturnine American, with no apparent sense of humour. ' Idle also said that I didn't talk very much .

Idle remembered tensions between the directors and me during the shoot and he heard about other difficulties during the editing of the film. He recalled the disagreements we had over publicity as well.

Not that Eric was too concerned about the film publicity. At one Python meeting on July 24, 1974 when I explained the publicity efforts for the film, Eric refused to become involved in most of it. He said that interviews were useless and degrading. Eric Idle not doing an interview? What century was that?

Jones remembered that in Scotland tensions developed between me and the two Terrys. He thought I was distancing myself from the film, and complained about working with two directors who went in different directions. Jones also claimed that I said the film was a disaster.

Palin recalled that there were disagreements between me and the Pythons about publicity. They thought I was too negative and not in tune with them. They also thought I gave in to EMI as the film's distributor.

The 7th Python:

Cleese had some fun regarding the claim that I was to be treated as the 7th Python for financial purposes. He said "Mark Forstater wasn't even the 107th Python. He has a better chance of being accepted as the fourth Kennedy brother."

Idle claimed that they would never have called me the seventh Python. It was a laughable suggestion.

Gilliam also said the claim that I be would be treated equally to them 'as if he were the 7th Python' was a joke.

Bigging Up Chippenham Films/Julian Doyle:

Cleese remembered that Julian Doyle was much more involved in the shooting and editing of the film. Julian was eager and obliging and John cherished his counsels.

Idle recalled that either the two Terrys or Palin asked Chippenham Films to help make the film, but he didn't remember if he was part of these conferences.

Gilliam said that they employed Chippenham Films and as far as he understood it the 'profit share' was for both partners. He didn't know then that the written document was only with me. He didn't understand why there was only an agreement with me instead of Chippenham. But he added that I was in charge of the paperwork.

Cleese recalled that the Pythons had employed me a producer, along with my partner, and nothing else.

Idle remembered that Julian Doyle was much more conspicuous, was actively involved with the shooting and was generally adored.

N.B. Palin's published Diaries 1969-1979 never mentions Chippenham Films and the ever helpful Julian Doyle gets only one mention in regard to the shooting of Holy Grail. The film credits (prepared by Jones and Gilliam) do not mention Chippenham Films, not even a Thank You. I am credited as sole Producer and Julian Doyle as Production Manager.

How Did That Clause Sneak in there?

Idle said that the Pythons left me to do the documentation for the film. None of the Pythons were involved with that.

Jones said that after such a long time had elapsed, he couldn't blame anyone for the terms of the document which he signed for the company. They trusted me to instruct the lawyer to draft the Agreements, and trusted that we would get it right.

Only Graham Chapman, it seems, had nothing bad to say about me. But then, he was dead.

In the light of this cascade of who actually was Forstater and did he do diddlysquat my Barrister Tom Weisselberg put it this way in his opening remarks:

"The outrage expressed by a number of the Pythons in their witness statement as to the suggestion that Mr. Forstater was to be treated as the seventh Python is, with respect to them, misguided. There is no suggestion that Mr. Forstater would be writing jokes; what was being agreed was that Mr. Forstater would share equally with them in the product of the work that they were all together putting in to creating the film and that for that reason he asks for a share of the top half, and for that reason he was granted that share.

For financial purposes, in relation to the profit share, he is being treated like a seventh Python."

****

MY JOURNALS 2012

June 9 2012

The Pythons asked if we would agree to withdraw Claim 2, and I said yes to avoid possible heavy costs after the trial. They obviously twigged that if we do go to trial they will lose, but even if they win, how can I pay them?

Now I am hopeful that next week or so they might decide to settle the claim and avoid even more costs. That would be great.

June 11 2012

Spamalot returns to London in July for 3 months. Hope that brings in some dosh. I'm glad we never made an outright settlement at the mediation.

I saw Robert Young who told me the Pythons did a lousy deal with Eric and they are not getting any extra money. Eric even voiced God so he wouldn't have to pay anything to Cleese. It's a good thing the second claim has now been abandoned. I would not have found anything there.

June 26, 2012

On Friday late afternoon I got an email from Ian Miles. I avoided opening it until Monday. He was asking me to pay the £ 17,750 costs or he would seek bankruptcy in 7 days. I panicked and wrote back that I would give a proposal by Wednesday. Today I wrote back asking for clarification of how much spin-off income I am owed from the last statement. He was abrupt, so I consulted Lawrence. He told me that as we had deferred Claim 2- Spamalot- costs to the judgement that Ian Miles shouldn't be asking me to pay this anyway, so I can invoice for the 7k that is owed. That would be such a boon. It would really get me through until December.

June 30 2012

Last week nerves came in due to PMP trying to bankrupt me over my debt to them. Lawrence says it will be thrown out. Also they have withheld lots of my VAT and also some ancillary income, so this won't look good to the judge.

I plan to write to Palin and Gilliam and ask them to stop the bankruptcy thing. It might not work, but I feel they should know.

July 7 2012

So much is happening all the time. Two weeks ago I had to deal with the Pythons threatening to bankrupt me, which they will still (may?) try to do.

July 26 2012

My ex started telling me about her memories of Terry G giving me the script and asking me to help them.

August 14 2012

Last night disclosure documents from the Pythons, including a letter in which Michael Palin writes to Anne Henshaw putting me in the discard bin with John Gledhill. Sad to contemplate this, but I have really lived with this rejection for 36 years now, and part of the reason for pursuing this court case was to examine, and exorcise this demon of rejection that has haunted me for so long. Yes this decision had a huge effect on my career, left me out of a number of films which would have made a huge difference to my bank balance and my name. But it was not to be and I have had to accept it, and to continue on my own, making my own name and surviving all this time. So really finally seeing this letter, cause of so much of my life and work, is a time to feel sadness and to reflect on what might have been. But I have done this for so long in the past that really I can no longer do it now, and in fact have no need to. Taking the Pythons on was to dredge up old history but I wanted to do it, I wanted to expose these old hurts to the light of day, and to kiss them goodbye..

If I really was the producer I thought I was, if I really did help make Holy Grail a success, then those qualities must be with me still, and so if I persevere I should be able to show myself that I can do this again- I can make films, I can write books.

Sunday, September 23, 2012

My witness statement is very solid now, with lots of documents attached and I am very confident about it. If I win the case I think it will be a watershed for me. I did make that film happen, I did achieve something significant and good for them, and I think I can really move on now, after 37 years of living under a shadow. Now I can step out from that shadow and stand in the full yang glare of the sun, This is who I am, and this is what I do, and this is what I am capable of, and I will continue to back my hunches, my ideas and my gut instinct.

So even though I will be 69, I am youthful in spirit, youthful in body and am in good health and can continue for the next maybe 10 years to continue to produce films and work and be.

Friday October 5, 2012

Got the Python Witness statements this week. No surprises, pretty weak I think. No statement from Anne Henshaw. Will they really want to be in the witness box? Cleese, Palin, Idle, Goldstone? I don't think they will look too good. Gilliam has announced a new film October 22, so I don't think he will be able to attend.

I still don't know if they will want to settle before the court date. I would prefer them not to, since I would like the press to report what they have done.

Sunday October 7, 2012

Whatever the outcome of the trial, there has been a great benefit for me in taking on the Pythons. I re-valued what I accomplished in 1974/5. I helped create a good successful film, a classic. And I was instrumental in making it happen, although my problem with the Pythons meant that I could not take part in the success of the film.

A shadow fell over me, and it was a shadow partly of my own making, a sense that I had failed in keeping in with them, had failed as a producer. Now, I can see that I did not fail, but I was inexperienced and trying too hard, was probably judgemental, was a bit insecure and so on. These are normal human failings and I don't think I could do it this way now, but as Terry G said a couple of years ago, they were naive, and I too was a bit naive and inexperienced. But I did not fail, I succeeded.

I helped them make a film that was meant to cost £169k and finally cost £229k, 38% over budget, but which has returned over £ 20m in profit. Nearly as good as Apple if you bought early.

So I now feel able, I trust much more in my own judgement, my intuition, not that I am always right, but by and large I feel able to trust my feelings - I have cleansed my heart and I am clearing my body of all the old obstructions that have held me back for so long.

Friday November 23, 2012

On Wednesday I met my new barrister Tom Weisselberg. I liked him a lot- dynamic, intelligent, forceful. He wrote an excellent skeleton, raising the point about John Cleese not turning up and also Anne Henshaw's absence. He suggested I start reading my Witness Statement and the pleadings to ready myself for the cross-examination. He said Richard Spearman was an ethical. soft-spoken and intelligent QC. He will try to trip me up, especially in relation to the oral agreement. I need to do my homework.

The Witness Statements and especially the Python skeleton have set out their stall in such a way as to make it obvious the questions they will ask, so I have started to write up my answers and I will discuss this with Lawrence on Monday. We think the trial will start on Tuesday.

At the beginning of the week I felt very weak and slightly depressed. I felt that I might lose, after being so bullish about it for many years. I never thought the Pythons would come to court. I almost didn't want the mediation to succeed because I wanted my day in court, yet now when it appears that this is about to happen, I feel apprehensive. But after the meeting with Tom I felt better, more optimistic and I feel confident in him. Now that I am writing my responses I am also feeling more confident in myself that I will be able to handle the examination. I will certainly prepare myself.

I assume the press will be there. I hope so.

Sunday November 25

Last night at my ex-wife's. Explained to her and my daughter Asha about why I took on the Pythons. They understood and changed their view of my case from one of scepticism about why I was doing it to one of sympathy. Asha brought out a set of affirmation cards she uses, asked me to close my eyes and choose the card I felt attracted to. So I ran my hands down the cards and felt a kind of spark at a specific card and so picked it. It was related to the solar plexus (a problem area for me) and it had a set of 'I know' answers, the first was: 'I know I will not let anyone take advantage of me.' It was so apt.

I spent yesterday and this morning going through all the pleadings, diaries, skeletons and witness statements, writing notes to remind myself of how I need to respond to the cross-examination.

I found a number of points that were useful, the best one being that Richard Spearman, their QC, has repeated the error that Lambeth made - re: Anne's letters in 1977 - about how the NFTC pays the 50% of Python merchandising profits. This may be important.

I am happy with the work I am doing.

Tuesday Night November 27th

1.30 am. Can't sleep. Thinking of the case, thoughts rolling. Want to sleep but can't. I worked out I am owed about 248k by the Pythons, at the moment, With interest and costs it would be well over 300k if I win. I must win.

My future depends on it. Must try to sleep now.

Thursday November 29

Heard today that we have Judge Norris who is in his early 60s and a stickler. Lawrence was hoping for someone younger but we have who we have. There is a procedural battle going on over the Amendments. Hopefully the Judge will allow them and ask us to continue with the trial. Otherwise he may throw it out, which would be no justice at all.

I have been working all day on my preparation - it's now 4.0 PM- and have cancelled a meeting and a screening to work on it all night. My friend Ruth suggested I make 3 x 5 cards with my notes on them. I am doing that and I hope to finish later tonight. I can then read them before going to bed, in the morning on the train etc. Good advice.

I reread the I Ching to see what it said about the case. Hexagram 45 - Gathering - a good hexagram. It says that a king puts together an altar where people gather. He makes a sacrifice. It joins people, the living and the ancestors, the dead. It says that it is beneficial to see a Great man. I doubt if my Judge is that Great Man. Perhaps the Great Man is me - I need to be able to see myself as a Great Man, a leader, who has lost ego, and has made a great sacrifice, one who has communed with his ancestors.

You sharpen your sword and go into battle feeling dreadful, full of fear and shaking like a leaf.

Head held high, horns held high, sabre ready. I must be a warrior of light and right.

**

PART FOUR: The Trial: The law is an ass (or a twat)

Day 1- Is This The Right Room For An Opening Argument

Jarndyce and Jarndyce drones on. This scarecrow of a suit has, in course of time, become so complicated that no man alive knows what it means.
Bleak House

The trial started on November 30th 2012 in the Rolls Building, a huge new court complex off Fetter Lane in London. I wasn't surprised to see photographers and camera crews standing outside waiting to take the Pythons' pictures - Palin, Jones and Idle had turned up. The snappers recognised me (I don't know how) and asked me to stop for a few pics.

The court rooms are light and airy. We were in one of the larger ones because The Daily Mail, the Press Association, the Financial Times, a reporter from Sky, and others were there. A couple of friends of mine also arrived to show support, and I sat with my two lawyers – Lawrence Abramson and Stephanie Bonnello, just behind my two barristers – Leading barrister Tom Weisselberg and Junior Mark Vinall. The Pythons also had two barristers- Junior Amanda Michaels and Leading Richard Spearman QC; their manager Roger Saunders sat near the three Pythons.

Gilliam cited filming in Romania as his reason for not appearing, and Cleese, because he lived in Monaco, was 'beyond the seas.' The Pythons never seem to have heard of that modern device- the video link. If we could manage it for Simon Olswang from Israel, why couldn't they sort one out for Cleese?

Basil Fawlty in one of his more exasperated with the world moods could have written his Witness Statement. Only Cleese was exasperated with me.

A friend who was in court heard gossip that the Pythons were only there because of their costs. When they finally woke up to what was happening in the case, they realised that their legal bill was enormous, and if they settled with me they would have to pay my damages and costs as well as their legal costs. They decided to go to court to try to win the case, so that they would not have to pay these costs. The law makes fools and monsters of us all but I have to rely on that law.

I have asked my barrister Tom Weisselberg QC to make a few comments on some of the case's problems, as he saw them:

Memory

It is notoriously difficult to piece together memories, particularly about events which at the time seemed to be of little consequence. The Pythons were being required to recall events that took place in 1973 not long after I was born (in 1971), about an agreement that had no humour value and in respect of particular financial terms that were pretty difficult to understand even for a qualified lawyer. It was always unlikely that the Pythons would have any real recollection

My aim in cross-examination was therefore always to take those Pythons who attended the trial away from post facto assertion as to what they would never have accepted and to demonstrate the limits of their recollection.

In contrast, as the Producer, Mark <u>could</u> be expected to have a better memory of such things as agreements and contractual terms. This was particularly the case given his post-agreement conduct – namely, within a couple years of the agreement, raising invoices which claimed exactly what he said had been agreed.

The big moment had now arrived. We all stood for the arrival of Judge Norris. He was a slightly florid man in his 60s, who looked like a friendly uncle. I was also sorry to learn that he was a Cambridge man. Given the fact that he was 10 years younger than the Pythons, it would be easy to surmise that he had probably been a fan in his teens. Not a good sign for me, I thought.

We had been given an advance copy of the Defence team's skeleton argument for their opening remarks. Snakes don't have good memories so it is apt the main defence seemed to be amnesia. None of the Pythons recalled any meeting or discussion about my 1/7th share, none of them remember agreeing to it, none of them would have wanted to give it to me, and therefore it must have been put in by 'mistake'. I thought this was very weak, given the hard evidence that existed:

My Producer's Agreement, signed by Terry Jones

The confusing Third Schedule, where the merchandising share was given, had changes initialled by Michael Palin

The 1977 letters from Anne Henshaw to me

The 1979 memo from Anne to their accountant

The fact that Anne Henshaw, their former manager, and a close friend of Palin and Jones, had decided not to be a witness for them, was a very poor omen. I suspected inevitably that she did not want to lie on oath, so the poor woman had to be subjected to their QC labelling her a secretary who was 'confused' about the arrangement we had made in 1974. Richard Spearman, QC, leading barrister for the Pythons, wrote that her response in the letter to me of 1977 "demonstrates that Anne Henshaw had not properly understood the contractual position." He characterised Anne as a ditzy dogsbody which was demeaning to her. But then going to law is a brutal process. You try to shred me; I try to shred you.

In civil cases, the Barrister for the claimant goes first. Tom Weisselberg spent the whole of the first day taking the Judge through all the important points and documents in the case.

The Pythons' claims that my $1/7^{th}$ share was a 'mistake', and their contention that I was responsible for all the documentation for the film came close to insinuating that the lawyer for the film – Simon Olswang - had included this $1/7^{th}$ share without having any permission to do so. This point came up very quickly in court after my barrister kept referring to the difference between the 1/7th and 1/14th interpretations. One of the defence barristers objected, saying:

We say that the agreement is mistaken but not mistaken in giving him $1/14^{th}$ as opposed to $1/7^{th}$; it is mistaken in giving him $1/14^{th}$ at all because it was never intended he should have any share in the top half. That is our position.

MR. WEISSELBERG: What is difficult about that submission is the very fact of Mr. Palin signing the amendments to the profits of the film schedule. So there is no explanation as to $1/14^{th}$ because, on my learned friend's case, it was always a mistake that there should be any share at all. In the context of the manuscript amendments made by Mr. Olswang and annotated by Mr. Forstater and Mr. Palin, it is odd that if no agreement had been reached between Mr. Forstater and the Pythons that Mr. Forstater should be entitled to share in the top half, that Mr. Forstater should have been content for Mr. Palin to have his attention particularly drawn to those provisions and for him then to sign his initials in respect of amendments to that schedule.

There is an unspoken but inferred allegation that in some way Mr. Forstater may have done something wrong in relation to this agreement. It remains to be seen --

MR. JUSTICE NORRIS: I had not read the arguments as suggesting that there was some impropriety on your client's part. I had read the case as being (not trying to put words into anybody's mouth) that there is a muddle and one has to try to fathom out whether in truth on the evidence you can find out how the muddle came about and what the agreement should have been; otherwise one is left with a muddle. That is as I had understood the competing positions, but with no sense of any allegation of misrepresentation, deceit, lack of frankness or anything like that. Am I correct?

MR. SPEARMAN: Your Lordship is entirely right.
MR. WEISSELBERG: It is of great assistance that your Lordship and my learned friends have confirmed that is not their case, either up one's sleeve or at all.

Trials are brutal. When I was cross-examined by Mr. Spearman, I thought he came very close to making this insinuation, and I tried not to be rattled.

Spearman   Is it possible that that is why you started invoicing for the 1/7th of the top half?
A   I started invoicing for the 1/7th of the top half when statements arrived from the NFTC showing revenue, and I invoiced for that - for my share of that revenue.

Spearman   Is it possible that that is because it is basically a deal you wished you had got but you hadn't got. You thought it was only fair, so you invoiced?

I summoned all my courage to reply:

A   Well, I think you're coming close to what, in the very beginning of this trial, you denied was the situation - that somehow I contrived or colluded with Simon Olswang to give myself a share of income that I shouldn't have had. I think you're getting a bit close to that, Mr. Spearman.

Spearman   I do not think I have ever suggested that, but I will leave your answer where it is and your Lordship can make what he will of it in due course.

In his opening remarks my barrister said history showed how, in regard to my producer's fee, my profit participation and the 1/7th share that I was being "treated, for financial purposes, like the six Pythons.".

He also showed the Judge the memo from Anne Henshaw that I had found during disclosure:,

Mr. Weisselberg: There is one other letter from Mrs. Henshaw that I want to show your Lordship now, which, again in our submission, supports Mr. Forstater's case. This is not a letter that was sent to Mr. Forstater; it is sent to "Dear Anton", who I have assumed is an accountant. At 1(c): "I confirm that with regard to spin-off rights Mark Forstater receives, in addition to his share of the profits from the film pot, 1/7th of the 50 per cent payable to Python (Monty) Pictures".

MR. JUSTICE NORRIS: That was accurate because that is what he was invoicing?

MR. WEISSELBERG: That is what he was invoicing, but that was also what   Mrs. Henshaw was confirming to the accountant. One assumes that the way that that request would have come about was an accountant saying we have got this invoice here for $1/7^{th}$, why is he getting $1/7^{th}$? Mrs. Henshaw comes back to say: he has got $1/7^{th}$ because I can confirm that that is what he is entitled to get.

MR. SPEARMAN: My Lord, that is an interesting piece of speculation, but it is no more than that.

Never ask a question in court if you don't know the answer is a maxim of my learned friends. The law is full of irony so my barrister regretted what we did not really regret.

MR. WEISSELBERG: Regrettably, Mrs. Henshaw is not being called by my learned friend ......it is surprising that she is not coming along to explain what her understanding was of what went on in 1974. But what I will be submitting is that your Lordship is entitled to look at this 1979 letter and also the 1977 material that I showed your Lordship a moment ago to say that the Pythons' manager appears to have understood that Mr. Forstater was entitled to $1/7^{th}$ of the top half in circumstances where she was the Pythons' informal manager if not their formal manager at the time of the agreement being concluded.

He added that: " that was what everyone understood Mr. Forstater would be entitled to receive."

Here are my journal entries after the first day in court:

Friday November 30 2012

Came out of court. Went to Tom and Mark's Chambers, then walked with Stephanie and James to their offices.

Was intending to get the 98 bus home, but I had no food at home and no one to hang with, so I went to Joy King Lau for a shredded duck.

I read the Standard where the case was on P 5.

BBC Radio wants to speak with me, but Tom said not to talk to the press. I guess I can wait until after my cross-examination, which will be Monday and maybe some of Tuesday,

Photographers at the court exit this morning x 2 and then at night x9.

Can I win if I win? The minimum should be at least 250k otherwise how can I pay off my bank and creditors?

Sunday December 2 2012

Tomorrow is the big day, seven years in the making and it all comes down to this- 4-5 hours in the witness box, explaining my case. My barrister thinks the Pythons are all saying they don't remember the important meeting (and I do) and Anne Henshaw isn't here to corroborate either side, then the Judge will have to believe me, especially since the deal was put into writing and then acted on for 30 years, and confirmed on 2 occasions by Anne Henshaw. I hope they are right - I will do my best and not try to be too clever!

Day 2

Day 2 began with Richard Spearman QC giving his opening remarks. He went through numerous Python documents from 1974/5 to show that there was no reference in them to any meeting or discussion about any 1/7th share. When Anne Henshaw was noted as being present at these meetings he tried to minimise her role. She was not behaving in a managerial or quasi managerial role:

Mr. Spearman: It is all basically getting the members of the group in, asking them how they see things unfolding, and discussing financial information. There is nothing about her negotiating, taking a managerial role at all. ... It was basically a financial advisory role. It was a sort of company secretarial and accountancy role. Some of it is absolutely straight accountancy material.

He went on to discuss the 1977 letters between Anne and myself over the book publication.

Mark Forstater Productions Ltd
9 Cliff Road, Camden Square, London NW1
Telephone: 01-267 6178
Cables: Markfilm London NW1
Telex: 22861 ATTF150

Ann Henshaw
Python Productions Ltd
20 Fitzroy Square
London W1

23 June 1977

Dear Ann

MONTY PYTHON AND THE HOLY GRAIL (Book)

I have received the letters from Python Productions and the NFTC regarding the proposed book deal.

It seems to me that the deal being offerred by Python Productions is a fair one for the investors and has been justly managed by the Pythons.

However, this new deal does affect me directly. Since in the original deal negotiated I was allocated 1/7th of the Python's share of any spin-offs. Under this proposed deal I lose that share. Would the Pythons be willing to bring me in on the Python Productions side so that this 1/7th share remains the same?

If you can find a way to accommodate me I would be more than happy to approve the deal and to recommend it to any investors who seek my advice.

Yours sincerely,

MARK FORSTATER

Mark Forstater Productions Ltd
Reg. No. 1206966 (England)
Reg. Office: 7 Fitzroy Square, London W1P 6BB
Directors: M I Forstater (USA), M P Forstater (USA)
G C Wheatley, R J Harris, M Hatton

Where she confirms my 1/7th share he says that she is just repeating what I have written:

Mr. Spearman. Then she is mistaken, my Lord, in the last part where she is, in our submission, repeating back his letter. "You will after all be receiving your investor's share plus a 1/7th of 50% of the amount paid to the NFTC, which would be the Python (Monty) Pictures" share because on our case, my Lord, the top half never went to the NFTC.

I have already shown the NFTC Statement which shows that the 'top half' - ie the 50% that the Pythons retained, did pass though the NFTC books. They passed the income on to the Python company and I invoiced my 1/7th to them. Lawyers can get it wrong.

Here is my journal entry after day 2:

Tuesday December 4, 2012

We broke for lunch and came back for Simon Olswang's testimony- via video from Israel. For a long time the video link didn't work - kept losing the picture and he couldn't see us. In the end we spoke to him via mobile phone. He was good, in particular about how he took instructions from Anne Henshaw thereby challenging the Spearman claim that she was a 'secretary'.

My WITNESS: Simon Olswang- The Video Link Sketch

I had two witnesses on my side: Simon Olswang, the lawyer for the film, and Selwyn Remington, who in 1974 was Simon's assistant at the firm of Brecher and Co. Simon lives in Israel now, so we had arranged for a video link to be set up in Tel Aviv. However, this soon turned into a quasi-Python sketch.

The video link had been set up during lunch, and we were due to start at 2:00 pm. However at 2:00 the video link was not working, and there was no picture and no sound.

I was worried I would miss having my most important witness heard. At last the video link started to work, and we could see Simon but could not hear him nor could he hear us. The technician finally managed to get the audio from Israel so we could hear Simon, but he couldn't hear us. Mark Vinall decided to phone Simon on his mobile and let Tom conduct the cross-examination in that way: We can bounce messages off Jupiter and send pebbles beyond the Solar System but getting a video link to work, please ..... We could see Simon and hear him on a monitor but he couldn't see or hear us, except through the phone.

2.30 p.m.

MR. WEISSELBERG: My Lord, thank you very much for your patience.

Judge Norris then let us have a dish of judicial humour.

MR. JUSTICE NORRIS: As you explained on Friday, it is all very straightforward!

It is wise to laugh at His Lordship's jokes so there were polite titters.

MR. WEISSELBERG: Absolutely. In my experience in the past it has been precisely that. What we are now doing is phoning Mr. Olswang and at the moment they cannot hear us, but they will hear us over the phone. Mr. Olswang, can you hear me?

MR. OLSWANG: I have just realised that the bundle has come apart so I am just repairing the bundle if you give me a second.

MR. WEISSELBERG: Mr. Olswang is on mute. I apologise for this. I understood that it was going to work.

MR. JUSTICE NORRIS: Provided we can extract something useful out of the process, let us just carry on.

MR. WEISSELBERG: I am grateful. Mr. Olswang, can you hear me?

MR. OLSWANG: Yes. I don't know who you are but I can hear you.

MR. WEISSELBERG: My name is Tom Weisselberg and I am appearing for the claimant.

MR. OLSWANG: Okay Tom.

MR. WEISSELBERG: In front of you, you have a number of bundles?

MR. OLSWANG: Yes.

MR. WEISSELBERG: Before looking at the bundles you will be asked to affirm.

THE CLERK OF THE COURT: Good afternoon, sir.

MR. JUSTICE NORRIS: Can you hear, Mr. Olswang?

MR. WEISSELBERG: Mr. Olswang, can you hear us?

MR. OLSWANG: I can hear you.

MR. WEISSELBERG: You are just going to have to promise to tell the truth, Mr. Olswang, so I would like you to listen to what you are about to be told and repeat back what you will then hear.

MR. OLSWANG: Yes. Okay.

<u>Mr. SIMON OLSWANG, Affirmed</u>
<u>Examined by Mr. WEISSELBERG</u>

Weisselberg   Mr. Olswang, it is Tom Weisselberg again?
A   Okay, Tom. I am just trying to organise the charger on my phone. Okay, I am all yours.

Weisselberg   I would like you to turn in bundle C please to tab 5?
A   Okay. Just please note that in the course of getting here the binder broke so it's a split binder and I am going to be in danger of losing pages, so I have to put the phone down.

(Tom handed over to Richard Spearman:)

Spearman   This is a trip down a long section of Memory Lane, Mr. Olswang. We are going back now to 1973. What I would just like you to look at, please, to start with is p.653.
A   I will put the phone down. (Pause) OK, I have that. No, sorry. (Pause) I have 653.

Soearman   I will just give you a minute to look at it. It is a letter from you to Mr. Gledhill. Your signature is on p.654. Has it gone off? I think it has. Are you back with us?

A   Sorry, we lost the connection. Can you hear me?

Sperarman   Yes, very well. Can you hear me?
A   Yes, and I now have 653.

***

Mr. SPEARMAN: I just want to take you through some of the documents. I am going to suggest to you, Mr. Olswang, that throughout this period you dealt with Mark Forstater and not with Anne Henshaw over matters connected with the film, any matters connected with the film.

MR. JUSTICE NORRIS: I think you have lost the video connection.

MR. SPEARMAN: Yes. I should say, my Lord, this happened a number of times before your Lordship came into court and we started up again but it has broken off again.

MR. JUSTICE NORRIS: Can we try to re-establish contact?

MR. SPEARMAN: Yes.

MR. JUSTICE NORRIS: Can we do that? (We need to wait for them to contact us) Do we? (Pause)

3.10 p.m.

MR. WEISSELBERG: My Lord, they are back.

MR. SPEARMAN: Are you back with us, Mr. Olswang?
A   I never left you.

Spearman   We left you. I am sorry. There is a parting of the ways here?
A   I can hear you and I can see myself, but not you.

Spearman   No?
A   Can you see me?

Spearman   Yes, very well thank you. Well, not very well right now; it is pixelated a bit but mostly very well.

A   Yes.
Spearman   No?

Spearman   Now, on the documents that we have got, the first contact that I can find anyway between Anne Henshaw and you that is recorded is page 664. Just to set this in context, Mr. Olswang, if you look at page 663 first, you will see that on 12th September 1974 you got a letter sent to you by Jim Beach, I think it is, of Harbottle & Lewis saying that Harbottle & Lewis has been formally instructed on behalf of the Pythons. Do you remember that? (Pause) I think we have lost you. Can your Lordship hear the answer? No. For a moment you will have to wait Mr. Olswang, because we cannot hear you and we need to get the site reconnected. Just one moment, Mr. Olswang.

UNKNOWN MALE SPEAKER: I am so sorry. Because we are doing this through a bridging company we need to wait for them to connect to us.

MR. SPEARMAN: Mr. Olswang, if you can hear me,

there is no point in speaking at the moment because we cannot hear you in court. If you give us a moment we will get reconnected. (Pause) Now, can you hear us? Could you unmute the microphone? Not on the phone, for the video conference facility?
A   Yes, yes.

***

A   Yes, I don't find it extraordinary. If you look at the first paragraph of this letter.....

Spearman   You have gone again, Mr. Olswang. If you wait a moment, your sound has gone. Have you touched the mute button again by mistake?
A   Ah, yes. How's that?

***

Spearman   Mr. Olswang, it is Mr. Cullen, representing the second defendant. Can you hear me? Mr. Olswang, can you hear me? It is Mr. Cullen who is representing the second defendant?
A   I am not quite sure whether you have finished with me or whether you wish me to stay on the line?

Cullen   Stay on the line, please. I have just got a couple of questions for you. Can you hear me?
A   Yes, but I hear whoever is speaking less well and I don't know who's speaking to me.

Cullen   It is Mr. Cullen who is for the second defendant.
A   Right. What is your name, please sir?

Cullen   Mr. Cullen.
A   Mr. Cole?

Cullen   Cullen. Do not worry about my name. Perhaps I will just ask the question.
A   I probably do not need to know your name, if you do not mind. That is what matters.

Cullen   Can you hear me now?
A   I can hear you well.
***

THE WITNESS: I am sorry that we had trouble with the two-way connection.

MR. JUSTICE NORRIS: Do not worry. We did not have to resort to pigeons so that is fine.

Ho Ho
Spearman was trying to show that Simon Olswang only took instruction from me on the film, and had no contact with Anne Henshaw. Simon's evidence was that he did deal with her, not on film matters, but on corporate and financial matters relating to the Pythons. Spearman also tried to rebut Simon's claim that I was to be treated as a '7th Python' in regard to financial matters in the film, but Simon confirmed,

What I now recall is the situation, and the situation was, as I understood it, that Mark Forstater was regarded as, for business purposes, the 7th Python.
I clearly recall that it was the intention of the parties that Mr. Forstater would be treated the same as all the other members of Monty Python here such that where they were to be entitled to deduct their 50% off the top, he was entitled to receive $1/7^{th}$ of this.

Simon's evidence, barring the technical fiasco, was very strong, and the Pythons decided not to cross-examine my second witness, Selwyn Remington. By doing this, they admitted Selwyn's Witness Statement as true, and the judge had to take it that way. Since Selwyn also confirmed that Simon spoke frequently to Anne Henshaw, and that he was instructed by Simon that I was to be treated financially as an equal to the Pythons, I felt this strengthened my case. It also showed that the Pythons were not happy with the way the trial was going.

I was called for cross-examination at the very end of the day.

DAY 3-

It's a weary world this Chancery! I am grieved that I should be the enemy of a great number of relations and others, and that they should be my enemies and that we should all be ruining one another without knowing how and why and be in constant doubt and discord all our lives.
Bleak House

If you read newspaper accounts of trials you inevitably get a précis – and nearly always a radical précis. Lawyers read law reports but they highlight the legal niceties of a case. For example if a building is shoddily built how shoddy does the builder have to be before you can sue him for negligence, malfeasance or outright fraud because he was not a builder at all but a jelly bean manufacturer? I have reported the way I was cross examined in detail not because I think I was clever in dealing with the Pythons' barrister but because readers may like to know what it feels like to be cross examined – and my cross examination lasted as long as four football matches. (At least I did not have to run about).

Spearman spent a lot of time on my relationship with Julian Doyle and Chippenham Films:

Spearman   You never told Mr. Doyle, did you, that you had signed the agreement, the producer agreement, in your name alone and not in the name of Chippenham Films?
A   I had no need to because Chippenham Films was not involved in the production. When I say in the production, I mean as a corporate co-producer or involved in some kind of enabling or financial way.

Spearman   You were taken on, you and Mr. Doyle, together as a partnership as you had been on previous occasions. That is my suggestion to you.
A   If you look at the credits of the film, which were put together by the two directors, Terry Gilliam and Terry Jones, there is no mention of Chippenham Films. There is no credit to Chippenham Films. And no one ever either spoke to me or wrote to me in the terms that Michael Palin is using here. No one ever said to me, "Chippenham Films is making this film". In fact, if you look at Michael Palin's diary entries, he introduces me as the producer to John Cleese. The company, at a meeting, proposing that in all future films I will be their producer. There is no mention of Chippenham Films at all. I am afraid this is re-writing history.

Spearman   All right. Let us just look then at p.652 in Bundle D2. This is an undated draft letter. "Dear Mr. Forstater: In view of your endeavours in the setting up of the second Monty Python film we wish to put in writing our firm intentions concerning the relationship between our two companies. The film will be produced by Python Productions in association with Chippenham Films, and you personally will be the nominal producer subject, of course, to satisfactory negotiations being concluded between us. We confirm that you are authorised to do all

you think fit to bring about the production of the film and to keep us informed of all negotiations you undertake. We on our part will consult closely with you and no negotiations will be finalised without our mutual agreement". Do you recollect - that is only a draft - getting a letter in those terms at any stage?
A   No. I never got a letter like this. I see this is a draft letter. It is undated and unsigned. You know, it just never appeared.

Spearman   So that would have been a complete departure from the real position on your case. Is that right?
A   That is right.

Spearman   I suggest, in fact, that letter reflects the real position.
A   Well, if Chippenham Films had been involved in the film as a co-producer you would have thought that Chippenham Films would be mentioned at least once in all of these diaries of Michael Palin and Terry Jones. It is not mentioned once and in the film's credits it is not mentioned.

Spearman   It is not mentioned in the credits because the agreements - the agreement that you negotiated and you signed - provides that you will be credited as the producer.
A   Yes, but the two Terrys made the credits. If they wanted to give Chippenham Films a credit as a producer, because they felt that it was right, that was totally in their charge. They had total freedom to create a title subject to obviously legal obligations. But if they wanted to give even a "thank you" to Chippenham Films they easily could have done that. They did not do it because it was not part of the mix.

Spearman   The reality is different, I suggest. What happens is they trusted you to look after, in fact, their interests - that is the Pythons' interests - as well as Julian Doyle's interests. They did not concern themselves with the documents. They trusted you to get on with that and you negotiated the agreement between yourself and the Pythons, with the help of your solicitor, Mr. Olswang, and you got a credit as producer because that is what the agreement provides for.
A   Mr. Olswang is not my solicitor. He was a solicitor for the company. The letter you showed me before from Michael Palin, he said that Julian's remuneration was very fair.

Spearman   Yes, he is not saying it is unfair but he is saying ----
A   If it is not unfair it must be fair.

Spearman   He is saying it is a matter that he left for you and Julian Doyle to sort out between you, but he expected you both to be remunerated.
A   And he says it is fair.

Spearman   As a production team.
A   They wanted Julian involved in the film and Julian was involved with the film. He was the production manager. It was an important job. He did it very well. Because he did it so well he put in extra times doing many other things that a production manager normally would not do. I felt that he deserved a share of profits and therefore I gave it to him.

Spearman   It was always the intention that he should have a share of the profits, not at your behest but because that was the deal that was done between Chippenham Films on the one hand and the Pythons on the other.

A   No one conveyed to me, either in writing or orally, that there was a such a deal. It just never existed.

Spearman also wanted to stress that I was the main person liaising with Simon Olswang on the film's documentation,

A   In relation to the film, for example as you pointed out insurances for the film, financial matters relating to the film, investment - all these matters were things that a producer deals with and I did deal with them. But when it came to the Pythons' own share of fees, profits etc, this was not - you know, this was not my area for informing Simon Olswang. This was really where Anne Henshaw had her place. I mean, she was their - from my point of view she was their manager. Any matters that related to their involvement was..... Really her involvement was there to reflect that and to protect that.

Spearman   Well, what were they asking you to do then? We just looked at the diary entries. They wanted you to do negotiating. They wanted you to take charge of documents. If it was not their involvement, what were they asking you to do? Whose interests were you looking after?

A   I was looking after the interests of the Pythons in terms of how the film was going to be financed and structured, but in terms of their own involvement in terms of their earnings, their profit share, you know, their own individual positions, that was not for me to negotiate. That was for Anne Henshaw to inform Simon Olswang and myself on their behalf. I wasn't negotiating for them as writers, performers, directors. I was trying to put the entire film together.

Spearman   Can I suggest to you that that is a nonsense for two reasons. First of all, when you are negotiating the financing and so forth, you have obviously got to have regard to who is going to get what out of the money that is coming in?
A   Yes, but it wasn't my job to say: Okay, Terry Jones, you'll get this and John Cleese, we'll give you that. I wasn't dictating what their fees were. This was something that had to be negotiated in terms of all of us. Michael White, the main financier, Anne Henshaw representing the Pythons, the Pythons themselves and myself. This is all a mutually agreed situation. There is no way for me to dictate how the Pythons should be paid or what their profit share was. If it was, I should have walked away, you know, under your terms, I would have walked away with 50% of the profits for myself, if no-one else was looking at the documents.

Spearman   I do not think they would have quite let you get as far as that, Mr.   Forstater, but there we are.

Spearman was trying very hard to establish Anne as a bookkeeper or secretary who had no more authority than a private.

Spearman. The sort of role that Anne Henshaw was performing in the period we are talking about is illustrated, I suggest to you, by page 660A. It is not a letter that went to you. It is a letter from Mr. Gledhill to the bank. "Could you please note for your records we now have new accountants. There is some expansion with the company and they are: Henshaw Catty... The person who is dealing directly with our affairs there is Anne Henshaw." She dealt, I suggest, with accountancy and book-keeping matters, and also organising and minuting meetings that happened. That was her role?

A   To my memory she did much more than this because if Gledhill was being pushed away and was not doing his managerial role, who was doing it? I mean someone had to do it. The Pythons were not doing it themselves, and I thought she was there. She was involved. She was at the end of a telephone. She was their manager. John Gledhill wasn't at this point.

Spearman   He was, you see. We can look over all these entries if you want, but the position is that of course there was dissatisfaction with Mr. Gledhill. You were part of the reason for it. I do not attribute blame to you in that. I mean you came in and made criticism of some of the things that he was doing, but he was never replaced as a manger until June?

A   Perhaps in terms of the actual contract that could be correct. From the papers it does look to be correct, but in reality - I don't know from what date - but sometime during the time that I was involved, probably late '73, John Gledhill was just not a figure who was involved in any of these discussions. Anne Henshaw was, and the meetings I attended were all at the Henshaws.

Spearman   We can take some time if you want, Mr. Forstater, but the diary entries, the minutes, are littered with references to Mr. Gledhill?

A   Yes, but are they not all about how they are going to pay him off and what kind of deal they should give him?

You know, it's not that he is running the meetings and is coming up with suggestions and doing activities for them as a manager. I think it is mainly about how they are nice guys; they don't want to say to him, "Go away", and they are trying to work out a reasonable deal to pay him off.

Spearman   They are building up to what eventually is a termination package, but until it happens he is still the manager - and not just in name, but in practice?
A   That's just not the impression that I got from these documents, or from my experience there.

Spearman   Which documents do you get the impression from that Anne Henshaw then is the manager?
A   There was - one of the meetings where there's a discussion about the music and about the role of Nancy Lewis.

MR. SPEARMAN: Just to remind you, your witness evidence in para.16 is: "From early 1974 she [Anne Henshaw] was acting in a managerial representative role (Michael Palin diary entry 4th March 1974, 11th March 1974) and was eventually appointed the Pythons' manager later in 1974." So you have answered me in a way which accords with your evidence. This, I think we can say perhaps, is the high water mark of your case that Anne Henshaw was in a managerial/representative role at this time. Let us just look at it. First of all, the 4th March entry.

"We were due to meet with the Henshaws and Nancy (Lewis) and Ina before lunch. We finally got there at 1 o'clock. There were some sandwiches and white wine.

Under discussion was Nancy's official future with Python. At a recent meeting we decided to put Nancy in charge of our new music publishing company Kay-Gee-Bee Music Ltd, also to give her control of records and recordings and all future contracts (now that Mark is in charge of our film section! Nancy's appointment will further restrict the sphere of Gledhill's influence.)"

Where do you get out of that that Anne Henshaw was acting in a managerial/representative role?

A   Well, I mean, John Gledhill was not at that meeting or lunch, the Henshaws are. Anne Henshaw is, from what I gathered from Michael's diaries, taking on more of their – trying to sort out their kind of mess is more or less how he put it. Michael Henshaw was really, from my point of view, only dealt with their accounts as far as I knew, because he wasn't involved in any of the meetings that I had with them. I was introduced to him but he was not at any of these meeting that I had with them and Anne Henshaw was.

Spearman   First of all, this of course is something that you did not know about at the time, is that right? You only know about this from the documents, is that correct?
A   That's correct. What I'm saying is that the documents reflect my experience of dealing with her on a daily basis.

Spearman   Going round to her house and having some sandwiches and white wine and talking about record deals, that sort of thing?
A   Well, talking about the film, yes.

Spearman   But you see there is nothing here to suggest that she has got any managerial role, is there? There is a meeting at the Henshaws, a decision is taken to put Nancy in charge of music publishing. There is nothing to suggest that she was involved in that decision, is there?
A   From this diary entry?

Spearman   Yes.
A   Wasn't there a memorandum from this meeting that does seem to me to reflect more her involvement?

Spearman   It is a diary entry you rely on in your witness statement so let us deal with that first. I am suggesting to you there is nothing there to suggest she has got a representational or managerial role.
A   Except that this is - in Michael Palin's published diary he mentions who Anne is at a certain point in early 74, and that note isn't here in this transcript of the diaries.

Spearman   You are saying there is a published diary entry that relates to this date, is that right?
A   Yes, a note from him explaining who she was and what she was doing.

Spearman   We have not got that.

At this point my barrister referred the Judge to p 1107i and Spearman, since my learned friends are supposed to play fair to each other, read the footnote.

MR. SPEARMAN: I can read your Lordship the footnote, my Lord. It is from the published diaries. It says this: "Michael Henshaw had been my accountant since 1966. His wife Anne was helping sort out Pythons' affairs." My

Lord, that is a footnote which explains the reference to the word "Henshaws". So you are saying if you look at this, you look at the footnote, you can see that Anne Henshaw was acting as a manager. Is that what you are saying?
A   All I'm saying is that Michael's reference to sorting out their affairs seems to me to be more than just a bookkeeper.

Spearman They had plenty of financial affairs to sort out, did they not?
A   Yes, they had indeed.

Spearman   But nothing to do with managerial matters.
A   I assumed from my experience that she was acting in a managerial role.

Spearman   You can see at the end of the 4th March diary entry that what is being talked about is Nancy's appointment, she is going to be in charge of the new music publishing company "which further restricts the sphere of Gledhill's influence". So you can see from that, can you not, that Mr. Gledhill was still in the saddle, so to speak, but his territory was being cut into by Nancy being appointed?
A   Yes.

Spearman   Let us look at the next diary entry then: "Another Python meeting at the Henshaws. Anne was there smoking, slightly nervously as usual." I am not going to read all of this. I will let you read it to yourself. (Pause)
A   Again, I think that at the end of that diary entry this reflects my understanding: "Full marks to Anne who is working hard to try and sort us out." I think this, yes, I

mean, she is trying to sort out their affairs which they felt Gledhill had left in a terrible state, as their manager.

Spearman   But what she is doing is, if you go back – I do not think you are doing yourself much justice, Mr. Forstater – what he is doing is first of all talking about the so-called Gledhill retirement scheme, right?
A   Yes.

Spearman   Which is obviously which is, for that purpose, the Pythons on the one hand and Gledhill on the other and what they are going to offer him. Secondly, top of p.967, she is taking Mr. Gledhill to task over their figures. "I detected almost visible discomfiture when Anne mentioned the figures for UK and Canadian tours." So in other words, she is helping them with the negotiations for terminating Mr. Gledhill's retainer, and she is helping them with the arithmetic.
A   Yes.

Spearman   That is not a managerial function, I suggest. It is a straightforward accountancy function that she is performing for them.
A   My experience of her was that she was involved in much more than that.

Spearman   I suggest to you there is nothing in there to indicate she is performing any sort of managerial function at all. A meeting has been convened; she, one assumes, has drawn up the agenda; she has drawn up the notes. What is happening is whoever attended this meeting (we can personnel, no doubt, somewhere) are being asked for what they want to do about various things; she is recording the approach that those people are adopting. For example, bottom of p.1002 about the calendar which Eric Idle is talking about. Then she is giving, if you like, straight accountancy/bookkeeping input. For example, at the top of p.1003, what the company's corporation tax position will be.

A I think that there are some areas in this agenda, and actually it is not the agenda but it is the notes of the agenda. I mean, in "Item 3 Point 5", p.1002, obviously they are discussing Nancy Lewis' fees and it seems to me that this is a managerial role. They are negotiating. They are talking about how this could be negotiated, what this fee could be and the variations that could be applied. I think that is something that clearly a manager would be involved in because they would have to be then, once that discussion took place, it would have to be communicated to Nancy Lewis. Presumably she might not agree. They might have to negotiate with her further and then report back to the Pythons whether that negotiation was successful or not. It seems to me that is not a bookkeeping or a secretarial role. Secondly, in number 6, talking about next year's activities, I just think this is not just, you know, putting things in a calendar.

Spearman Why do you say that?

A I say it is a discussion about what they are going to be doing and what they want to do, so I think that that has to involve a discussion about what they should be doing, what they want to do, where they are headed. It seems to me that is more than just recording dates. That has an involvement of, you know, where is the group going, what can we achieve, you know, who will go along with any of those things. This is a group of six very different individual people, as you can see. John Cleese and Eric Idle are kind of on the periphery. They do not really want to be involved. There is a core of Python sort of engagement which is Michael Palin, Terry Jones, Terry Gilliam and Graham Chapman, to a degree. So that to get these people together to do something is quite a difficult task. The manager is the only link between all these six and acts as a hub, and I just cannot see that someone who is just doing bookkeeping is going to be able to do that and keep them functioning as a creative and productive group.

Spearman So in Item 6 you read in that she is getting these disparate six individuals together and coordinating their activities for the coming months, do you? Is that what you read into 6?
A I would say that she would have to do that in order to get them to actually have a calendar that could be kept to.

Spearman So the simple possibility that it is just a short record of what they were telling her they had in mind is not one that attracts you, Mr. Forstater? You read into it a managerial role, do you?
A Given the nature of this group and the personalities involved, I would say that was correct, but that is my impression. My interpretation.

Spearman Your interpretation.
A Yes.

Spearman Right, very well. All I can say is that we must agree to differ. What I suggest this shows is, like all the other minutes, she was organising meetings; they were expressing, whoever turned up, views, and she was recording what the views were, what the issues were, but never taking a managerial role about anything in all of this. Very well. Again we can go over it but would you accept from me that there is not a single document in these bundles which shows Anne Henshaw acting as a communications link with either you or Mr. Olswang until we get to a much later date, around about August 1974?

A   I have not looked through the documents but I accept it.

So we differed on what makes a manager a manager. There was formidable brain power in that room- Oxbridge men, expensive lawyers, Terry Jones has a PH.D - yet curiously no one dipped into the many textbooks on management which presumably define the subject.

Spearman also questioned me about how the 1/7 share found its way into my Agreement,

Spearman   Let me then ask you this about your witness statement, where you say in para.17 that after the accord that you say was reached under which you would get a 1/7th of the top half, you did not give any instructions to Simon Olswang about the wording of the third schedule and you assume that Anne Henshaw did. May I just ask you this, on what on earth is that assumption based?

A   I had asked them for a share of their 50% of the merchandising and it was agreed, but I would not - this is I think what I expressed to you before - it is not my role to tell Simon Olswang how to share out the Pythons' interests and their money. That was their shareholding. It was not my role to tell Simon Olswang, "Will you carve out a 1/7th of that for me, please?" That would have to come from them. It would not have been right for me to tell Simon Olswang, "Oh, I have this share. You know, just please write it into my agreement". I just would not have done that. It was not right and it was not how it was done.

***

Spearman.   You say this, five lines up from the bottom, "I did not instruct Simon Olswang about the wording of the Third Schedule and do not recall any discussion with him about it. So I assume that Anne Henshaw gave him instructions." Your witness statement is clear, is it not, that you did not give the instructions to Simon Olswang?
A   Yes. I don't think I did give him the instructions.

Spearman   Let us leave the Pythons' side of it. It is unfair for you to give the instructions, you say, because it is part of their income stream they have given up to you. What about being fair to yourself? You have gone and negotiated a seventh of the top half. You want to be sure, presumably, that you get that, and that is enshrined in your contract. Correct?
A   Yes.

Spearman   So if you would not instruct Mr. Olswang on their behalf, why did you not instruct him on your behalf?
A   I just don't remember.

Spearman   Can I suggest a simple answer: because it never happened, and it was never agreed?
A   Well, that is a very simple answer.

****

Spearman questioned me on my differing explanations over the years regarding how the 1/7th share was created and documented.

Spearman.   This is the first of a number of versions you have put forward over the years as to how the 1/7th of the top half was either made or recorded. You say at 723: "I believe the agreement for my merchandising share was not part of the original documentation, but was agreed on side letters at a later date, when it became clear I had been missing out on the ancillary income." Your original case is it was in side letters and it was not at the time of the original agreement at all; it was at a later date. Is that right?

A   Well, again, I don't have the agreement in front of me when I'm saying this.

Spearman   I understand that.

A   So I am trying to remember how was this 1/7th expressed in a document, and I knew that it had been done somehow at a separate occasion. I remembered that Michael Palin and I, and I believe Anne Henshaw, had gone to Simon Olswang's office and in his office had initialled or signed something. So I had a memory of that but I did not know whether that was a side letter and, to me, I am not a lawyer, so a side letter or an appendix or a third schedule are all the same kind of thing. They are not the kind of main agreement. They are kind of appended or ----

Spearman   Mr. Forstater, I am sorry, I must - I am sorry, I did not mean to cut across you. I must disagree with you about that. You have been a producer for a long, long time. You must have negotiated an awful lot of deals in your day, have you not?

A   Yes, but I am not a lawyer. I let my lawyers do that. I do not put the documents together, legal documents together, and in my mind, you know, I am a layman. A side letter, an appendix, these all are, as it were, extra or separate from a main body of an agreement. So in my mind I obviously was trying to figure out where was this agreement and I thought, okay, it was not in a body of a document but it was separate. It was a side letter.

Spearman   We have got your answer that for you a side letter and an appendix or a schedule are the same thing, but would you agree with me about this, that what you were saying here, at p.73, was that the agreement, in your recollection at that time, was made at a later date than the documents were signed?
A   Yes, that is what I remember here and, of course, in fact I think that turns out to be correct. I do not think that is incorrect.

Spearman   I am afraid it is because what you are saying here is - I will just read it to you again - "I believe the agreement for my merchandising share was not part of the original documentation but was agreed on side letters at a later date when it became clear I would be missing out on the ancillary income". What I suggest you are saying there is that the original documentation is made; later on it becomes clear you will be missing out on ancillary income, and then a side agreement is made in side letters. That is what you are saying in that email. That is my suggestion to you.
A   You know, the actual events of 30 years before, you know, it is very hard to be absolutely certain of what happened and when. Clearly this idea of missing out on ancillary income was really the earlier discussion. It was not part of a later fact. What I am saying about, I give the later date, is that it did turn out, when I finally did get a copy of the agreement, there was a third schedule, which was an appendix, and it had some handwritten amendments which were clearly made at a later date and so I think obviously this is just fragments of memory that

are there and not the complete picture. But the fragments are actually correct. The complete picture is not there in my memory at this point but the fragments I think actually are pretty good.

Spearman   That is a matter for his Lordship in due course but it is reassuring to know your views on it. Let us go on, shall we? Page 725, Mr. Saunders comes back to you and says he cannot seem to find the side letters amending the agreement.

A   Yes.

Spearman   726 you say you doubt you kept them, they go back such a long way.

A   Yes.

Spearman   Then 727 you come up with what is, I suggest, your second version of events on this. You say you cannot find any papers and you say, "Since you have no letters regarding this agreement it is very possible this was done purely verbally".

A   Yes. I finally realised I do not have the documentation. He said to me that he cannot find this reference to 1/7th of 50%, which is what is in my mind, in the agreement or in this third schedule and he cannot find any side letters. So I am trying to figure out where is this 1/7th of 50%, where is it expressed if it is not in any documentation which I thought it was in documentation, and it is not in documentation then, you know, what is going on? So I said, well, then perhaps, if it is not in any documentation, perhaps it was only done verbally. Because we did have a verbal agreement but in my mind it had gone from a verbal agreement to a document but he cannot find a document. So I am kind of floundering around trying to figure out where is this 1/7th of 50%

located. I have no papers to look at. He has an agreement sitting in front of him and I am just in the dark.

Spearman   Yes. You are floundering around but the floundering goes on because, if you go to p.732, this is 31st October this time, again I suggest to you, you use the same point as you used in your email back at p.723 - I am reading from the second paragraph, Mr. Forstater on p.732 - "I made the point at the time that as the producer of the film I should share in the Python share of this revenue as if I were a Python, i.e. a seventh member of the team, and should therefore be entitled to a 1/7th share of the Python (Monty) revenue".
A   Yes.

Spearman   It is even clearer, I suggest, there that the basis is that you are part of the same team and therefore you get a 1/7th.
A   The line you have just left out, "This was accepted and was enshrined in an appendix".

Spearman   No, I had not left it out. I had stopped.
A   Sorry.

Spearman   Do not worry. You will have your chance to answer that in a minute.
A   I made a reference to the appendix to the agreement. This means that at this point I actually have the agreement, otherwise I would not make a reference to it.

Spearman   That may be true but the point I was asking you was about the fact that you were saying that the reason why you were entitled to a 1/7th share was because you were a seventh member of the team. That is what you were saying.

A   Once I had the agreement and was able to read it I could see. It reminded me of my position as a deferee with the other six and that that position kind of brought back - I mean, just getting any document tends to bring back with it, you know, some memories of the time and helps to bring back information that may have been buried and so I realised that that position of being a deferee with the other six, of taking that risk with them, was in effect being a seventh Python with them for that area of risk at that time. That is why I wrote it in this way to Michael Palin.

Spearman   You are not talking about sharing risk and things like that. You are talking about being a producer and a seventh member of the team, are you not?

A   Yes, but it was that element of risk as well as the positive elements of bringing the entire film together and producing it with them, that to me was how I would characterise myself at that specific period of time, as a seventh member of the team.

Spearman   At this stage you say that the agreement you invite his Lordship to find was reached and was enshrined in an appendix.

A   Yes.

Spearman   Then you say on the next page, again the second paragraph on the next page: "I do not know if your memory goes back this far, but I believe the true nature of our agreement at the time was I should be treated as a seventh Python for this revenue which I did help to create". Let me ask you about that. The whole point about the top half is that it is to cater for a situation where the Pythons

make a material contribution to certain merchandising and spin-off income. Yes?
A   Yes.

Spearman   So the reason why there is a distinction between that type of merchandising and spin-off income and ordinary merchandising and spin-off income is that it is got the extra material contribution by the Pythons in it. So why should you be treated like them for that revenue stream? I understand why you should be entitled to a share of the profits of the film. I understand why you should be entitled to a share of merchandising and spin-off as well as just the film. But why should you be treated the same as them when you are not making the extra material contribution, which is the whole reason why the top half is created?
A   I have to go back to the answer I gave you previously, that the producer is a co-creator of the film itself, and without the film there is no spin-off. So in that sense the producer really should share in all the revenue that comes from the film and its spin-offs.

Spearman   But you are always going to get a share in this spin-off revenue. You are going to get the bottom half of it and that is going to be shared like everything else. Why should you get a share in the top half?
A   I felt that I deserved that share as the person who helped to bring the film into existence.

Spearman   So you deserved to participate equally with the people who are going to make a material contribution even though you are not making any material contribution?
A   Yes.

Spearman   And it is right, is it not, as a matter of arithmetic, that the end result, if you are right, is that you will get a bigger part of that revenue stream than if it was just a merchandising or spin-off where they did not make a material contribution?
A   Yes, I would get a larger share.

Spearman   You think that is right as well, do you?
A   Yes, I do.

Spearman   What is the logic of that?
A   Again it is the same logic, that if they are getting a larger share of that merchandising income the producer should not be left behind. As it worked out, in fact, they put other companies of their own in the position off the top so that my 1/7th and the investors' share was diluted and that the people who actually did the work took a share through these other companies, leaving the top half, 50% of the top half, for all the Pythons who did not do anything and myself. But the net effect of that was actually to dilute my share and the investors' share, but I did not want to go into that with Michael Palin because it is, you know, water under the bridge.

Spearman   You could not go into it, could you, because you agreed to it?
A   I agreed to it but I knew that it was -- well, I did not want to cause any disruption. I thought we would perhaps work in the future together. I did not think it was worth making a fuss about it but it was clearly designed to -- After all, the 50% split, 50/50, was for their contribution, for the work they were doing, but now another company was being put in front which was making the contribution.

So it was really, you know - It was not the way it was designed in the trust deed.

Spearman   We will come to that in a minute. Let us deal with this first though. Your answer to his Lordship is that in your view it is fair, based on your creative role in assisting to bring the film into existence, that where there is a revenue stream where the Pythons, and not you, make a material contribution you should end up with a greater participation in the revenue that is produced than where there is a revenue stream where they do not make a material contribution?
A   Yes, in the same position, in the same place as them. You have missed out one of these emails in this exchange.

Spearman   Yes, let us go back and look at it?
A   It's the one of 6th October. Is that the one? I sent - the last one you looked at was ----

Spearman   Your counsel will take that up with you in re-examination. I do not want to ask you about that?
A   Fine. Can I just say that after I told Mr. Saunders that I didn't have a copy of the agreement, he didn't volunteer to send me one. I didn't ask for one. I think I was too shocked, but he didn't offer to send me one.

Spearman   Mr. Forstater, what sort of point is that?
A   Eventually my solicitor asked for it in October and we got it.

MR. JUSTICE NORRIS: This is October?
A   Yes. From the beginning of this exchange, it goes back to the 6th or 9th September.

Spearman   Yes?

A   9th September all the way through to, I think, October we did not have a copy of the agreement. It was only after - sometime after the 20th that we got an agreement and therefore I could actually see what it said. All this time we were without.

MR. SPEARMAN: Mr. Forstater, we looked at it. Mr. Saunders' email of 28th September, the bottom of 723, top of 724. He says he has read the agreement and he says what it says. It was open to you, quite obviously to say: "Well, I haven't got it. Can you send it to me?" and you did not do that?

A   Yes. I didn't do that and I don't know why I didn't ask for it, other than the fact that I was just very - I really was quite disturbed by this. After 30 year of having my invoices paid suddenly they were saying, you know ----

Spearman   The reason, I suggest, why you did not do it is because your first reaction was to say: "Let us not worry about the agreement. It was all agreed in side letters." That is why you did not do it because you adopted the stance that it was agreed in side letters at a later date. That is what you did - on page 723?

A   I just - from what he had said to me, I assumed that he was reading the agreement from the appendix correctly and he could find no reference to 1/7th of 50%. That is what was in my mind because for 30 years I was invoicing on that basis and that is the basis on which we did the deal. Therefore, that's how I understood it. And so to have someone say: you should only get 7.149% just didn't make any sense to me. So I assumed that there was no reference in that agreement to this 1/7th of 50% and that is why I was panicking.

Spearman   You were right in that assumption because Mr. Saunders was telling you, entirely correctly, what the agreement says. It says 7.1429% on the top ----?
A   Yes. I did not even take the - I didn't even bother, which was later done, to say: Okay, if you divide 50 by 7, that's the percentage you get. I didn't take the time to do that.

Spearman   Because your reaction was: yes, it is not in the agreement. It is in later side letters?
A   Only because I assumed that he could not find that actual fraction, which is in my mind, in the papers. I was panicking that he couldn't find it.

Spearman   Let us go back to 733 for the midday adjournment and read you the end of 733. This is a letter you were writing to Mr. Palin and Mr. Jones in October 2005. You end the letter by saying this: "I am sorry to have to ask you to intercede on this but I really don't know what else to do. In the end my agreement is with you and the remaining Pythons and so I believe it's best you collectively make a decision." Now, all I would say about that is that that is what you wrote at the time. There is no mention at all, is there, of Anne Henshaw in any shape or form in this letter or any letter up to this time about this matter - the seventh of the top half?
A   Well, there is a reference to Anne Henshaw in this letter, is there not?

Spearman   Not to her agreeing anything?

MR. JUSTICE NORRIS: In the bottom paragraph on page 732 of the opening, "Brian Saunders and Anne James..." whoever she is "... now claim there was allowance made."
MR. SPEARMAN: Yes. That, Mr. Forstater, is not to do with the making of the agreement. That is to do with explanations that were being put forward to you as to why you were not entitled to 1/7th of the top half. It has nothing to do with the original making of the agreement, is it?
A   Obviously I didn't go into all the detail about Anne Henshaw because I didn't think it would be relevant at this point. I was just trying to remind them of what had happened and to tell them I have a problem, and could they please intervene because I - you know, I was just unhappy with what Mr. Saunders was saying, including this explanation of why it was 1/7th. That was also disturbing to me - this explanation that because they were taking this money off the top through these other companies that they allowed me to invoice for 1/7th instead of 1/14th. I mean I had never heard of that before at all and no documents have ever appeared to show that. That was just - well, I don't know what to say it was, but it certainly hasn't been evidence and it was not my understanding. If you can point me to a piece of paper that shows that, then I am wrong.

***

Spearman also asked me in detail about the letters between Anne and myself in 1977 regarding the book of the film. He got annoyed with my answers at one point and told me to stop arguing my case.

Spearman   You say "... the deal being offered by Python Productions is a fair one for the investors and has been justly managed by the Pythons. However, this new deal does affect me directly. Since the original deal negotiated

I was allocated 1/7th of the Python's share of any spin-offs. Under this proposed deal I lose that share. Would the Pythons be willing to bring me in on the Python Productions side so that this 1/7th share remains the same?" The answer you get comes at page 701 from Miss Henshaw on 28th July. It says this: "'[Because] the deal being offered by Pythons Productions is fair to the investors, but surely, by the same token, it is fair to you too. The Pythons are not aware of any exceptional circumstances, for example participation in the production of the book, which might suggest that you should receive part of Python Productions' share." Now, do not worry, I have not forgotten the last sentence. I will come to that?
A   Sure.

Spearman   You get that and you do not disagree with that, if I understand it correctly; you accept that?
A   I have accepted it although I am aware that as with the Kay-Gee-Bee share the Pythons have made a deal with their own company for their material involvement in the book, which is above the 50/50 split - in other words... As you know ----

Spearman   Yes?
A   So I am aware of this and I'm not happy about it, but you know I don't want to make a fuss and I let it go.

Spearman   I understand that up to a point but the logic of what she is saying applies equally to your claim to have a 1/7th share in the top half, does it not, because the reason she is giving that you, Mr. Forstater, are not participating in the production so there is nothing exceptional which means that you should have a share of the revenues, but that is exactly, on your case, the deal you had negotiated with regard to the top half - namely that even though you did not make a material contribution you got a share of the revenues?

A   Well, it seems to me that if Anne Henshaw - if she says that there is a meeting of the Pythons where this is going to be discussed. Is that right?

Spearman   I think it is implicit. I do not know that she says it. You can see it has been discussed in 701?

A   I mean, if there was a meeting and she put forward my proposal ----

Spearman   Maybe 698. "I will bring this question up with the Pythons when they meet."?

A   So Anne Henshaw was a very thorough person and I assume that when she met with them and explained that I was asking a 1/7th share of the book, in order to present that properly she must have said to them: "He already gets a 1/7th share anyway of this 50%." If she didn't say that, she misrepresented me very badly. She does not come back to me and say, "They don't remember giving you this 1/7th of the 50% share. Where has this come from?" In fact, as you said there is another paragraph which refers to it. So I think they had to know at this point that that 1/7th of 50% existed if she expressed my approach properly.

Spearman   I think you may do yourself more justice if you answer my questions rather than try and argue your case. My question was not about that at all. My question was: the reason that she gave why you should not receive part of Pythons Productions' share of the book is a reason that would have applied equally to why you should not receive 1/7th of the top half, because it is a question of extra work by the Pythons in which you are not participating and generating revenue. That is the same situation as applies to the top half?

A   I agree with you that that could have been applied in 1974.

Spearman   My only question is: when you get this, if you are right about your agreement to have a seventh of the top half, why did you not write back and say "That won't wash. I don't need exceptional circumstances, for example, participation. The deal is I am treated the same as the other Pythons financially whether I make a contribution or not. So can I please have my contribution, my share?"

A.   I didn't feel like going into a discussion about it. I wasn't prepared to take this further or legally. It just was not something that.... I gave into it and I wasn't going to fight it. So I wouldn't have written a letter like that.

Spearman   Okay. Now, let us look at the last sentence on 701. She says, "You will after all be receiving your investor's share plus 1/7th of 50% of the amount paid to the N.F.T.C., which will be Python (Monty) Pictures' share."?

A   Yes.

Spearman   Python (Monty) Pictures' share was never paid to the NFTC, was it?

A   It was. That's why when I got this letter I thought well surely now Mr. Saunders will realise that this is black and white. This is exactly my case. When you see a statement from the NFTC, especially the first one which we found to look at, and under the trust deed, divisible receipts include the 50% that's payable to Python (Monty)

Pictures. It is paid. In other words, the NFTC receives all the income except for some deductions that are taken off the top, and then from the net that the NFTC receives from the record album, they pay out to various parties who need to be paid out. They pay out 43% to Kay-Gee-Bee Music and then from the balance they pay 50% to Python (Monty) Pictures and the other 50% goes into the pot to pay the investors. It's divisible receipts. It's the way the trust deed sets it out and it's very clear that that money is received by the NFTC and paid out to all. That is why I could work out my 1/7th share from the statements because it says, "To Python (Monty) Pictures Limited, 50%" with an amount, and then I would then invoice 1/7th of that amount, plus VAT.

Spearman   I think there may just be a difference between us on that, so we will have to leave that. What I suggest to you happened here (but perhaps you cannot answer one way or the other) is that if, as I suggest, Anne Henshaw was not involved in any of the pre-contract financial negotiations, she gets your letter on p.697, it tells her what the original deal is, that you got 1/7th of their share of spin-offs and that is what she writes back to you on p.701 saying you are not going to get anything for the book, but after all you are still getting 1/7th of the spin-offs.
A   Yes.

DAY 4

Two things grow weaker with the years: teeth and memory.
Jewish Saying

Celia: Griffin, don't ask.
Griffin: Don't ask - you don't know, or - I don't want to know?
Celia: Just don't ask.

The Player (Robert Altman)

Michael Palin, Terry Jones and Eric Idle had been in court to hear my cross-examination. I was aware of some sniggering coming from their section of the courtroom and I had heard Eric Idle say '1/7th' in a funny voice, which also elicited some laughter from them. Now it was their turn. Idle took the stand. I have put Palin and Idle's full witness statements in the Appendix again because we so rarely see such statements in full.

Tom Weisselberg QC related his strategy in cross-examination:

I thought that it was important from the outset to diffuse the creative outrage that the "Seventh Python" comment had engendered (or had been prompted to engender) and to show that difficulties that had arisen during the making of the film were irrelevant.

Thus in opening I made it clear that the "Seventh Python" comment only related to financial share – in that film alone. I also expected vitriol (particularly from Eric Idle) in relation to Mark and the process by which the film had been made – but thought that any bile could be used to undermine any evidence given by him. I would be able fairly to say to the Judge that Eric Idle's evidence was infected by after-acquired dislike.

I was also concerned not to appear hard on a "national treasure" (Michael Palin). The aim was to be gentle on him in cross-examination and to get concessions as to a lack of recollection rather than to inflame him. With Terry Jones, I was similarly concerned not to get him angry and sought to winkle useful information out of him rather than using a bludgeon. I expected Eric Idle to be very hostile and angry. He was.

Palin said that he remembered very little about the time, and it was mainly his diary items that reminded him of what actually happened. He answered in a deliberate, slow and cautious way. I got the sense that he wanted to make 100% certain that he didn't say the wrong thing.

I had written twice to Palin requesting him to get the real deal from Anne Henshaw, since I was certain that Anne would have remembered the deal we made. I didn't know if Palin had actually asked her, since he never wrote back to me with anything concrete, so I was wondering what he would say about it. In the trial he was asked about his relationship to Anne:

Weisselberg: Did you discuss your evidence with Mrs. Henshaw?
Palin: No.

Weisselberg: You have never discussed the issues relating to this case with Mrs. Henshaw?
Palin: No.
Weisselberg: Why not, Mr. Palin?
Palin: There was no reason to.
Weisselberg: So even though Mr. Forstater says that there was an agreement between you and other of the Pythons in relation to his share of the top half, that Anne Henshaw was at a meeting with you, you have never discussed his claim with Mrs. Henshaw at all?
Palin: I cannot remember that meeting, if that meeting ever took place, whether we discussed it.

Weisselberg: My question was you have never discussed it with Mrs. Henshaw at all?
Palin: Not to my recollection.

Later Weisselberg returned to Anne Henshaw's role:

Weisselberg You are still a director of two companies with Mrs. Henshaw. When did you last see her?
Palin I should think probably a year ago.

Weisselberg   You said that you have not talked about Mr. Forstater's claim to her at all. Is that right?
Palin I have avoided talking to her about it because I felt it was a Python matter and not something I personally wanted to get into.

Weisselberg   So you did not ask her to give evidence in these proceedings?
Palin: I might have asked her if she had any views on what was going on. That was all. That may have been a long time ago, but I always insisted that if she had anything she wanted to say she should go through the normal process and talk to our solicitor. I recollect that only came up once.

Tom Weisselberg also wanted to talk to Palin about his signing various documents relating to the production,

Weisselberg Mr. Palin, you are familiar with what I mean when I talk about "the top half", are you not?
A   Yes.

Weisselberg Your diary makes no reference as to the circumstances in which the top half came to be created, does it?
A   Not as far as I know.

Weisselberg   The agenda and the minutes that you may have heard being referred to in court, they make no references to the circumstances in which the top half came to be created, do they?
A   No.

Weisselberg   In fact, the agenda and minutes make no reference as to the terms of the financing that was to be provided for the film at all, do they?
A   No.

Weisselberg   In those circumstances do you have any recollection of who first suggested that the top half be created at all?
A   I really have no recollection.

Weisselberg   One assumes it was suggested by one of the Pythons but you do not know?
A   I do not know.

Weisselberg   So you do not know who raised the concept of the top half with the investors?
A   I am afraid I do not.

Weisselberg   And you do not recall how the top half came to be negotiated with the investors or the clause providing for the top half came to be negotiated with the investors?
A   No.

Weisselberg   In addition to the top half, each of the Pythons had a profit share, did they not?
A   Yes.

Weisselberg   Do you have any recollection of how the percentage that you came to get was negotiated?
A   No.

Weisselberg   Do you even remember what percentage you ended up getting?

A   I remember it was about 6%.

Weisselberg   Do you remember how it was decided that Mr. Forstater would get the same percentage as you?
A   No.

Weisselberg   But he did get the same percentage as you, did he not?
A   Yes.

Weisselberg   You do not have any recollection of how either the top half came to be negotiated or how the profit share came to be negotiated but it is right, is it not, that by the time the agreement came to be signed at the end of April 1974 you knew that you were having a share of the top half and you knew you were having a percentage profit share?
A   I really cannot remember about the top half. It is something I do not remember the full details.

Weisselberg   But at the time the deal was done would you accept that you must have known that you were getting a share of the top half and getting a share of the profits, roughly 6%?
A   It is a long time. I cannot remember that we absolutely knew that. We were working on other things at the time.

Weisselberg   Mr. Palin, you are an Oxford graduate; you have a degree in Modern History. Are you suggesting to his Lordship that you would have had no idea about those financial terms of the deal that was being done with the investors?
A   No, I am not suggesting that. I am just suggesting

that I have absolutely no recollection of knowing the details at the time or how I came to hear about those details.

Weisselberg   You would assume, would you not, that someone must have told you about the terms of the deal?
A   Probably.

Weisselberg   But you cannot recall who that person was?
A   No.

Weisselberg   Would you also have read at least your agreement before you signed it?
A   Sorry?

Weisselberg   Would you have at least read your agreement before you signed it?
A   Well, not necessarily.

Weisselberg   So someone might have just passed you a document and you would have put your signature on it without looking?
A   It is possible.

Wcissclbcrg   Do you remember that on 1st November you had a book launch and Mr. Gledhill gave you a document to sign it, you sign it and everyone becomes very annoyed. Do you remember that?
A   I remember it from the diaries.

Weisselberg   So at that stage you were very concerned about signing documents without having read them, were you not?

A   I did not personally become very annoyed because I think I must just have let it through without really properly checking what it was.

Weisselberg   But by April are you saying that it is likely that you would not have looked at even your own agreement for signing?

A   It is possible.

Weisselberg   But likely?
A   I have no recollection.

Weisselberg   Is it unlikely? I accept you have no recollection, Mr. Palin, but you know what you are like and what I suggest to you is that it is likely that you read your agreement before you signed it. Shall we have a look at it just so that you might be helped? It is D1, p.368. If you look, it is an agreement dated 25th April. Your name appears at the end of the first paragraph. Do you have that at 368?

A   Yes.

Weisselberg   Halfway down para.1 ----
A   I cannot quite see where my name appears.

Weisselberg   At the very end of the first paragraph. Do you see, it says "Michael Palin" in capital letters.
A   Oh, yes. Right, yes.

Weisselberg   In para.1, about four or five lines down, there is again in capitals "Monty Python", and it originally said "meets the Holy Grail". Do you see someone has crossed out "and" and you have put your

initials, have you not?
A   Yes.

Weisselberg   So someone showed you that that was a change and you would have looked at that, seen what the nature of the change was and put your initials on. Yes?
A   Yes, I should think that is likely. I mean, again I have no recollection of reading the whole thing but I am sure that is likely because I have initialled it.

Weisselberg   So it is likely, is it not, that you would have read what was being changed before putting your initials on it?
A   Yes.

Weisselberg   Over the page, at p.369, you see at the very top the payments that you were going to be getting as fees. Do you see that?
A   Yes.

Weisselberg   Would those figures, at that stage of your career, have been significant amounts of money?
A   Yes.

Weisselberg   So you would have looked to check to see what fees you were getting?
A   I do not know. I may well not have looked to checked. I am afraid I did not read all the legal documents very often. I have given a summary by somebody mostly and agreed with that.

Weisselberg   Then look at 378, there is another amendment. This is the fifth schedule of the agreement and someone has written "So far as reasonably possible on

all paid advertising", and again those are your initials, are they not?
A   Yes.

Weisselberg   You would have read what was being said there and then put your initials on it?
A   Yes.

Weisselberg   Then if you look at p.379, there is your signature and you have got a witness and that is Mr. Olswang. Do you see that?
A   Yes.

Weisselberg   Do you know whose signature that is above your signature?
A   Terry Gilliam.

Weisselberg   So it appears that Mr. Gilliam was at 78 Brook Street in front of Mr. Olswang to sign the agreement and it is likely, is it not, that you were there at the same time?
A   I have no recollection but maybe.

Weisselberg   Do you have any recollection of being at Mr. Olswang's offices in Brook Street?
A   No.

Weisselberg also wanted to establish how Palin responded to the letters I wrote him, asking him to intervene.

Weisselberg   What was the position that your agent was adopting - Mr. Saunders?
A   Mr. Saunders, as far as I remember, questioned the right of Mr. Forstater to have the $1/7^{th}$ share.

Weisselberg   Was it he who first suggested that Mr. Forstater should not have a 1/7th share?
A   He suggested he should not have it. He was not entitled to it.

Weisselberg   Was he the first person to suggest that?
A   Yes, I think so.

Weisselberg   What Mr. Forstater does is he then writes to you. One sees the letter in Bundle D2, p.732. Would you turn that up, please?
A   Yes.

Weisselberg   Do you remember receiving that letter?
A   No, I do not remember receiving it but I obviously have received it.

Weisselberg   If you look at the bottom of 732, what Mr. Forstater is saying is: "Roger Saunders and Anne James now claim there was an allowance made that I could invoice for 1/7th because other Python companies, Kay-Gee-Bee Music etc., were taking so much of the merchandising revenue off the top before my share was applied. Their current argument is that since the Spamalot revenue does not have any monies coming off the top to other Python companies that I need to reduce my share to what is written in the appendix. In response I have to say that this is the first time I have ever heard of this allowance argument and was certainly not aware of it at the time. I do not know if your memory bank goes back this far, but I believe that the true nature of our agreement at the time was that I should be treated as a seventh Python to this

revenue which I did help to create". Mr. Palin, if one looks back at 732, is the explanation being given or being said by Mr. Forstater to have been given by Mr. Saunders and Mrs James a correct one? Do you recall whether there was an allowance made that Mr. Forstater should invoice for a $1/7^{th}$ because other Python companies were taking so much of the merchandising off the top?
A   I am sorry, I do not recall that arrangement.

Weisselberg   In your witness statement you say, at para.31, that you do not recall whether you replied to him directly. If you go to p.738, there is a letter from you: "Dear Mark, I am afraid I am lost in all this. Roger Saunders is now our manager and should know all the contact details. We barely get together these days to discuss our own future plans so I am only being realistic to say that it may take quite a while to get the group to consider this. But the most I can do is to query the situation with Roger Saunders and try to make sense of it all". You expected Mr. Saunders, did you, to find out what had been agreed in 1974?
A   Well, he had raised the whole issue in 2005 so I felt that it meant very little to me. The figure did not mean anything. I had not followed up the figures. I was probably doing lots of other things at the time and so my obvious reply was to put Mark in touch with Roger Saunders.

Weisselberg   Did you discuss with the other Pythons what they recalled having occurred in 1974?
A   No.

Weisselberg   Have you ever discussed with them what they recall?

A   Well, only recently.

Weisselberg   Did you exchange emails with any of the Pythons as to what they recalled?
A   Not as far as I remember, no.

Weisselberg   Did you exchange emails with Mr. Saunders as to what you recalled?
A   Again not as far as I remember.

Weisselberg   Did Mr. Saunders ask you what you recalled about the top half?
A   I am sorry to say, I do not remember him asking me that, no.

Weisselberg   Then if you go on to p.746, there is a letter from Mr. Forstater to you referring to an earlier letter from you which I do not think I need to show you.
A   Is that the one we have just looked at?

Weisselberg   No, it is a different letter. 742. Why not just see it very briefly?
A   Okay.

Weisselberg   742. "Dear Mark, Thanks for your letter. I've raised the question of your royalty with the Pythons, well, all but Cleese who has been inaccessible for a while in New Zealand. They said that they would like Roger Saunders to investigate the situation and after your letter arrived I contacted him to see how things were going. He has a lawyer looking into things who should report back in a week or so. All the best".
A   Yes.

Weisselberg   So you were leaving it to Mr. Saunders and the lawyers to find out what had gone on in 1974. Is that right?
A   Yes, the whole question of the share and what happened there, yes, was going to be looked into by somebody else because I do not think the Pythons could remember anything about it really.

Weisselberg   What Mr. Forstater then says at 746 is that over 30 years ago he had agreed with Anne "approved by the group that I should receive equal shares of the merchandising revenue with the six Pythons". He is saying that he agreed with Anne (that is Anne Henshaw). Why, when you got that letter, did you not go and ask Anne Henshaw what agreement, if any, she understood to have been entered into?
A   I can only think there was just too much going on at the time and I did not actually follow this one up.

Weisselberg   Because what you reply to Mr. Forstater, at 747, is: "I have been away filming the Eastern European series and have rather small windows in between each shoot. The general feeling amongst the Pythons was that the lawyers should examine the detail and come to some conclusion as to the share of merchandising revenue to which you are entitled". Did you tell the lawyers to go and talk to Anne Henshaw?
A   No.

Weisselberg   If you look at 748, Mr. Forstater says - and one sees this at the bottom by the second hole-punch - "It is now down to the lawyers but I am not certain they will find the objective truth. Often they find what they are asked to look for and fit the facts to a preconceived notion.

It is easy for Roger to try to re-write history because he wasn't around 30 years ago. However, Anne was and she knows where the bodies are buried. Have you ever asked her frankly to tell you the truth in this matter?" So again you received that letter but you did not ask Mr. Saunders or the lawyers to ask Anne Henshaw for what had been agreed. Is that right?

A   That seems to be right, yes. Yes. There were many, many other things going on. This is a pursuance of an issue which I felt should have been sorted out and did not really want to have a sort of hands-on involvement with.

Weisselberg   What you hoped would happen Mr. Palin, is this right, is that the lawyers and Mr. Saunders would investigate what had happened 30 years ago and would ask Anne Henshaw for what had happened?

A   Well, I wanted them to investigate what had happened all those years ago, yes. Whether they asked was obviously up to them, but yes …

Weisselberg   Do you know what Anne Henshaw would say happened in relation to the $1/7^{th}$? Do you know what her position is?

A   I'm afraid I don't, no.

Weisselberg   So you have decided to defend these proceedings, you are a director of PMP and you do not know what Mrs. Henshaw might think was agreed back in 1974?

A   Well, at this time Roger Saunders was dealing with it. It had been our management for a few years. I was leaving it to him to discuss with whoever he wanted to discuss it with. I didn't have much contact with Anne

James at this time about any business matters at all because Python had dismissed her as manager in 1997.

Weisselberg   So if Mr. Saunders wanted to be a hawk, he should be a hawk and you would allow him to do whatever he wanted to do, is that right?
A   I believed he would get to the facts of the matter. He had raised something which seemed to be a problem.

Weisselberg   Sorry, there is one more letter I need to show you, Mr. Palin, which is at 852. That is a letter from Mr. Forstater to you dated 4th December 2008. He notes that he has just received a letter from your solicitors rejecting your proposal for an equal share of the merchandising in *Spamalot* revenue. "As you know, I put this proposal forward in an attempt to avoid going to court. However, this response leaves me with no alternative. Before I do that I want to explain to you directly about my proposal." Three claims, the first claim he sets out in paras.1 to 5. Those are the allegations that we have discussed in some detail. What I would like to draw your attention to is para.5 over the page at 853. What Mr. Forstater says is: "To back up my original claim I cite correspondence between Anne Henshaw and myself regarding the proposed publication of a book of the film. In that correspondence I wrote to Anne on June 23 1977 seeking to clarify how my merchandising share would work with the book. I wrote to her [and this is in the bundle]. In the original deal negotiated I was allocated 1/7th of the Pythons share of any spin-offs. Under this proposed deal I lose that share. Would the Pythons be willing to bring me in on the Python Production side so that my 1/7th share remains the same?" That is the document I showed you a moment ago. Then "Anne wrote

back to me on July 28th 1977 confirming: "You will after all be receiving your investors' share plus 1/7th of 50% of the amount paid to the NFTC which will be Python (Monty) Pictures' share." He says at the end of that paragraph: "I attach the letters for you". The second quotation comes from the document that we looked at earlier on: p.701 of D2 which, as I told his Lordship, was a pleaded document. I think your evidence, Mr. Palin, was that the first time you had seen it was in the box?
A   I am sorry, what are you referring to? I am slightly lost.

Weisselberg   Sorry, Mr. Palin. You see the words in bold?
A   Yes.

Weisselberg   "You will after all be receiving your".
A   Yes, I understand.

Weisselberg   That comes from the letter I showed you a moment ago from Anne Henshaw dated 28th July 1977. What Mr. Forstater says is "I attach the letters for you". Do you want to have one more look at the letter that he attached, which is at 701. I think you told his Lordship that the first time you had seen it was today in the witness box. In light of Mr. Forstater's letter do you want to reconsider that answer? Do you recall seeing that letter?
A   I don't recall reading the attached letters that Mark sent to me on 4th December 2008 I'm afraid, I just don't recall it.

Terry Jones spent less time in the witness box, and covered many of the areas as Palin's, so I don't intend to reproduce it or comment on it. However, Eric Idle's cross-examination was quite a performance.

Weisselberg   And Chippenham Films was never the producer of the film, was it?

A   According to the contracts, but according to our desires Chippenham Films - it was always Mark and Julian, and in particular Julian.

Weisselberg   Well, Mr. Forstater was the producer of the film, was he not?

A   He was until about half-way through and he fell apart.

Weisselberg   He was the main producer and he got ----?

A   In credit indeed.

Weisselberg   And he continued to work on the film and deal with the distribution issues; he dealt with EMI?

A   Up to a certain time, yes.

Weisselberg   Do you have a particular animus against Mr. Forstater, Mr. Idle?

A   Only recently.

Weisselberg   Is that because of the fact of these proceedings?

A   It's ingratitude.

Ingratitude seems often to be on Idle's mind, and I look forward to his performance of King Lear.

But he didn't just pin it on me; he also said of his fellow Pythons, "I'm making them money, and the ungrateful bastards never thank me. Who gave them a million dollars each for 'Spamalot'?" So ingratitude must mean, for Eric, that people who have helped him become a multi-millionaire have failed in their duty to thank him for allowing them to do so.

The following short excerpt bears token to Eric's voice here, and it echoes some of the sketches he wrote.

Weisselberg   What I am suggesting to you, Mr. Idle, is that in the context of what was in the parties' minds when you came to conclude the agreement in April 1974, there was a possibility that Mr. Forstater could be involved in the book production in the same way as one looks at the involvement of Mr. Beach and Mrs. Henshaw.
A   But we do not see his name here.

Weisselberg   No, he was not actually involved because ----
A   Because?

Weisselberg   I am asking you to think back.
A   Yes.

Weisselberg   When you agreed to give him a share in the top half ----
A   Which we never did.

Weisselberg   -- which the document gives him ----
A   So you say.

Weisselberg   -- at that stage it was possible, was it not, that Mr. Forstater could assist in the production of the book?
A   No, I still find it absurd.

****

Weisselberg   Do you think that your position in these proceedings ----
A   Yes.

Weisselberg   -- is being inspired by, I will put it bluntly, a dislike of Mr. Forstater?
A   I am hopeful that I am trying to be as honest as far as I possibly can be and that my dislike, as you put it, of Mr. Forstater does not influence my honesty in reporting to you the answers to your questions.

Weisselberg   But you have no recollection, do you, one way or the other as to whether or not Mr. Forstater was entitled to 1/7th of the top half?
A   I had no recollection until quite late on at which you ...

Weisselberg   You challenge, as do your colleagues, the suggestion that there was an intention to treat Mr. Forstater as a seventh Python.
A   When I first heard about that I found it remarkable.

Weisselberg   From a financial perspective, Mr. Idle, in circumstances where he has got the same percentage profit share as you.
A   Well, he is sharing it with Julian Doyle for a start and there are eight profits shares, not seven.

Weisselberg   He is deferring his fee under the agreement in the same way as you.   Mr. Olswang and Mr. Remington have given evidence that they understood that he was to be treated as, for financial purposes, a seventh Python.
A   They are his solicitors, right?

Weisselberg   No, Mr. Olswang was your solicitor, Mr. Idle.
A   I think that Mr. Forstater brought him into our lives.

Weisselberg   Mr. Olswang and Mr. Remington were the solicitors who worked on papering the deal on behalf of the company.
A   With whom my friend and lawyer, Jim Beach, took issue.

Weisselberg   Mr. Beach did not take issue with the top half, did he?
A   Perhaps he had not seen it.

Weisselberg   You do not know.
A   I do not know.

Weisselberg
   What I suggest to you is that Mr. Forstater was indeed being treated for financial purposes as if he was the same as you.
A   Certainly the same and I believe in the eight-way split, below the line, or whatever you call it, the bottom half, then, yes, he was being treated the same as to the other seven people.

Weisselberg   Mr. Idle, it is right, is it not, that since *Spamalot* has made so much money there has been a fair amount of publicity as to which Python thinks that they have had the better of the financial deal?
A   We have squabbled since we first met. We are brothers, we are children, and we are comedians. But we love each other and we get on very well. The press does like to exaggerate these things and I have emails from John

Cleese only yesterday.

Weisselberg   You have complained that some of the other Pythons have been ungrateful as to the amount of money that you have managed to generate for them.
A   I may at some times and -- I have been promoting this thing since 2004, so I have answered a tremendous amount of questions and there is a selection of responses that have been selected.

Weisselberg   If you look at Bundle D3, p.1047.
A   So what is this from?

Weisselberg   I am not sure which newspaper it is from.
A   Isn't it rather relevant?

Weisselberg   But what one sees in the paragraph on the subject of money: "He is candidly regretful about his decision to hire a lawyer to represent the Pythons' interest in *Spamalot*. Over a recent lunch with Observer writer Simon Garfield, he pointed out" - that is you - "that with a third share the others are being paid over the odds without doing very much". Is that something that you said to the Observer writer, Mr. Idle?

A   It reflects possibly a bitterness I was feeling at the time. Insofar as I gave them Marcia Brooks, my lawyer, because I was concerned about conflict of interest, and she negotiated against me the highest percentage that has ever been received in Broadway history. Normally they would have been entitled to X% and John du Prez and I had to settle that they would take Y%.

Q   I think the terms of the deal are confidential. Certainly I have understood that they are.
A   Then forgive me, I just breached confidentiality inadvertently.

Weisselberg   So, Mr. Idle, what I suggest to you is that at a time when *Spamalot* is making lots of money; where there is a degree of tension between you and the other Pythons; the request by Mr. Forstater to be paid more could not have come at a worst possible time. Is that right?
A   Are we to reveal how much he has received from *Spamalot* or is that also confidential?

Weisselberg   I am not seeking to suggest that it is confidential.
A   I mean, I think he has received over a quarter of a million pounds from *Spamalot* and about half a million pounds since 2005 for *Monty Python and the Holy Grail* and *Spamalot* and the whole box. So I feel, yes, he is slightly ungrateful.

Weisselberg   That is exactly the word that you used in relation to the other Pythons.
A   Well, the ingratitude matters to me frankly.

Weisselberg   Mr. Idle, if you look at p.1070, this is an extract from a report from CNN and you are quoted as saying: "I am making them money and the ungrateful bastards never thank me', Idle joked. 'Who gave them a million dollars each for Spamalot? It was Idle. Who adapted Monty Python and the Holy Grail ... Spamalot.'"?
A   I think you see I am trying to be amusing.

Day 5- The Trial

For a snake you should have no pity.
Jewish Saying

Day 5 dealt with the Claim that did not involve the Pythons, but also brought Roger Saunders and Ian Miles, the managers of the Pythons, to the witness stand. This is how Saunders responded about his dealings with Anne Henshaw, when cross-examined by my barrister Tom Weisselberg, QC:

WEISSELBERG: I would like now to turn to the claim that Mr. Forstater has to an entitlement of 1/7th of the top half.

WEISSELBERG: That claim came to your attention as a result of the monies that were generated by the *Spamalot* musical?
SAUNDERS : Yes.

WEISSELBERG : A deal is done with Ostar in 2002 which provides for the Pythons to share in the revenue that was generated? .... I am afraid to say, you will need to say "yes".
SAUNDERS : Sorry.

WEISSELBERG Either "yes" or "no", if you agree with me. The transcript, which at the moment I do not have a copy of ----
SAUNDERS : It provides for the film to share in revenues that are generated.

WEISSELBERG The agreement is concluded in December 2002?
SAUNDERS : Yes.

WEISSELBERG   And *Spamalot* opens in February 2005?

SAUNDERS :   *Spamalot* opened in December 2004 in Chicago and it opened in March, I think, 2005 on Broadway, yes.

Weisselberg :   Mr. Forstater queries the amounts of monies that he is receiving in an email that he sends to you on 9th September 2005. If you go to that email, please, which is in D2, p.720. I would like to look first at your email to him which prompts him to come back to you. What you say is: "Dear Mark, The last statement, dated 31st July, which includes income to 30th June shows Spamalot income is under two headings", and then "$94,000 was sent to the NFTC in August and will appear in the next statement. Income will be paid over quarterly thereafter. The show is doing huge business now and plays regularly to full houses. Recoupment is expected before the end of the year, at which point the royalty goes up. The US tour starts on March 7th and the special Las Vegas tour is scheduled to open in January '07 so everything is looking good at the moment". What Mr. Forstater replies to say is: "Thanks for pointing this out otherwise I would have missed it. My deal with Python (Monty) Pictures is that I invoice a 1/7th share of all merchandising and spin-offs that are earned by Python (Monty) Pictures such as the book and record revenues and have been doing this since 1996. The deal is that Python (Monty) retains 50% of this merchandising income and I invoice for a 1/7th of it". Mr. Saunders, he refers to invoices. Did you seek to go and look at some of the invoices?

SAUNDERS : I did not have any of the invoices. Ian Miles - the invoices went to him and he dealt with them.

WEISSELBERG Did you ask Mr. Miles to dig out the invoices and show them to you?
SAUNDERS :   Well, I mean, later on in the process, yes.

WEISSELBERG: So in response to this you did not immediately go and ask to look through the invoices?
SAUNDERS :   I think I looked at the agreement. I mean, I am sure I looked at the agreement and I probably spoke to Ian Miles and looked at the invoices as well.

WEISSELBERG   Do you have any direct recollection of that being in fact what you did?
SAUNDERS :   I certainly did both of those things.

WEISSELBERG   There is a reference to an invoice and so my automatic reaction would be to go and look to see what he had been invoicing for, but is that not your automatic reaction?
SAUNDERS :   I think I probably spoke to Ian Miles on the telephone and said, "Is this what is happening? I have had these conversations and emails from Mark Forstater". I probably forwarded this to him. "Has he been paid 1/7th of this income that he is referring to?"

WEISSELBERG   I will be corrected if I am wrong, but I do not think that we have seen any emails from you forwarding anything from Mr. Forstater to Mr. Miles.
SAUNDERS :   Well, then I probably spoke to him on the telephone.

WEISSELBERG   Do you keep internal notes of conversations that you have about those types of issues?
SAUNDERS :   No, I do not think so.

WEISSELBERG   Did it surprise you that Mr. Forstater was claiming a share of this revenue stream?
SAUNDERS :   Yes.

WEISSELBERG   Did you think that, "I am going to have to protect my client's interests and will seek to do whatever I can to make sure that he cannot get that share"?
SAUNDERS :   No, definitely not.

WEISSELBERG   So what you said is, I think when I first asked you, that you would have gone back to the agreement. Did you go back to the agreement?
SAUNDERS :   Yes.

WEISSELBERG   Let us pick up the agreement, shall we? If you go to D1 and look at p.323, if you look at the last two lines of that there is a reference to 7.1429%. Do you see that?
SAUNDERS :   Yes.

WEISSELBERG   Did you ever think to say, "Well, what is 50% divided by 7?", so 50% being the top half. The top half divided by 7 is 7.1429%. Did you ever do that calculation?
SAUNDERS: No, no. I read the agreement and I read it again and every time I read it it identified this share of income and identified that he should receive a 1/14th of it.

WEISSELBERG   In circumstances where he had said that he had invoiced for a 1/7th for many years, did that

then mean that you thought, "Well, I need to go back and look at the invoices to see whether in fact he has been"?
SAUNDERS   Yes.

WEISSELBERG   When did you do that, immediately that you did the calculation?
SAUNDERS   Yes, I would. I am sure I did, yes, speak to Ian.

WEISSELBERG   So you go to the agreement. You say, "Well, it is not a $1/7^{th}$, it is a $1/14^{th}$". Do you also notice the manuscript amendments?
SAUNDERS   Yes.

WEISSELBERG   Do you know why the manuscript amendments were made?
SAUNDERS   No.

WEISSELBERG   Do you ask anyone as to why the manuscript amendments were made?
SAUNDERS   Who? Who would I ask?

WEISSELBERG   I do not know. That is why I am asking. Did you ask anyone?
SAUNDERS   Such as? I mean ----

WEISSELBERG   You have been sent an email relatively out of the blue by Mr. Forstater who is saying, "I invoiced for a $1/7^{th}$".
SAUNDERS   Yes.

WEISSELBERG   You do a calculation which leads you to conclude that 7.1429% is a $1/14^{th}$. You tell his Lordship that you did not do the calculation that 50%, i.e. the top half, divided by 7 is the same percentage. You have been

told that there are invoices. You see that there are manuscript amendments. You have no direct knowledge of what had been going on at that time because you were not around, so what I am keen to know is did you ask anyone what had been going on and what this was all about?
SAUNDERS   Well, yes, of course.

WEISSELBERG   So my question was, who did you ask?
SAUNDERS   I obviously spoke to Ian about it. Shortly afterwards, I cannot remember when exactly, I made efforts to speak to Anne Henshaw about it. I think that is probably what you are getting at, isn't it?

WEISSELBERG   No. I want to know who you spoke to. Did you speak to the Pythons?
SAUNDERS   I did, yes.

WEISSELBERG   What did they say?
SAUNDERS   They had no recollection of there being such an agreement.

WEISSELBERG   When did you speak to them? Did you speak to them immediately after getting the email from Mr. Forstater?
SAUNDERS   No, probably not because I needed to sort of try and work out why it was that he had been paid a $1/7^{th}$ of this income that he had been invoicing for when his agreement plainly to me said he was only due a $1/14^{th}$. So I probably made efforts to - I mean, I did make efforts to try and find any files that were around. I obviously looked at the agreements, looked at whatever files there were in the office and tried to make sense of this discrepancy.

DAY 6- The Trial

If your friend becomes your enemy, he will be your enemy for life.

Jewish Saying

Day 6 brought Julian Doyle and John Goldstone, who was executive producer of the film, to the stand.

I was particularly annoyed with Julian being their witness, because I felt he was being a Judas. I had treated him well on the Holy Grail, had given him a large percentage of my profit share, and he, his ex-wife and a number of his associates managed to find useful roles on subsequent Python films.

Weisselberg   You knew, you have told his Lordship, in May 1974 that you were going to be paid less than Mr. Forstater. Did you ever ask to see the agreements that were being concluded?
A   No. I never saw it until 2011 when they came to me and said would I make a statement and they said, "Oh there's..." I said, "Well what's it all about?" And they said, "Oh it's about Spamalot" and I said, "Well, we get money from Spamalot. What's the problem?" and they said, "Oh, there's extra money going to Mark for Spamalot" So I never even knew that Mark was getting extra money from this other source. And then the solicitor says, "You know, you're entitled to that. As partners you should be having 50% of that." So I said, "Ah I don't care."

Weisselberg   You did not think you were entitled to that share, did you, because you were not partners?
A   I was told. I didn't even know about that share. I was told when.... When   they said, "Oh we've got a dispute about Spamalot" I said, "Well, we get money from Spamalot through our percentages" and then they said,

"Oh, no. There's another lot of money that Mark's getting. He's had, you know, several hundred thousand pounds." And they said, "Do you know you're entitled to that?" And I said, "Oh, no. I don't care."

Sure, he didn't care. Tom Weisselberg wanted to discuss the credits of the film,

Weisselberg   There we see your titles on the opening credits as being, first, production manager - do you see that?
A   Yes, I do.

Weisselberg   And then three lines up from the bottom "Special effects photography - Julian Doyle"?
A   Yes.

Weisselberg   Those were the credits that were given to you on this film?
A   They were put there by Mark.

Weisselberg   But Mr. Jones ----?
A   I never saw them.

Weisselberg   Are you suggesting that Mark Forstater wrote all the opening credits for the film?
A   He supervised them.

Weisselberg   But -----?
A   I mean I'm not saying that I wanted to do anything different. I didn't care. I didn't want to be a producer. I want to direct. I direct films. So I don't c care what was in there.

Weisselberg   If you look at p.1103 of the bundle, Mr. Doyle, you see there that Mr. Forstater is described as being the producer.
A   Yes, I gave him that title.

Weisselberg   You see that he was assisted by Earl J. Llama, Milt Q. Llama, Sy Llama, Merle Llama. Those credits were written by the Pythons, were they not?
A   Yes.

Weisselberg   You are a friend of the Pythons, are you not?
A   With some. I mean, I ----

Weisselberg   Which ones are you friends with?
A   With Terry - Well, I am friends with all of them but I have very little to do with John or - Eric I see sometimes and I cannot have much friendship with Graham anymore.

For the record, the opening credits were not supervised by me, but by the two directors of the film -Terry Jones and Terry Gilliam. That Julian Doyle gave me the title Producer is a staggering statement, and I have no idea where he pulled that from.

Weisselberg   You did not ask for Chippenham to be credited in the credits to the film, did you?
A   No. I didn't. Nobody asked for Chippenham. I didn't want Chippenham to be credited particularly.

Weisselberg   And that was because by that stage you were not really working as Chippenham Films any more with Mr. Forstater, were you?
A   We were drifting apart. That wasn't the reason it wasn't in the credits.

Weisselberg   Would you say that you had drifted apart by the time you came to complete the filming on the film?
A   Yes. Well, we were separate by the winter of '74. I don't know, I think he broke down or something. Something happened on the film. He became a different person and kept saying how the film was a flop and it was a failure and it was never going to make any money. Something happened, you know. I was very sad because we worked brilliantly together.

Weisselberg   Mr. Forstater does not accept that, Mr. Doyle, but I am not interested in that for the purpose of these proceedings. What I am interested in is to explore with you what you thought the role of Chippenham Films was in the filming of Holy Grail. What I suggest to you first is that you and Mr. Forstater were not in an exclusive partnership. You could do other things outside Chippenham Films, could you not?
A   Probably, yes.

Weisselberg   So you could do other work, for example, at the end of 1973 without involving Mr. Forstater in stuff that he was doing?
A   Possibly, yes.

Weisselberg   By the time you had done to make the feature film, I suggest that you and Mr. Forstater were already going your different ways?
A   No.

Weisselberg   And you didn't ----?
A   You can suggest what you like, but that's nonsense.

Weisselberg   You did not want to be a producer, did

you?
A   No.

Weisselberg   Mr. Forstater wanted to be a producer?
A   No, he didn't. And I can prove it.

Weisselberg   Well, Mr. Doyle, he becomes the producer on the film, does he not?
A   Yes, but he doesn't want to be a producer and I can prove it.

Weisselberg   I suggest to you ----?
A   He wanted to be a director.

Weisselberg   He is the producer on the film, is he not?
A   Okay.

***

Closing Arguments

Stay out of Chancery, whatever you do. For it's being ground to bits in a slow mill; it's being roasted at a low fire; it's being stung to death by single bees; it's being drowned by drops; it's going mad by grains.
Bleak House

I was a bit shocked at Spearman's closing argument. It was very personal and directed at my character. It is very hurtful to have this shit aimed at you, even if you know it is just a legal strategy. The Pythons needlessly put me in this position, and I think they should be aware of that. Their lack of engagement put me through years of struggle for nothing and in the end subjected me to an unpleasant character assassination. They were able to just walk away from it as if it didn't concern them. It only bothered them when they realised they were facing over

£1m of legal fees.

Spearman attacked my credibility (and Simon Olswang's) as a witness,

MF's credibility is at the heart of his case. It was already suspect in light of
(a) the lack of documentary support for his case and (b) his constant changes of story over
the years, Contrary to the suggestion in Closing, MF was a poor witness and his credibility was damaged beyond repair by the answers that he gave in cross-examination.

The claim based on rectification of the MF agreement should fail. In particular, the
claim relies upon the unconvincing and unreliable evidence of MF and Mr Olswang
and upon the unsustainable contention that MF was to be treated as a 7th Python.

MF's case rests heavily on the recollections of MF, Mr Olswang and Mr Remington.
However, both MF and Mr Olswang were very poor witnesses who lacked both credibility
and consistency.

Spearman then accused me of having a specific character 'trait',

Nevertheless, from an early stage MF considered that he had been "very foolish" and "had
ripped himself off" by not negotiating a higher fee for himself; he thought he
had "sold himself short".

PMP suggests that it is this trait in MF's character which has led him to adopt positions
concerning his financial entitlement as they may suit his claim, no matter how much those
positions fly in the face of other evidence and in particular what the documents show.

Spearman's cod psychology believes that this 'trait' of mine, which he can see in 1975 (almost 40 years ago) still dominates my character! This is what he said,

(a) MF has presented a thoroughly misleading picture to other people over the years and (b) has been dishonest in the way that he and MFPL have accounted for tax over very many years.

In this regard Spearman then went lawyerly and referred to the case of Royal Brunei Airlines v Tan [1995] 2 AC 378 where Lord Nicholls, a far superior legal animal, explains the two
main touchstones for dishonesty are:

(1) acting "with a lack of probity," that is,
"simply not acting as an honest person would in the circumstances" (at 389) and (2)
"Commercially unacceptable conduct" (at 390). Therefore, the starting point is to ask
whether someone has acted with a lack or probity, or whether his conduct is
commercially unacceptable. In either of these cases, a person will be held to be
dishonest. As Lord Nicholls pointed out: "In most situations there is little difficulty in
identifying how an honest person would behave" (at 389).

Accordingly, the test is an objective one. Therefore, a person need not have thought about what the
standards of honest behaviour are. Subsequent cases have confirmed that this
clarified view of Twinsectra represents English law.

So in the upside-down world of this particular Bleak House, a person seeking not to be cheated is accused of being dishonest by the people cheating him.

This is what I wrote in my journal when the trial concluded,

Friday December 7, 2012

Written closing statements over the next 2 weeks then an oral closing 3rd week in Jan, and then we wait for judgement.

I think we won, but there is always the possibility that the Judge will not be convinced. I find it hard to believe. The evidence on our side is OK, their defence is weak, the absence of Anne Henshaw should count a lot, but you can never know- I don't feel as buoyant and confident as I did yesterday and Wednesday.

Sitting in court I thought about how old friends- Gilliam, Palin, Julian were now adversaries, and how it was a shame that we had to become enemies in court. A useless battle.
Now it is 9:00 pm and I am sitting at home- I cried and I don't know why.
The trial has to go my way, otherwise I am in deep shit. The only way I can get myself back is if I win at least 250-300k, so that I can pay off my bank and get the creditors off my back.

Once this trial is really over I can just worry about health and work and not the law. A great weight will be taken off my shoulders. I thought last night I would sleep like a babe, but my mind was still working too fast so I didn't get a good sleep. I am tired now and hope to get some rest this weekend.

Saturday December 8, 2012

Was thinking last night about points to raise to Tom and Mark for the written closing. To do that, I had to re-read the opening submission (skeleton) by Spearman. A number of his points were demolished or watered down during evidence, so he is left with very little ammunition.
 for his defence.

Bob Storer thought the opening defence was weak. What kind of weapons does he have left to fight with? I think he has few and one of them might be memory. He may claim, for example, that as none of the Pythons remember the meeting, but that I remember it very well.

I've asked Lawrence to tell me what the procedure is, but it really struck me on re-reading the skeleton, that we have all our arguments intact and may even have gained new ones through hearing the witnesses, whereas I think his defence has gotten increasingly threadbare through our cross- examination - ie Simon, me and Selwyn's witness statement , which they have accepted as truth. So even if they don't recall going to Brechers for a meeting, Selwyn does recall it, and his version is admitted.

But only time will tell.

Sunday December 9, 2012

My dreams are still haunted by courts, evidence, documents, deadlines and so on. It will take some time to get the anxiety of this legal and emotional battle out of my system. I wish it would have concluded by year end, but that is not to be. I have to live with a bit more anxiety. I suppose when I see their submission I will know if there is any real danger there. Same with ours.

Wednesday December 12, 2012

I still dream about the trial and need to get it out of my system. I only need to go to court for one more day - January 22nd- and I hope that will be a positive outcome. I was looking back on the very beginnings of this dispute, when I saw the Spamalot and other merchandising income on the NFTC statement in 2005. I debated with myself whether to just invoice for the things I could assume were 50-50 deals- Spamalot etc and then wait for them to query my invoice, or I could email and ask which ones were invoiceable. I chose the latter but thought at the time it was a mistake. But in court I brought the Judge's attention to that email in which, before any dispute occurred, I gave Saunders a summary of my 1/7th position. It may well be that this summary may impress the judge and so something I thought was an error may turn out to be a stroke of luck. - or genius.

***

The Judgement

I have the honour to attend court regularly. With my documents. I expect a judgement. shortly. On the Day of Judgement.

Bleak House

On July 5, 2013 Judge Norris finally handled down his judgement. He found in my favour on the Rectification claim against the Pythons, but went against me on the third claim, He also hit me with costs on the abandoned second claim, so the result was a very mixed bag.

When my daughter Maya read the judgement, she rang me to say that the Judge didn't like me. She's right, the judgement does read like that, and I don't know why. This is what he said about me in regard to the Python claim,

Mr Forstater gave his evidence in a measured way, although it was clear that the events under consideration had been the absorbing focus of his attention since about 2005 to such an extent that it became extremely difficult to separate recollection from reconstruction

He noted that the Pythons QC accuses me of "changing his story to fit the documents", but had this to say about it,

The strength of that criticism is moderated by the fact that in 2005 Mr
Forstater was called upon to recollect how a bargain had been made in
1973 or 1974, and to so do unexpectedly (after 30 years' of acceptance of his invoices) and without the assistance of documents. I do not find it surprising that his initial recollection had to be modified as further pieces of the jigsaw came to light.

The Judge summed up his findings about the evidence that we presented,

In my judgment (1) the rendering and payment of invoices plainly claiming 1/7th of the Top Half in the period immediately following the making of the MF Agreement; (2) the continuation of that practice for almost 30 years (3) the rejection of Mr Forstater's claim to special treatment in relation to the music and publishing companies on the grounds that he was already entitled to 1/7th of the 50% that was payable to PMP and (4) the confirmation to PMP's accountants that that was the actual arrangement in place (without suggesting that the actual arrangement was incorrect) are (on their face) strong corroboration of the oral evidence tendered by Mr Forstater.

I turn to consider what (if anything) should be made of the absence of Anne Henshaw at the trial of the action. She herself fell out with the Pythons as a group in an acrimonious split in 1997. But she remained a friend of Michael Palin and of Terry Jones, and a Director of two of Mr Palin's companies. No real account was given as to why PMP did not call her to give evidence, given her continued friendship with Michael Palin and Terry Jones.

That she may have relevant evidence to give was apparent from the original pleaded case (though the real significance of that evidence was only brought on to the face of the pleading by the re-amendment at the start of the trial). But a challenge to call her had been squarely put in correspondence by Mr Forstater himself, and I must examine the consequences of PMP choosing to duck that challenge.

a)   Mr. Forstater's oral evidence was capable of belief, though not convincingly strong.
b)   That evidence would receive corroboration from the invoices and from the 1977 correspondence (unless those matters are capable of explanation).

c)   The person best able to explain the conduct of PMP in paying the invoices (and why that was treated as unremarkable) and in refusing to treat Mr Forstater in a special way in relation to the new music and publishing companies (on the ground that he was already entitled to a one seventh share of the Top Half) was Anne Henshaw.

d) When the issue arose in 2005 (after the acrimonious split) Anne Henshaw was prepared to accept as possible Mr Saunders' speculative account of why Mr Forstater was in fact paid a one seventh share of the Top Half.

e) Anne Henshaw retained close personal contacts with Michael Palin and with Terry Jones (even though she had years ago fallen out with the other Pythons): she knew of the dispute and was contactable, but was not called.

f) I may at the least infer that Anne Henshaw had no evidence that she could offer or which PMP wished to adduce to displace the inferences that might plainly be drawn from the terms of the invoices and the fact of their payment and the terms of the 1977 and 1979 correspondence.

g) This undoubtedly strengthens Mr Forstater's case because it means that that subsequent conduct can be treated as strongly corroborative of his oral account.

h) The failure to call her also means that there is no evidence-based challenge to Mr Forstater's assertion that he was told by Anne Henshaw that his request for a one seventh share of the Top Half had been approved by the Pythons; and that also strengthens his case.

I therefore find and hold that there is evidence of a sufficiently convincing quality to persuade me on the balance of probabilities that immediately prior to the signature of the MF Agreement there was a consensus that Mr Forstater should be entitled to a $1/7^{th}$ share of the Top Half. The Third Schedule to the MF Agreement does not so provide. That is not because there was any change of mind. As I assess the evidence the Pythons continued at that point to be "a soft lot and not at all business-like" and to be genuinely enthused at having secured the services of Mr Forstater: and Mr Forstater continued to be concerned that he got the maximum from his relationship with the Pythons and that what he had obtained should not be whittled away. So the consensus was *intended to be recorded in the MF Agreement. It was not so recorded because of a mistake in the drafting by Mr Olswang or his firm. The MF agreement should be rectified (by doubling the percentage of the Top Half to which Mr. Forstater is entitled).*

Hooray!

The Judge did not give them the right to appeal. So after 7 years it came to an end.

My Last Journal Entries

Money has a way of changing people... or doing them in.

Jerry Lee Lewis

Monday July 1, 2013

At about 4:15 I got a call from Lawrence- the judgement was in. The Judge gave me the Rectification claim. We see the Judge Friday

Tuesday July 2nd, 2013

It's slowly starting to sink in that winning the Python case means that I will be able to pay off the bank, and this means the immediate threat to sell the house is gone. The relief of knowing this is slowly starting to sink into my being. I feel a bit more relaxed. This is such a change that I can finally breathe freely after 8 years. Such a long time to live with this thing.

I was hurt by their actions in 1975 and lived with that pain and disappointment for many years, and even after my successes I still had this feeling that my career would have been easier, greater etc had they not cast me off. Now having spent 8 years examining the past, understanding what happened in 1975, I have come to a new viewpoint - one that is more positive, more whole, that has filled in the gap left in 1975, and the fact that I have won the case gives me a feeling of vindication. They cheated me out of my creative inheritance and they tried to cheat me financially too. But I won the case and I have shown them to be thieves - corrupt.

Wednesday July 3, 2013

Conference call with Lawrence and the Barristers. PMP had asked for an adjournment. so the discussion on costs will be delayed. Lawrence thinks till October. That leaves me with a huge hole in my budget.

Thursday July 4

Independence Day. Tomorrow is the hearing. This case has lasted 8 years and it has caused me a great deal of stress and financial worries and problems. I'm glad it is al last over. I'm pleased but also sad. Sad that our friendship has come to this. I don't feel anger at the Pythons- I think they were led into this by their manager and lawyers.

Sunday July 7, 2013

There were 3 snappers waiting for me outside the Rolls Building. "Why aren't you smiling?, said one. "I'm waiting to hear what the Judge says." "We think you know," he says.

I met Lawrence in the lobby and we went in together. Outside the court Simon Rocker of the JC met us. Inside we saw that Brian from the PA, an FT reporter, a Bloomberg reporter and a UK Law reporter were there. The Judge was announced and gave his judgement in 2 minutes. It was over.

Outside the PA guy and one of the others asked me questions, and Simon suggested going for a coffee to talk. Outside the court, the photographers were still there and one did an interview on his video. We were happy. A reporter from Sky News was there and Nigel asked if he wanted to do a live interview. He rang his desk and they said come to Millbank by 12:45 for a live Sky News Interview.

At a cafe we chatted and Nigel got a phone call - there was a camera team from the PA who wanted to talk. We went back to see them and then an ITN guy showed up and also wanted to chat.

Nigel and I did Sky News, then went to have a sarny. I had gotten an email through David Roper of Heavy Entertainment that Jay Patel of BBC News wanted to contact me. Nigel rang and Jay said he could try to see if he could book a studio at Broadcasting House, so Nigel and I decided to cab it there. On the way they rang and said can you divert to the Playhouse Theatre (Spamalot) where a camera team would do an interview for BBC local news.

So we got BBC, Sky and ITN, FT etc. Next day all the papers wrote about it, and the news spread to North America, - NY Times, Israel, Poland, Russia, Oz, Thailand, Holland etc.

Tuesday July 9, 2013

Yesterday afternoon an email from Lawrence: a Daily Mail journalist, Frances Hardy, wants to interview me. Seems she has been working on an in-depth piece on the case. Of course this is exactly what we have been waiting for- the chance to be in a mass market paper. Prayers answered?

Nigel tells me the Daily Mail wants to dish the dirt on the Pythons. I am not interested in that, but if you read the letters I sent Palin and knowing the Judge's decision, you would have to ask, why didn't he intervene? That's the question I also have: why did they let it go on so long? Why did they ignore the evidence? Why did they leave it with the lawyers? I have re-read the letters and they are strong. I think I will follow this line. The Pythons relied too much on their manager and lawyers and did not ask enough questions or get involved.

Wednesday July 10, 2013

I am going to meet a Daily Mail journalist, to get some free publicity and right some wrongs.

TWAT'S LAST THOUGHTS

Of course you don't understand this Chancery business. I don't know who does. It's about nothing but costs now. That's the great question. All the rest, by some extraordinary means, has melted away. The costs were three times the legacy. My whole estate has gone in costs.
Bleak House

It is now June 2015, nearly 10 years after this dispute began, and the section on the judgement makes clear what I won and what I lost. I won my claim for Rectification, but the costs awarded against me for the abandoned second claim, (relating to the financial structure of Spamalot) and the loss of the 3rd claim wiped out any financial gains I made, so I did not emerge well financially from the litigation.

However, my personal need to reconsider the events of 1974-5 gave me a new understanding of my previous relationship to the Pythons, and this has been a great benefit to me. I feel able now to close that part of my history and really put it behind me. Fighting the Pythons helped me regain my old sense of self-respect. I now look forward to life and work with renewed energy, and I believe without this trial (both the good and bad aspects) I would not be in the fit state I now find myself. It took either courage or madness to pursue this case, but whichever one it was, I feel better for having risked so much.

A few years ago my health suffered because of the stress I was under. My digestive system decided to behave as no system should and my blood pressure and cholesterol levels rose. But since the case ended I have used the tools of meditation and exercise to repair my health, so that I am beginning to feel stronger and nearly as energetic as I was before this case took over my life. I continue to have love and support from my two families, even though this case impinged on their lives too. The end result is that I am older, poorer, and - hopefully - wiser.

Judge not lest ye be judged. Well I have been judged and I suppose I need to issue my own judgement on the Pythons based on my recent experience with them. I don't feel anger towards them for what they did. It is always difficult to know what others feel but I suspect the Pythons do not feel at all guilty and that the fantastic five never stopped to consider the cost to me – financially, emotionally and physically – of having to pursue this avoidable and wasteful legal battle. My claim was £ 300,000, which for the six pythons (five living plus Graham's estate) amounted to £ 50,000 each, not nearly enough to give them any sleepless nights. In any case, this money was not coming out of their bank accounts but was revenue directly from the Spamalot box office.

I also don't blame Anne Henshaw for not appearing since to do so meant that she would have had to admit to being either incompetent or confused about the arrangement we had made in 1974. In fact, her absence spoke volumes in court.

Inevitably, I feel the need to speculate on the unanswered questions I had during these ten years: why did they pursue it and why didn't any of them intervene? Roger Saunders, in his cross-examination, said that Anne Henshaw, "wasn't prepared to deal with the situation. I mean her attitude was: this is your problem. I'm not going to lift a finger to help you." The reason she was unwilling to help, again I suspect but here with some knowledge, was that the change of Python management from Anne Henshaw to Saunders was acrimonious. Anne left in anger and Eric Idle was the Python who particularly wanted Saunders to be running their affairs. Since Eric's Spamalot had brought in the latest windfall I believe he was in the driving seat.

Eric is a litigious person. When a programmer created a software language called 'Python' he wrote,

"Well, I feel very litigious. I feel we should stop them, sue them, burn them, bury them or dump them in the Thames."

The self-styled Greedy Bastard is also fond of money. On an internet site I read that John Cleese has said of him that "Eric Idle gives selfishness a bad name." So I believe that Eric has been my nemesis.

I also wonder why Michael Palin never asked Anne Henshaw to tell him the truth; was it that he was afraid to hear it, because he would then have to confront Idle and tell him that they were wrong. I had hoped that Palin would take the trouble to ask Anne for me, since he was a friend of hers and in business with her.

As for the others, Cleese never bothered to turn up for the trial; Gilliam, my former roommate, concentrated on making movies and opera and Terry Jones took what seems to me a very medieval attitude: do not disturb the universe. I can't figure out what I did to incur the wrath of the Pythons, other than help them all make £ 1.5m each. I did nothing except ask for what I had been given. Why did this go on for seven years?

The Pythons left the dispute to their lawyers and managers to deal with, until the costs of doing so became so high that they had no alternative but to fight in court. If they won the case they would not be liable for their costs, which would be mine to bear. But having lost the case, and having to face costs of about £ 1.3m, they then told the press that they were doing the 02 reunion shows to pay off 'losses' that they had, or to pay Cleese's alimony or Jones' mortgage. At least Idle was honest enough to say that it was to pay their legal costs, but he always added an insult by calling me a twat or an idiot or a loser and never admitting that they actually lost the case.

Soon after the trial concluded John Cleese stated in an interview that they had sacked their managers. About time too. Am I an idiot or twat for pursuing this case for 7 years? Am I an idiot or a twat for trying to get my hands on what was mine? For sticking up for myself? For not wanting to meekly turn the other cheek? Perhaps I should start a pressure group: Twats for justice for Twats?

A number of years ago I attended a couple of Transformational Breathing workshops. Transformational Breathing uses a technique of sustained breathing through the mouth to break through any blockages or obstructions that stop you from having a full open breath. These blockages are as much emotional as physical. When I was going through this process, the facilitator asked me to try to open my heart. After the session, I thought about the process of opening the heart, and how you would go about it. What would you have to do on a mental or emotional level?

I decided to ask the I Ching, 'Will I be able to open my heart?' Throwing the stalks I got the answer Hexagram 35: Advance; The 5th line, (in the Taoist I Ching) reads,

Regret comes from the heart/mind not being open. If one knows how to empty and open the heart, one can thus seek from others, and so be able to fill the belly. Once one has filled the belly, fortune, misfortune and stopping at sufficiency are all in the palm of one's hand. One can thereby be free from worry about loss or gain, and go straight ahead without doubt, going ahead in advancing the fire and working with good result beneficial in every way. This is the illumination of becoming empty to bring fulfilment.

If my heart is not open enough, then it must be crammed full of old and new desires, and to open my heart means that I have to empty it. The failure to achieve a desire leads to feelings of loss, lack, bitterness and regret. Even if we manage to accomplish our desires and have a feeling of joy these feelings do not last. We know that life is transient and impermanent. We lose even the things we have gained, so that loss is also part of success. All desires, whether fulfilled or unfulfilled, lead to feelings of attachment and dependency, to a sense that we can only feel whole when we can bring outside or external things into our being, our heart.

So my heart was full of the corpses of desire. I harboured past feelings of hurt and betrayal, as well as the seeds of new desires that I want to pursue. If I could empty the heart of these old feelings and reduce my present desires, then I can make room in my heart. Through a kind of fasting of the heart it's possible to create an emptiness that will allow other and better feelings, like compassion and love, to take up residence.

The Taoist meditation practise that I use is called Zuowang - sitting and forgetting. I do this to try to transform my body and mind. The forgetting part is to remove old slights, pains, hurts and betrayals, so that my heart empties out its old attachments and can become a storehouse for new feelings. Unless I houseclean my heart, I will be dragged down by my past, and this means I will not able to move forward in a unified way. I will remain a victim of self-doubt and low self-esteem, and will not be able to utilise my energy in a powerful way.

After I became ill, I studied how stress affects the mind and body. One aspect of stress that is not well known relates to memory. When you remember a stressful event, your mind initiates the same stress response in your body that the original stressful event produced. So to keep hold of your old painful experiences is inviting disease. Therefore to meditate - to sit and forget - is my healthy response to old trauma and pain, since living with it will continue to make me ill.

Do I need to forgive the Pythons? From their perspective I don't believe they thought they did anything wrong. There is a quote from The Great Gatsby that fits this situation:

They were careless people ...they smashed up things and creatures and then retreated back into their money or their vast carelessness, or whatever it was that kept them together, and let other people clean up the mess they made . . .

So I think it is more sadness I feel than anything else. These were friends and colleagues, and for no good reason we have become enemies; those relationships are now gone and lost forever. I don't like to think of them as old cynical businessmen who can't be bothered to give a damn; I'd rather remember them as the idealistic rule-breaking young blades who wanted to stick two fingers up the establishment, and who created a form of anarchic silliness that gave pleasure to generations.

 On July 5 2013, the NY Times wrote an article on the trial. This anonymous poem was added as a comment to the online article. I quite like it:

With a little grudge, with a little grudge
Open your purse 'cause you've been defeated
With a little nudge from the trial judge
You're worth's slightly worse but not depleted

Sorry if it's dumb to say
You've done all right in your lives
Really, is the sum you'll pay
Worth such a fight in your lives

And though you feel rotten that he has won
Still I say don't appeal, say that the deal is done
Is it just a grudge, just a little grudge
Hope the little nudge from the judge
Helps erase the grudge

And thus, through years and years, and lives and lives, everything goes on, constantly beginning over and over again, and nothing ever ends.

Bleak House

****

Appendix 1: Cross Examination of Eric Idle by Tom Weisselberg

Mr. Weisselberg Mr. Idle, you do not keep a diary, do you?
Mr Idle No.

Q   Would it be right to say that your recollection as to how the financing of *The Holy Grail* was undertaken is very, very limited?
A   I don't think so.

Q   In your witness statement you refer in a number of places to Mr. Palin's witness statement?
A   Yes.

Q   Why did you not set out your own recollection?
A   Because we started to do that and it seemed they were entirely compatible, so to save time and space and energy at trial, we combined.

Q   So you were working together to produce a witness statement. Is that right?
A   Only through our solicitor.

Q   So you did not sit down together and ----?
A   Sadly not.

Q   And Chippenham Films was never the producer of the film, was it?
A   According to the contracts, but according to our desires Chippenham Films - it was always Mark and

Julian, and in particular Julian.

Q   Well, Mr. Forstater was the producer of the film, was he not?
A   He was until about half-way through and he fell apart.

Q   He was the main producer and he got ----?
A   In credit indeed.

Q   And he continued to work on the film and deal with the distribution issues; he dealt with EMI?
A   Up to a certain time, yes.

Q   Do you have a particular animus against Mr. Forstater, Mr. Idle?
A   Only recently.

Q   Is that because of the fact of these proceedings?
A   It's ingratitude.

Q   You left the financing side of the film, back in 1973, to Mr. Gilliam, Mr. Jones and Mr. Palin of the Pythons. Is that right?
A   The financing of the film was like all films. Several people were working on it at the same time. There was Jill Foster. There was our manager and there was a group working under Graham Chapman, Tony Stratton-Smith, who were approaching rock groups. So this is all on-going at the same time.

Q   One of those people working on the financing of the film was Mr. Forstater?
A   Eventually, yes.

Q   He initially started working on the film before you and Mr. Cleese had had your say. Do you remember that?
A   No, I don't remember that.

Q   What Mr. Palin's diary shows, and if you take up bundle D3, is that you met Mr. Forstater on 1st November 1973. That is page 962. Do you see the entry for 1st November. "Surprise, surprise. A cordial, relaxed, totally constructive meeting at John's. All of us present, and Mark as well." Was that the first time that you met Mr. Forstater?
A   It's the first time I probably recall, but we had worked on three previous films which he apparently was one, which I only remember Julian Doyle from.

Q   And if you look back at 961, I made the point a moment ago that Mr. Forstater had been working as a producer before you had agreed to it. If you look at the entry for 30th October, "Tonight a long phone call from John Cleese. He proposed asking John Goldstone to our Python meeting ... So John is hardening against Mark for some reason. He talked with little humour, he seemed rather cross and lashed out at Terry over his failure to consult John when Mark was 'appointed' producer..." Were you involved in the decision, before 1st November, to - quote "appoint" - and I do not just that is a formal appointment - but to get Mark to do producer-type functions?
A   I don't recall but I do recollect generally at the time being in favour of Julian and Mark working on it certainly.

Q   In paragraph 11 of your witness statement, Mr. Idle, you say at tab 9, page 227, paragraph 11 - do you see that?
A   Not yet.

Q   Bundle C, page 227?
A   I am getting there. Yes.

Q   Tab 9, page 227, paragraph 11, you suggest there, "It was only when I went on location in April [1974]that I recall becoming aware of Mark Forstater..."?
A   Yes.

Q   That is not right, is it? Do you remember you met Mr. Forstater before in November 1973?
A   I remember now I have read Michael Palin's diaries and testimony.

Q   So without the diary ----?
A   That was my recollection of Mr. Forstater largely on location.

Q   You say that, Mr. Idle, but presumably you have read all of Mr. Palin's witness statement before you signed off on yours; and Mr. Palin sets out in some detail the meeting on 1st November?
A   Are you suggesting I should have changed my evidence?

Q   Well, Mr. Idle, what you have done is you have prepared your witness statement together with Mr. Palin ----?
A   Not together. We were advised that our opening remarks were necessarily replicating the same ground.

Q   And what you could have said, was it not, that "I now recall that I met Mr. Forstater on 1st November 1973"?
A   But I have no recall of that meeting.

Q   A moment ago you said that based on the diary entry you do recall meeting him on ----?
A   I am believing the diary entry. I do not recall it directly.

Q   So you have no independent recollection of that fact?
A   Correct.

Q   Do you have any independent recollection of any meetings with Mr. Forstater during the period from November to April 1974?
A   No, because what you have to remember is that from the February 26th of 1974 we were on stage every night at Drury Lane for four weeks, and that my wife was also in that production, and I had a young baby. So we were very busy every night.

Q   And you were attending meetings ----?
A   Well, some of those meetings were quite short, and some I remember being held in the lobby of the Drury Lane Theatre

Q   You were attending meetings in relation to the finances of the film, were you not?
A   Not specifically. Not that I recall, no.

Q   Do you recall receiving any updates as to how the

financing of the film had been done?
A   We were not concerned- the lazy Cambridge side - with the actual details of the financing. We tended to leave that to the two Terrys to get on with, and Mark Forstater.

Q   You also left it to John Gledhill?
A   John Gledhill was our manager. He was our manager throughout Drury Lane. We were on every night. He arranged for tickets for everybody, made sure we were comfortable in the theatre. So he was actively our manager.

Q   Do you believe he was looking at the terms of the financing?
A   I have no idea, but I would expect so.

Q   Anne Henshaw: do you remember having meetings with Anne Henshaw?
A   I remember going to Michael and Terry's accountants, Henshaw Catty & Co, Michael Henshaw was their accountant and I believe that Anne Henshaw came in and began to give us some kind of secretarial assistance because we were very chaotic. It's a bunch of comedians, and so people did not tend to take minutes properly like a regular business, and she began to do this and organise us, answering questions and so on financially.

Q   She was doing more than a secretarial function, was she not, Mr. Idle?
A   Such as what?

Q   She was providing you with advice in relation to deals that you might or might not want to ----?
A   I doubt she would have been doing that at the time. She was quite young.

Q   Let us look at bundle D3, Mr. Idle?
A   All right.

Q   Let us turn to page 1001 please in D3. That is an agenda for a meeting with Python Productions to be held on 11th March at 22 Park Square, East at 4 p.m. Do you know whether you attended that meeting, Mr. Idle?
A   I have no recall.

Q   According to Mr. Palin you did. Just before we look at the context of the meeting itself, can we go back to Mr. Palin's diary and go to page 966. Keep your finger in page 1001 and just go back to page 966. At the bottom of the page: "Monday 11th March: Another Python meeting at Henshaw's. Anne was there, smoking slightly nervously as usual, John C, Eric and myself and John Gledhill..." ?
A   Mmh.

Q   "John G had come to give us his reactions to the proposed 'Gledhill Retirement Scheme'." I was interested in the agenda and the notes to it. If we look at page 1001, at the bottom of the page there, starting "Obviously..." That is some detailed analysis of what type of deal would be appropriate to enter into with Nancy Lewis, who was then going to be involved in the music side of the Pythons' business. What I suggest to you is that it is likely that that is advice that was being given to you by Mrs. Henshaw?

A   No, on the contrary. We were very grateful to Nancy Lewis. She had been working for Buddha Records in America. She had been responsible for getting us broken in America, and getting us a record deal, and we were obviously trying to find some way to recompense her or give her some role. We were not accepting advice from Anne Henshaw. What would she know about it?

Q   She became your business manager, did she not?
A   Eventually, yes, at the end of that year.

Q   In the middle of that year, I think.
A   Well, June we fired John Gledhill. Nobody seems to recall when Anne came on board, but she began to impress us with her skills and her bookkeeping and keeping notes which we'd never done before.

Q   Are you suggesting that what appears at the bottom of 1001

"What has to be borne in mind is that the base worked from is the company in London, and working on your previous budget to give 15% of 80% would only allow 5% to cover overheads, commission to UK agent. Normally something would be paid to the negotiator or coordinator at the London end, because whereas your US representative would not be involved in any UK contracts, the London end would at least be involved in coordinating supply information etc".

Are you suggesting that that is material that came from one of the Pythons, Mr. Idle?
A   I have no idea where it came from. I don't really

recall discussing Nancy Lewis' proposed deal at this time. We were on stage every night.

Q   What I suggest to you, Mr. Idle, is you may not remember discussing it, but what this suggests is that Mrs. Henshaw was providing you with advice by 11th March 1974.
A   Where do you find that suggestion?

Q   I am suggesting it to you on the basis of who else would you suggest was producing this type of information?
A   I have no answer to your question.

Q   You also got Mr. Beach involved in the structure of the finances, did you not?
A   Yes.

Q   Who was Mr. Beach?
A   Mr. Beach worked for Harbottle & Lewis.

Q   Was he your personal lawyer?
A   He was my personal lawyer and eventually he became the Python lawyer after Mr. Olswang was removed.

Q   You passed to him the documents in draft that were going to be concluded in relation to the financing of the film, is not that right?
A   I don't know that. You must obviously – he's a lawyer.

Q   Let us look at what Mr. Palin says. Before we do that, do you have any recollection of a meeting at which

Mr. Beach and Mr. Olswang discussed the terms of the Michael White deal?
A   I don't know any details. I believe they came to a meeting at Terry Jones' house on the frenetic last day when we were all trying on costumes and trying to finalise things. It was complete chaos at the time, so we were not in their discussions.

Q   You were not?
A   I certainly wasn't. I doubt whether anybody else had the time to be in them.

Q   Let us look at what Mr. Palin says about that meeting. It is at p.967 bundle D3. Do you have that?
A   I do.

Q   It is the entry for Monday April 29th. Mr. Palin is summarising what had happened earlier in the week:

"On Tuesday afternoon [you can take it from me that that is 23rd April] with the two Terrys about to leave for Scotland, Eric's lawyer, Jim Beach, decided that our contract should never be signed - it contained, or rather didn't contain, clauses which could lose us a lot of money. So we sat round a table at Terry's and our solicitor Simon Olswang and Jim Beach fought politely with each other on our behalf. I must say Jim did draw attention to certain dangers in the contract but these mainly centred around Mr. White's control of the final cut. What Jim was most worried about was what happened when or if the film ran over both the completion guarantee and the contingency money. Then there was then nothing in the contract to stop Michael White stepping in and dictating crippling terms as a price for more money. So we decide to insert a clause saying that any further investment will be treated in pari passu with the rest of the investors. So that little battle was over. The room was still full of lawyers" and it continues on.

    Mr. Idle, do you have any recollection, apart from that diary, of that particular incident?
A   Not of that incident, no.

Q   Mr. Beach there is discussing the terms of the deal with Michael White. Did you pass that document to him?
A   I don't recall doing that. I don't see why I would have had it in my hands.

Q   So someone else must have passed it to him, is that what you are suggesting?
A   He must have got it from Simon Olswang.

Q   Did you ask Mr. Beach to look at the agreement for you?
A   I am assuming that I did, because otherwise he wouldn't be there.

Q   But you have no recollection one way or the other?
A   No, I mean, none of the others would have invited him. I would certainly have invited him, possibly because I had some issues or anxieties about the deal.

Q   Is that because you would have looked at the document and read it?
A   Not necessarily.

Q	How would you have found out?
A	I don't really know. I mean, we were very casual about reading and signing documents. We were more concerned at getting the script out and getting the film made and being on stage.

Q	There must have been some reason why you passed it to Mr. Beach?
A	There absolutely must have been, but I can't tell you at this point what triggered my anxiety.

Q	So it is either reading the document.
A	Very unlikely.

Q	Or being told about the contents of the document by somebody?
A	Quite possibly, or the other Pythons.

Q	Do you remember, do you have any express recollection of ever being told about the terms of the financing deals by anybody?
A	Before the film was made?

Q	Yes.
A	I recall Michael White coming in, which made me very comfortable because I liked him, I trusted him. I recall Tony Stratton-Smith coming in with all this rock and roll money: Pink Floyd, Led Zeppelin, Genesis, and that was quite amusing. That was almost because we were on in Drury Lane and they came to see us. So in a sense, we were the rock stars and they were in the audience.

Q	But do you remember any discussion about what

percentage Mr. White was going to get?
A   No.

Q   Any discussion about what percentage you were going to get?
A   No.

Q   Do you remember any discussion as to what percentage Mr. Forstater was going to get?
A   No.

Q   No percentages at all?
A   You have to understand that percentages were a dream in the future. I think we got £2,000 to make the film. That wasn't expensive, but that's all we were counting on. That was what was going to pay us.

Q   And there was a deferred fee, was there not, as well?
A   I imagine we deferred because of the contingency.

Q   Do you have any recollection of how that deferral came to be agreed?
A   No.

Q   If Mr. Beach was provided with the Michael White agreement, would you expect all the draft agreements to have gone to Mr. Beach?
A   I can't answer that. I mean, I would have just said I have some anxieties and he would have got hold of whatever he could.

Q   Do you remember asking Mr. Beach to explain to you the terms of the deals?

A   No, we didn't have time for that.

Q   Do you remember disagreeing with any particular term of any of the deals that were on the table?
A   I think the only thing I disagreed with was when one of the producers asked us to share bedrooms on location. That was a little disagreeable.

Q   Contractually nothing?
A   I don't think we were contracted to do that!

Q   At some point someone went to Michael White and asked for the creation of the top half. You know what I mean by the top half?
A   I do now.

Q   Do you know who went and asked for the creation of the top half?
A   I have no clue.

Q   Do you have any recollection of any discussion amongst the Pythons as to the need to create the top half?
A   In terms of contract no, but I do know that I had edited both of the Python books which were to become enormous best sellers and we had done several records which were actually more valuable than what the BBC was paying us. And of course Drury Lane was paying us extremely well.

Q   You viewed White and Goldstone as being outside the Python tent, is that right?
A   Yes, they were part of the financing, sure.

Q   You had a good relationship with them, you had a

good relationship with the Tony Stratton-Smith lot, but they were outside the tent?
A   I'm not quite sure what your tent is, but --

Q   You needed to negotiate with them, you needed someone to negotiate with them on your behalf?
A   We assumed, perhaps arrogantly, that things were taken care of, and particularly when the two Terrys were in charge of directing the film, we were absolved of main responsibility in that area.

Q   It was for the two Terrys to get on with it and make it happen?
A   Certainly in the directing world, yes.

Q   And also with structuring of the financing?
A   No, I mean, John Gledhill was our manager and the manager too would have been involved in the contract and looking over our specific details and protecting us from various things like people exploiting things they shouldn't.

Q   Do you remember having any discussion with John Gledhill about the precise terms of the agreement?
A   No.

Q   Mr. Forstater does share in the top half?
A   I have subsequently learned this.

Q   You do not know on what basis the creation of the top half was presented to the investors, do you?
A   Nor how he got to be in there.

Q   You do not remember, or do you remember, a

conversation about Mr. Forstater's share in the top half at all prior to 2005?
A   No.

Q   You have no memory as to how the top half was presented to investors?
A   No idea.

Q   The mechanism that was used after the film was made to produce a book and an album involved the insertion of companies above Python (Monty) Pictures Ltd?
A   Were the companies already created?

Q   We have seen Kay-Gee-Bee was being created at the time.
A   That was newly being created, yes. But the book company?

Q   Python Productions had been around for some time.
A   For some time because we already had a record of producing two very big sellers books.

Q   Are you able to tell me why Kay-Gee-Bee Music was inserted above Python (Monty) Pictures Ltd in relation to the album?
A   I have no idea. I know the album didn't sell anything.

Q   And in relation to the book, are you able to tell me why Python Productions was inserted above Python (Monty) Pictures Ltd?
A   I imagine that was just the company we used to

create other things than films or records.

Q   Did Mr. Cleese contribute towards the production of the book?
A   Neither he nor I contributed very much to that book. It was largely, I think, Terry Jones edited it. I had edited the first two books.

Q   Despite the fact that you did not contribute to the production of the book, you shared in the top half revenue?
A   We shared in the Python revenue, that was the way we did it. It was always swings and roundabouts; somebody would work harder on other things and others would gain the benefit, but it worked out in the end.

Q   In February 1974 there is a board minute that reflects an intention to work with Mr. Forstater in the future. I have dealt with that with both Mr. Palin this morning and Mr. Jones this afternoon. Do you want to see the document or are you familiar with the document I am talking about?
A   I'm familiar with the document and I was aware that Michael was being ironic. Let me just say, it was hardly certain that we were actually making this film in April, let alone any future films. So the idea we would put him in charge of future films must have been slightly in jest.

Q   I was maybe taking things slightly too fast, Mr. Idle. I think Mr. Palin was talking about his exclamation mark in relation to film section. I am interested in, if you look at bundle D3 p.999, that is a memorandum of suggested terms of agreement with Mr. Gledhill. The first paragraph says that any future films should also be made through Python (Monty) Pictures Ltd with the intention of working with Mark Forstater.

A   I think the main point is it would be made through Python (Monty) Pictures. I mean, there may have been an intention – I was surprised at that.

Q   You do not remember it?
A   I do not recall it.

Q   It is unlikely to have been untrue, is it not?
A   Oh no, I don't believe it's untrue. I mean, somebody's intent may have been to work with Mark Forstater in the future.

Q   When it came to producing merchandise – the book or the album – it is possible, is it not, that Mr. Forstater could have assisted with that production? He could have assisted the people who were creating --
A   No, it's not possible.

Q   Why do you say that?
A   Because he has no comedy in him.

Q   Not to create the material itself, but to assist those people, arranging meetings, talking to people.
A   When you make a book you don't have meetings. I mean, it's absurd!

Q   You say you do not have meetings, Mr. Idle, but if you take up Bundle D2 and turn to p.693, in order to justify the inclusion of Python Productions Ltd. in the structure above Python (Monty) Pictures Ltd., for the production of the book, one of the documents that was

produced by Anne Henshaw on behalf of the company was a long list of meetings in respect of the book.
A   What year is this?

Q   This is in 1977, and one sees that from 689.
A   It is referring to 1977 or a previous year?

Q   It is referring to that year.
A   Or the previous year as it is December.

Q   But it is showing a large number of meetings involving the Pythons and other people to produce ----
A   But it does not say all the Pythons. It says "Pythons".

Q   No, but then on some occasions, for example on 14th December, you have TJ, GS, DB and TJ is Mr. Jones.
A   Right.

Q   So what I am suggesting to you is that in relation to your comment that, "Well, you do not have meetings in relation to books", I do not think that is quite right.
A   I do not see my initials anywhere there.

Q   No. You see references to "the Pythons", but if you say that you had no involvement at all and you should not be included within that then so be it.
A   In this *Holy Grail* book I had absolutely almost nothing to do with it.

Q   What I am suggesting to you, Mr. Idle, is that in the context of what was in the parties' minds when you came to conclude the agreement in April 1974, there was

a possibility that Mr. Forstater could be involved in the book production in the same way as one looks at the involvement of Mr. Beach and Mrs. Henshaw.
A   But we do not see his name here.

Q   No, he was not actually involved because ----
A   Because?

Q   I am asking you to think back.
A   Yes.

Q   When you agreed to give him a share in the top half ----
A   Which we never did.

Q   -- which the document gives him ----
A   So you say.

Q   -- at that stage it was possible, was it not, that Mr. Forstater could assist in the production of the book?
A   No, I still find it absurd.

Q   My next area relates to whether or not you and Mr. Cleese needed to be in agreement with Mr. Forstater getting a share of the top half.
A   It was always agreed -- We would never have a meeting without everybody being in consensus. Python has adopted for many years a veto issue where any one person can stop an agreement being made, and this was beginning to hold true, and so it is entirely impossible that people would have made agreements on our behalf without coming to us first.

Q   What about payments? Would you ever make a

payment without all of you agreeing?
A   New payments or residuals?

Q   New payments.
A   I do not know what you are referring to.

Q   Would you make new payments to people without all of you agreeing?
A   If some of us disagreed we certainly would not.

Q   If you look at Bundle D3 and go to p.1011, that is an agenda for a meeting that was to take place on 5th June.
A   Yes.

Q   Then at p.1011A is the minutes of the meeting.
A   Yes.

Q   Mr. Cleese is not present at that meeting, is he?
A   Apparently not.

Q   At item 2 the meeting decided that the percentage should be paid directly into the company, and that is item 2 that relates to the -- Well, "it was decided that the percentage should be paid directly into the company and then 5% out to each of the directors leaving 0.4% in reserve and also to enable some payment, an acknowledgement of their contribution to the film, to be made to the following".
A   Yes.

Q   So a decision is being made to make payments out without Mr. Cleese being there, is it not?
A   We were paying all of the people who worked on

the movie, which I believe is unique in cinema history: people on sound, people doing camera, and I am sure we had John's consent to do that.

Q	If you look at 1012, there is a meeting attended by a number of people but not you nor Mr. Cleese, and then at item 2 it was decided "the board decision of 5th June 1974 should now be given effect". Then, "The list of other personnel to receive deferred fees were drawn up as follows". So again we have got a decision being recorded at which you and Mr. Cleese were not present. Is that right?
A	This is a continuation of the same discussion about paying the people who had worked for us on the movie extra money, which we had agreed in principle to do and was one of the nice things Python did, I think.

Q	What I suggest to you is that as at February/March 1974, in circumstances where the two Terrys who were, as you have said, being left to deal with most of the film work, and Mr. Palin agree to give Mr. Forstater a share of the top half, that is something that they would have felt able to do. Is that not right?
A	Not right at all, no. It would have been unconscionable.

Q	If Mrs. Henshaw told Mr. Forstater that that was something that the Pythons agreed, would you accept that Mr. Forstater was entitled to think that that was right?
A	If I had ever learnt such a thing we would have fired her.

Q	You say that now, Mr. Idle, but that is, is it not, with a great degree of hindsight as to ----

A   That is the only sight I have.

Q   -- as to your view of Mr. Forstater's contribution to the film and his attempts to claim a $1/7^{th}$ of the share of the *Spamalot* revenue?
A   I am sorry, would you repeat that?

Q   Your position as to the fact that you would have fired Mrs. Henshaw and the virulence with which you are suggesting that Mr. Forstater was not entitled to the $1/7^{th}$ arises out of your view of Mr. Forstater's performance during the film and his attempt, in these proceedings, to claim a share of $1/7^{th}$ of the top half.
A   I was asking you whether -- Am I supposed to agree with you?

Q   I am asking you if that is right.
A   I did not get the question.

Q   Do you think that your position in these proceedings ----
A   Yes.

Q   -- is being inspired by, I will put it bluntly, a dislike of Mr. Forstater?
A   I am hopeful that I am trying to be as honest as far as I possibly can be and that my dislike, as you put it, of Mr. Forstater does not influence my honesty in reporting to you the answers to your questions.

Q   But you have no recollection, do you, one way or the other as to whether or not Mr. Forstater was entitled to $1/7^{th}$ of the top half?
A   I had no recollection until quite late on at which

you ...

Q   You challenge, as do your colleagues, the suggestion that there was an intention to treat Mr. Forstater as a seventh Python.
A   When I first heard about that I found it remarkable.

Q   From a financial perspective, Mr. Idle, in circumstances where he has got the same percentage profit share as you.
A   Well, he is sharing it with Julian Doyle for a start and there are eight profits shares, not seven.

Q   He is deferring his fee under the agreement in the same way as you.   Mr. Olswang and Mr. Remington have given evidence that they understood that he was to be treated as, for financial purposes, a seventh Python.
A   They are his solicitors, right?

Q   No, Mr. Olswang was your solicitor, Mr. Idle.
A   I think that Mr. Forstater brought him into our lives.

Q   Mr. Olswang and Mr. Remington were the solicitors who worked on papering the deal on behalf of the company.
A   With whom my friend and lawyer, Jim Beach, took issue.

Q   Mr. Beach did not take issue with the top half, did he?
A   Perhaps he had not seen it.

Q   You do not know.
A   I do not know.

Q   What I suggest to you is that Mr. Forstater was indeed being treated for financial purposes as if he was the same as you.
A   Certainly the same and I believe in the eight-way split, below the line, or whatever you call it, the bottom half, then, yes, he was being treated the same as to the other seven people.

Q   Mr. Idle, it is right, is it not, that since *Spamalot* has made so much money there has been a fair amount of publicity as to which Python thinks that they have had the better of the financial deal?
A   We have squabbled since we first met. We are brothers, we are children, and we are comedians. But we love each other and we get on very well. The press does like to exaggerate these things and I have emails from John Cleese only yesterday.

Q   You have complained that some of the other Pythons have been ungrateful as to the amount of money that you have managed to generate for them.
A   I may at some times and -- I have been promoting this thing since 2004, so I have answered a tremendous amount of questions and there is a selection of responses that have been selected.

Q   If you look at Bundle D3, p.1047.
A   So what is this from?

Q   I am not sure which newspaper it is from.
A   Isn't it rather relevant?

Q   But what one sees in the paragraph on the subject of money: "He is candidly regretful about his decision to hire a lawyer to represent the Pythons' interest in *Spamalot*. Over a recent lunch with Observer writer Simon Garfield, he pointed out" - that is you - "that with a third share the others are being paid over the odds without doing very much". Is that something that you said to the Observer writer, Mr. Idle?
A   It reflects possibly a bitterness I was feeling at the time. Insofar as I gave them Marcia Brooks, my lawyer, because I was concerned about conflict of interest, and she negotiated against me the highest percentage that has ever been received in Broadway history. Normally they would have been entitled to X% and John du Prez and I had to settle that they would take Y%.

Q   I think the terms of the deal are confidential. Certainly I have understood that they are.
A   Then forgive me, I just breached confidentiality inadvertently.

Q   So, Mr. Idle, what I suggest to you is that at a time when *Spamalot* is making lots of money; where there is a degree of tension between you and the other Pythons; the request by Mr. Forstater to be paid more could not have come at a worst possible time. Is that right?
A   Are we to reveal how much he has received from *Spamalot* or is that also confidential?

Q   I am not seeking to suggest that it is confidential.
A   I mean, I think he has received over a quarter of a million pounds from *Spamalot* and about half a million pounds since 2005 for *Monty Python and the Holy Grail*

and *Spamalot* and the whole box. So I feel, yes, he is slightly ungrateful.

Q That is exactly the word that you used in relation to the other Pythons.
A Well, the ingratitude matters to me frankly.

Q Mr. Idle, if you look at p.1070, this is an extract from a report from CNN and you are quoted as saying: "I am making them money and the ungrateful bastards never thank me', Idle joked. 'Who gave them a million dollars each for Spamalot? It was Idle. Who adapted Monty Python and the Holy Grail ... Spamalot.'"?
A I think you see I am trying to be amusing.

Q You are, Mr. Idle. (Laughter) But it is right, is it not, that in circumstances where Mr. Forstater comes and asks for more money and the Pythons are at each other's throats in relation to money, Mr. Forstater's request could not have come at a worse possible time?
A Actually I didn't know of Mr. Forstater's request until much later and it was only about dividing his share of the income that was coming from the Python stream. It was nothing really to do with me. I wasn't involved in the negotiations of that. I mean he was just claiming a larger share of the third of the pot that went back to Python (Monty) Pictures, or NFTC.

Q Did you ever seek to find out from Anne Henshaw what she understood had been agreed back in 1974?
A I don't think she was terribly fond of me. We fired her in 1997 for the second time.

Q And made her a director of one of your companies?

A   That was astounding to me. I have no recollection why that should have been, or who would have done such a thing.

MR. WEISSELBERG: My Lord, I am very grateful. I have run on but I Thought we would run completely on and make me stop at 4.30.

MR. JUSTICE NORRIS: That is why I did not do it.

MR. WEISSELBERG: I have now finished.

MR. JUSTICE NORRIS: Thank you.

MR. SPEARMAN: My Lord, I have no re-examination unless your Lordship has any questions.

MR. JUSTICE NORRIS: Thank you for giving your evidence. You are free to go.

Appendix 2: Cross Examination of Michael Palin by Tom Weisselberg

MR. WEISSELBERG: Mr. Palin, we are looking at p.280 where your statement of truth appears. If you flip the bundle round, there is a footer on it which says " ".
Mr. Palin Yes.

Q   What is Mayday Management?
A   Mayday Management was a company originally begun by Anne Henshaw James and Steve Abbot. It is now still in existence. Steve Abbot works for Mayday and he represents me.

Q   It is right, is it not, that Mrs. James is also a director of Mayday Management?
A   Yes.

Q   So am I right in thinking that you sent this statement of truth from the offices of Mayday Management?
A   Yes.

Q   Did Mrs. Henshaw help you send the statement of truth from Mayday Management?
A   No.

Q   Did you discuss your evidence with Mrs. Henshaw?
A   No.

Q   You have never discussed the issues relating to this

case with Mrs. Henshaw?
A   No.

Q   Why not, Mr. Palin?
A   There was no reason to.

Q   So even though Mr. Forstater says that there was an agreement between you and other of the Pythons in relation to his share of the top half, that Anne Henshaw was at a meeting with you, you have never discussed his claim with Mrs. Henshaw at all?
A   I cannot remember that meeting, if that meeting ever took place, whether we discussed it.

Q   My question was you have never discussed it with Mrs. Henshaw at all?
A   Not to my recollection.

Q   We will come back to that in due course, Mr. Palin. I would like to ask you some questions about your diary entries and really your approach to how you come to prepare your diary. It is right, is it not, that you do not record everything that happens to you?
A   That would be a very long diary.

Q   You are not a politician who is concerned to track the nuance of your life or your political life in great detail?
A   I am not a politician, no.

Q   You do not record in painstaking detail the work that you are doing, the jokes you are writing, for example?
A   Well, there is no particular scheme of how I write

the diary. It is an account of what I have done, as far as I can remember, in the previous day and, of course, the significant issues will generally come to the top, not always. It depends how much time one has to write it.

Q   You do not write it every day, do you? I am sorry, I will start it again. In the period that we are interested in, so 1973 and 1974, you were not keeping a diary every day?
A   Largely but not always.

Q   Would it be right that you tend to record matters that are amusing, interesting or full of human interest rather than the commercial side of your life?
A   No, I do not think that is true.

Q   Would you say that you tend to record difficulties rather than agreement in your diary?
A   Again I am not sure that is true.

Q   When you came to prepare your witness statement you drew very heavily on your diary, did you not? If you have still got your witness statement open, if you turn to para.18 of your witness statement, p.269, there what you do is that you say that: "You see from my diary that by the end of October Mark and Julian's position in relation to the film had still not been agreed", and you set out the diary entry that you have for a particular telephone conversation with Mr. Forstater. Do you see that?
A   Yes.

Q   You do not say that you have any independent recollection of that call. Is it right that what recollection you have of that call is based entirely on what your diary

entry says?
A   Yes.

Q   So if it is not in your diary in relation to that call you do not remember it?
A   No.

Q   Mr. Palin, you are familiar with what I mean when I talk about "the top half", are you not?
A   Yes.

Q   Your diary makes no reference as to the circumstances in which the top half came to be created, does it?
A   Not as far as I know.

Q   The agenda and the minutes that you may have heard being referred to in court, they make no references to the circumstances in which the top half came to be created, do they?
A   No.

Q   In fact, the agenda and minutes make no reference as to the terms of the financing that was to be provided for the film at all, do they?
A   No.

Q   In those circumstances do you have any recollection of who first suggested that the top half be created at all?
A   I really have no recollection.

Q   One assumes it was suggested by one of the Pythons but you do not know?

A   I do not know.

Q   So you do not know who raised the concept of the top half with the investors?
A   I am afraid I do not.

Q   And you do not recall how the top half came to be negotiated with the investors or the clause providing for the top half came to be negotiated with the investors?
A   No.

Q   In addition to the top half, each of the Pythons had a profit share, did they not?
A   Yes.

Q   Do you have any recollection of how the percentage that you came to get was negotiated?
A   No.

Q   Do you even remember what percentage you ended up getting?
A   I remember it was about 6%.

Q   Do you remember how it was decided that Mr. Forstater would get the same percentage as you?
A   No.

Q   But he did get the same percentage as you, did he not?
A   Yes.

Q   You do not have any recollection of how either the top half came to be negotiated or how the profit share came to be negotiated but it is right, is it not, that by the

time the agreement came to be signed at the end of April 1974 you knew that you were having a share of the top half and you knew you were having a percentage of the profit share?
A   I really cannot remember about the top half. It is something I do not remember the full details.

Q   But at the time the deal was done would you accept that you must have known that you were getting a share of the top half and getting a share of the profits, roughly 6%?
A   It is a long time. I cannot remember that we absolutely knew that. We were working on other things at the time.

Q   Mr. Palin, you are an Oxford graduate; you have a degree in Modern History. Are you suggesting to his Lordship that you would have had no idea about those financial terms of the deal that was being done with the investors?
A   No, I am not suggesting that. I am just suggesting that I have absolutely no recollection of knowing the details at the time or how I came to hear about those details.

Q   You would assume, would you not, that someone must have told you about the terms of the deal?
A   Probably.

Q   But you cannot recall who that person was?
A   No.

Q   Would you also have read at least your agreement before you signed it?

A   Sorry?

Q   Would you have at least read your agreement before you signed it?
A   Well, not necessarily.

Q   So someone might have just passed you a document and you would have put your signature on it without looking?
A   It is possible.

Q   Do you remember that on 1st November you had a book launch and   Mr. Gledhill gave you a document to sign it, you sign it and everyone becomes very annoyed. Do you remember that?
A   I remember it from the diaries.

Q   So at that stage you were very concerned about signing documents without having read them, were you not?
A   I did not personally become very annoyed because I think I must just have let it through without really properly checking what it was.

Q   But by April are you saying that it is likely that you would not have looked at even your own agreement for signing?
A   It is possible.

Q   But likely?
A   I have no recollection.

Q   Is it unlikely? I accept you have no recollection, Mr. Palin, but you know what you are like and what I

suggest to you is that it is likely that you read your agreement before you signed it. Shall we have a look at it just so that you might be helped? It is D1, p.368. If you look, it is an agreement dated 25th April. Your name appears at the end of the first paragraph. Do you have that at 368?
A Yes.

Q Halfway down para.1 ----
A I cannot quite see where my name appears.

Q At the very end of the first paragraph. Do you see, it says "Michael Palin" in capital letters.
A Oh, yes. Right, yes.

Q In para.1, about four or five lines down, there is again in capitals "Monty Python", and it originally said "meets the Holy Grail". Do you see someone has crossed out "and" and you have put your initials, have you not?
A Yes.

Q So someone showed you that that was a change and you would have looked at that, seen what the nature of the change was and put your initials on. Yes?
A Yes, I should think that is likely. I mean, again I have no recollection of reading the whole thing but I am sure that is likely because I have initialled it.

Q So it is likely, is it not, that you would have read what was being changed before putting your initials on it?
A Yes.

Q Over the page, at p.369, you see at the very top the

payments that you were going to be getting as fees. Do you see that?
A   Yes.

Q   Would those figures, at that stage of your career, have been significant amounts of money?
A   Yes.

Q   So you would have looked to check to see what fees you were getting?
A   I do not know. I may well not have looked to check. I am afraid I did not read all the legal documents very often. I have been given a summary by somebody mostly and agreed with that.

Q   Then look at 378, there is another amendment. This is the fifth schedule of the agreement and someone has written "So far as reasonably possible on all paid advertising", and again those are your initials, are they not?
A   Yes.

Q   You would have read what was being said there and then put your initials on it?
A   Yes.

Q   Then if you look at p.379, there is your signature and you have got a witness and that is Mr. Olswang. Do you see that?
A   Yes.

Q   Do you know whose signature that is above your signature?
A   Terry Gilliam.

Q   So it appears that Mr. Gilliam was at 78 Brook Street in front of Mr. Olswang to sign the agreement and it is likely, is it not, that you were there at the same time?
A   I have no recollection but maybe.

Q   Do you have any recollection of being at Mr. Olswang's offices in Brook Street?
A   No.

Q   Thank you, Mr. Palin. You can put Bundle D1 away. I would like to ask you some questions about your first feature film And Now For Something Completely Different.
A   Yes.

Q   Did Mr. Gledhill negotiate the terms of the deal with the investors in relation to that film on your behalf?
A   I am afraid I do not know.

Q   You were not satisfied with the terms of the deal that ended up being concluded. Is that right?
A   I do not know.

Q   What I suggest to you is that you, when it came to making your second feature film, felt that that first film was unsatisfactory in that you had not been given creative control of the film. Would you agree with that?
A   That is my memory of it, yes.

Q   Do you remember what financial interest you had in the film?
A   I am afraid I do not.

Q	Do you have any recollection of discussions of the financial terms of that film?
A	I have no recollection.

Q	When it came to making the second film is it not right that you were determined to try and retain control of the production process?
A	Yes.

Q	That was an issue that you were very concerned about?
A	Yes.

Q	Do you recall any particular discussions that you had with anyone about that concern?
A	I do not recall exact discussions but I know it was an issue that was raised amongst the Python team.

Q	How do you know, if you do not recall any particular discussions, how do you know it was raised amongst the Python team?
A	I think I refer to it in my diary at some point and being concerned about keeping control of the production, and so I assume that that must have come from me not talking to myself but me talking to somebody else.

Q	So because it is in your diary you assume it is true? It happened rather.
A	I assume it happened.

Q	You are considering making your second feature film and you are beginning to have doubts about Mr. Gledhill, is that right?
A	Yes.

Q   Is it right that you have concerns about Mr. Gledhill from two perspectives, first as a producer of the film, is that right? You have concerns about him being the producer of the film. We are talking ----
A   Yes, that was one ----

Q   -- September/August 1973.
A   Yes.

Q   So you have concerns about him being the producer of the film?
A   Yes, I think we probably did.

Q   You also had concerns about him being your manager?
A   Yes, we were certainly worried about his performance.

Q   Would it be fair to say that at that stage, i.e. September/October 1973, his kingdom stood on brittle glass? He was in danger of falling through and not being held on as your manager?
A   Yes, that is a very interesting way of putting it and probably true.

Q   Given your experience with the first film and given your concerns about   Mr. Gledhill as being the producer, by September/October 1973 you were very concerned to make sure that you had someone on the production side that was on your side. Is that fair?
A   Yes.

Q   And it was very important to you that you had a

producer who you felt you could trust?
A   Yes.

Q   You wanted someone who would be batting for you?
A   We wanted someone who we could trust.

Q   And who would take the fight to the investors and protect your interest, is that right?
A   I do not think it was quite as straightforward as that. We had Mr. Gledhill, he was still our manager. We had issues with Mr. Gledhill. We were looking for some good advice on the new film.

Q   It was more than advice, was it not, Mr. Palin? You wanted someone to go out and find financing for you.
A   Well, yes, there were people like Jill Foster who was working for me at the time who were looking for finance but, yes, that was part of it.

Q   In the end, by, I suggest to you, November of 1973, it was Mr. Forstater who you saw to be the person best placed to be the producer of the film.
A   Yes, I think that is borne out in one of the diary entries.

Q   He was the person that you felt you could trust?
A   I felt we could trust him, yes.

Q   He was going to be your team, the leader of your production team. Is that right?
A   Well, Chippenham Films were going to be the production team which was Mark Forstater and Julian

Doyle. It was always seen as a Chippenham Films contribution.

Q   You say that, Mr. Palin, but if one looks at your diary what one sees is no reference to Chippenham Films at all. One sees lots of references to Mr. Forstater being the producer. It is Mr. Forstater who was going to be the producer. That is right, is it not?
A   Yes. That does not mean that Chippenham Films were not involved. Julian Doyle was involved because he was going to provide production services and he was the partner of Mark. I am just saying that to make it clear, but certainly, yes, Mark was given the producer role.

Q   He was the producer initially, and you set this out, initially he suggests, according to your diary, that he and Julian Doyle should be the co-producers, does he not?
A   Yes.

Q   But that plan is not taken forward and Mr. Forstater becomes the sole producer of the film.
A   I think that was Mr. Forstater's decision. I mean, that was a decision taken between him and Julian.

Q   So Mr. Doyle does not become the producer but becomes the production manager. Do you remember that?
A   I do not know if he was given exactly that title but the share was that Julian would do the practical making of the film, providing the services, and that Mark would be the producer.

Q   The producer?
A   Yes.

Q   In fact, and I will take you to it if you want me to, but the credits for the film show Mr. Doyle being the production manager and the special effects photography man, and that is really what he was doing for the film, was it not, those two tasks?
A   Very important, especially production managers.

Q   In terms of raising money are you aware of Mr. Doyle doing anything to raise financing for the film?
A   No, I'm not aware of anything other than I know that Mr. Doyle was involved with Mark in approaching Michael White, I think, at some point. That is in the diary.

Q   If we go to your diaries, Mr. Palin, in bundle D3 I would like to show you the progression very briefly of Mr. Forstater's role as recorded in this diary. I would like to start, please, at page 958?
A   Yes.

Q   If one looks at the paragraph between the two hole punches: "Home to a barrage of phone calls. Gledhill has two bites on the film. It's amazing what pushing by Mark and Jill has done - but not good vibes. Somewhere along the line there must be a showdown. Too much tight-lipped co-operation. It must crack some time." So at that stage you saw Mark Forstater and Jill Foster as being important people in the securing or the attempt to secure finance for the film?
A   Yes.

Q   Then if you go on to page 959 there is an entry on 18th October. You say "Tony Stratton-Smith has still not confirmed his money for the film, and rumours are about that he doesn't have it. The latest likely backers are Michael White and John Goldstone, and they had been involved by Mark, after John said he'd spoken to them..." - that is John Gledhill, is it not?
A   Erm ----

Q   "... and they weren't interested."?
A   I think that was John, yes.

Q   "According to White-Goldstone, there was no approach from John."?
A   Yes, that' John Gledhill.

Q   Then we have looked at, very briefly, the conversation on 28th October which you see at page 960. At that stage Mr. Forstater, according to you, is saying that he wants to employ himself and Julian as co-producers, but we have established that wasn't the end position. What then happens between that conversation and the meeting on 1st November that you deal with at 962 - if I just summarise it - is that you are supporting Mark Forstater against Mr. Gledhill and Goldstone. Is that fair?
A   (No audible reply)

Q   For example you have a conversation ---?
A   Certainly - yes, against Mr. Gledhill, yes, in that case.

Q   And on 1st November we see the diary entry for the meeting at 962. Looking at the top, "Mark explained the film deal, thoroughly and efficiently, and also gave us a run-down on how he would hope to be involved in the film, and how much of a cut he would like." Do you remember what he said in relation to the cut that he would like?

A   No..

Q   Do you remember what he said he would hope to do in relation to the film?
A   No.

Q   So in relation to this meeting your recollection is pretty much based entirely on your diary entry. Would that be fair?
A   Yes.

Q   If one looks then into the third paragraph: "So at the end of what I had expected to be a bitter and acrimonious Python power struggle we had easy and complete agreement for Mark as Producer, and an equally complete determination to be strong with Gledhill." Then you say at the end of that paragraph, "It was the dissatisfaction with Gledhill as much as the satisfaction with Mark which had carried the day. I felt very pleased, and a little chuffed at having persuaded John two nights ago to meet Mark, before Goldstone." That is John Clccsc, is it not?
A   Yes.

Q   Then if you go to 963, which is another meeting on 5th November (one can see that from over the page at 962), I am interested in the last two lines of that entry. "However, the point seemed to have finally been made, that as far as we are concerned Mark is handling the film.

From that moment on, John G went quiet and Mark took over." Finally in your diary on this point, Mr. Palin, go over to page 966 to the meeting on 4th March. I am interested in the brackets at the end. It relates to a meeting that you are having at the Henshaws with Nancy Lewis. You say "(Now that Mark is in charge of our film section! Nancy's appointment would further restrict the sphere of Gledhill's influence.)" Is it right that at that stage you were considering Mark Forstater to be in charge of the film section?

A   No. I think the significant thing there is the explanation mark after "section" which suggests that it was a bit tongue in cheek. There was no film section. There was no music section. I think that was a little game we were playing at Python, suddenly becoming a major corporation with divisions. Hence, the reference to the film section with an exclamation mark.

Q   By that stage, Mr. Palin, you were considering making any further films with Mark Forstater. That is right, is it not?
A   I don't remember any decision to do that but if it is in the diaries, it must have been talked about.

Q   It is not in the diary, Mr. Palin, but if you go on to page 998 you will see a memorandum of a meeting that takes place a few days earlier on 28th February 1974. Do you have that?
A   Yes.

Q   The first point which follows the following words, "The directors came to the meeting having decided to reorganise themselves in the following manner: 1.. That any future films would also be made through Python

(Monty) Pictures Ltd. With the intention of working with [Mr. Forstater]." Do you have any recollection of the directors, i.e. you and the other Pythons, having reached that conclusion before the meeting on 28th February?
A   I don't, I'm afraid, and I see it as rather - it does seem rather unlikely that we would have made any forecast about future films. It was difficult enough getting this film made. That was what we were really all engaged upon. So the idea of future films being made through Python (Monty) Pictures with the intention of working with Mark Forstater doesn't ring awfully true to me of the Pythons as something that's been put in.

Q   So do you think that that is just wrong?
A   No. I don't think it's wrong. It's down there. We obviously - it is the memorandum. We must have had a look at it. We didn't cross it out, but I'm not sure how seriously we took it.

Q   Well, Mr. Palin, if you go on to page 999 you will see a document that we understand was given to Mr. Gledhill, and I will show you how you refer to this document in a moment, but the first point there is "... any future films would also be made through Python (Monty) Pictures with the intention of working with Mark Forstater." So it looks like that is what you were telling Mr. Gledhill?
A   Yes, and probably more discontent with Gledhill making quite clear what the position was than, as I have said earlier, a whole hearted commitment to Mark for our future film career.

Q   You say that but your diaries suggest that you would be supporting   Mr. Forstater. You are telling Mr.

Gledhill that Mr. Forstater would, in all - well, that the intention was that future films would be done with Mr. Forstater. It is right, is it not, that at that stage you were considering Mr. Forstater to be the person who was going to be the film guy within your set-up?

A   Well, that was the way I phrased it in the film section bit. As I have said, that was not something that was clearly worked out and was not subject to any sort of plans to feature films at all. It was just - it was something that must have been put in there to show that John Gledhill was no longer going to be involved in any films we made.

Q   Do you have any direct recollection of that, or is that something you are assuming now?
A   No, I have no direct recollection of that.

Q   In relation to the views that the other Pythons had towards Mr. Forstater, the initial link to Mr. Forstater came through Mr. Gilliam. Is that right?
A   So it says, yes.

Q   That Mr. Gilliam and Mr. Forstater knew each other from their time in the United States?
A   Yes.

Q   And prior to the start of the filming of *The Holy Grail* Mr. Gilliam was a supporter of Mr. Forstater. Is that fair?
A   Yes, I should think so.

Q   And Mr. Jones also came to be a supporter of Mr. Forstater?
A   Well, they both knew Mark, yes, and actually

worked with him.

Q   Would you say that they were the strongest supporters of Mr. Forstater to be involved as the producer for *The Holy Grail*?
A   Yes.

Q   Would you say you were as strong as them?
A   I took their recommendation, yes.

Q   Is one of the reasons that you were a supporter of Mr. Forstater was because you saw him as being a bulwark against the business like cohorts of Mr. White and Mr. Goldstone when they came on the scene?
A   I can't recollect thinking of it like that.

Q   If you look in your diary at page 964, there is a diary note for a meeting on 28th November where you say, "The film deal is still not finalised. Apparently our Fairy Godmother, Michael White, is being quite business-like with us - his cohort, John Goldstone, wants 12½% of the fee for a job whose function we cannot quite pin down, and Michael White wants his name prominently on the credits, plus various controls and final words on appointment of crew, productions staff, editing etc. So Mark has not signed yet." Then if you look over the page at 964, under the heading "December 1973", so it appears that you have not been keeping a daily record in December, but you have summarised some bits and pieces. What you say is: "On Thursday the 6th I was summoned to a meeting with Terry G and Mark to discuss with Tony Stratton-Smith his plan for raising finance for the film. As Mark is not entirely happy with the White-Goldstone deal, especially with the 12½ %

plus Producer's fee which Goldstone is asking, any alternative source of finance is useful." Then the passage I began to show you at page 965, the last three lines. "Tony asked one or two routine questions, but altogether his offer seemed a lot more attractive than White-Goldstone. All he wanted for supplying finance was 5% - but Mark, a steady negotiator to the end, got him down to 4½%." So, Mr. Palin, I suggest to you that at this stage, i.e. towards the end of 1973, you were looking at Mark Forstater as being someone who was negotiating on your behalf against the business-like cohorts of Mr. White and Mr. Goldstone. Do you agree?
A   Yes.

Q   Mr. Idle and Dr. Chapman - is it right that if you and the two Terrys were happy with Mr. Forstater at this stage, so by the end of 1973, they were happy with Mr. Forstater as well?
A   I don't remember. We certainly know that John Cleese was unhappy or less happy.

Q   I am coming on to Mr. Cleese in a moment. In relation to Mr. Idle and Dr. Chapman you do not know?
A   I have no idea.

Q   You have no recollection?
A   It's not in here so I have no recollection.

Q   Not in the diary and therefore no recollection?
A   No, no. No recollection.

Q   I will not accuse you of being Oliver North, Mr. Palin, but I take the point. Mr. Cleese: Mr. Cleese was

initially hostile to the involvement of Mr. Forstater, was he not?
A   Yes.

Q   You managed to engineer it so that there was a meeting on 1st November where Mr. Forstater turned up before Mr. Goldstone. Do you remember that?
A   I don't remember it, no.

Q   If one looks at your diary one sees that happening. It is at page 961. "Tonight a long phone call from [Mr. Cleese]." Then you set out what happened during the conversation. "He talked with little humour, he seemed rather cross and lashed out at Terry over his failure to consult John when Mark was 'appointed' producer - 'over the years Terry has quite a history of leaping in without thinking'..." Which Terry would that be, Mr. Palin? Would that be Mr. Jones or Mr. Gilliam?
A   Probably Mr. Jones.

Q   And you then continue to say: "Eventually I talked John down, saying that I didn't think it was wise to ask the advice of the man we should be bargaining with. In the end we agreed to ask Mark along first, just to give him a hearing - but even then I was made to feel I had wrung a major concession from John. John C who only two weeks ago made no secret of his contempt for Gledhill, now seems to be swinging behind him; it appears he will do anything that is hostile towards Mark." Then you say: "I cannot understand his attitude and, as John is less and less open with us these days, I feel there could be dozens of hidden motives." By that, Mr. Palin is it right that at this stage, i.e. towards the end of 1973 Mr. Cleese was, to put it colloquially, semi-detached from the rest of the Pythons?

A   Well, he was working, I think, then on his own new series, probably *Fawlty Towers*. We met, we talked. I wouldn't say he was totally detached, no. John has very strong views of his own and was expressing them, I think.

Q   What you recall Mr. Cleese going on to say is "Mainly, tho', I think he mistrusts Mark because he mistrusts Terry and sees Mark as his protégé and John is well-known to have an unshakeable respect for 'experience'..." What then happens is there is a meeting on 1st November which we have already looked at at 962 and Mr. Cleese comes round at least to that stage, doesn't he, and he agrees that Mr. Forstater should be the producer?

A   Yes.

Q   Then let's go into your diary in 1974 at page 966. In your diary you have a record of another conversation that you have had with Mr. Cleese. Do you want to have a moment just to read that to yourself?

A   Which page are we looking at?

Q   23rd January, just by the top hole punch?

A   Yes.

Q   Now, Mr. Cleese there is expressing doubts but as we have already seen by 28th February you were confirming that the directors had decided that any future films would also be made with Python (Monty) Pictures with the intention of working with Mr. Forstater. Now, what I suggest to you is by that stage, by late February, Mr. Cleese was fully on board with Mr. Forstater being

the producer for the film at the very least. Do you agree?
A   I can't remember exactly.

Q   Do you have any recollection of the conversation that you had with Mr. Cleese on 23rd January?
A   Only as is in the diary. I can't remember exactly details, except as they are down here.

Q   So what I suggest to you, Mr. Palin, is that by November 1973 from your perspective you thought that Mark Forstater would be producing the film for you?
A   Yes.

Q   And you considered that he was doing it as part of your team?
A   Well, he was producing the film. "Part of our team" - I don't know quite what that means, sorry.

Q   He was acting for you as against, for example, White and Mr. Goldstone, against Mr. Tony Stratton-Smith?
A   Mmh.

Q   He was protecting your interests, so Python interests, in relation to the production of the film?
A   Yes.

Q   Would you say you thought of him as being your man?
A   Could you explain that further? I am not quite sure what you mean.

Q   He was the person who was looking after your interests and going to be your guy on the ground in

relation to the production of the film?
A   He was going to be producer of the film, yes. That had been agreed.

Q   Initially he was going to be acting as the producer of the film just because a few of you had agreed that he should undertake that task. Is that right?   So Mr. Cleese exploded because Mark Forstater was doing the production work without him having been consulted. Do you remember that?
A   No, I think Mark became producer when we all agreed that he should be producer.

Q   And we have looked at some of your diary entries, but aside from your diary, do you have any particular recollection of how Mr. Forstater was allowed to find finance for the film and to work as a producer?
A   No.

Q   I would like to come back to the position of Mr. Doyle. If you look at bundle D1 - you can put bundle D3 away. If you look at page 314, that is the agreement between Mr. Forstater and Python (Monty) Pictures Limited. On that document in the first paragraph there is a reference to "The Company" in the second line and then a reference to Mr. Forstater in the third line from the bottom?
A   Sorry, we are looking at page 314.

Q   314, top paragraph?
A   Yes.

Q   An agreement made on 25th April. You see handwritten in the first line. Then in capitals

"BETWEEN PYTHON (MONTY) PICTURES LIMITED" and then three lines from the bottom Mr. Forstater's name?
A   Yes.

Q   This is the document that you initialled and one sees that at page 323. We will come back to talk about those initials in a moment. When you were given this document to initial, would you have looked at the first bit to see who it is an agreement between?
A   I don't know.

Q   You do not have any recollection?
A   No.

Q   But you would assume that you would. If you had been asked to put some initials on a document, you would be given it and you would be told who it is between?
A   Yes, I would assume that.

Q   So what I suggest to you is that when you came to put your initials on the document you must have known that the agreement was between your company and Mr. Forstater personally. Do you accept that?
A   At that time I don't remember reading carefully through all the documents that we had to, so I can't say that I read the whole document.

Q   I am not suggesting to you that you would have read the whole document through, Mr. Palin, but I am suggesting to you that when you are given this document to initial you would have known that it was an agreement between Python (Monty) Pictures Limited and Mr.

Forstater. Do you accept that?
A   I accept that's the likelihood, yes.

Q   We can put that away. I would like to ask you about the first meeting you had with Mr. White and Mr. Goldstone. Do you have any recollection of that meeting?
A   No.

Q   So if I told you it took place in Duke Street on 25th October, that does not ring any bells?
A   It doesn't jog my memory, I'm afraid.

Q   You do not remember who was there at the first meeting with Mr. White and Mr. Goldstone?
A   No.

Q   Do you remember Mr. Cleese agreeing that Mr. Gledhill could be called "the executive producer"?
A   I don't recollect that, no.

Q   Following that meeting, there is another meeting on 1st November and we have looked at your diary entries in relation to that meeting already. Do you remember where that meeting took place?
A   The meeting on 1st November? I have a feeling, from having read the diary, that it was Mr. Cleese's home.

Q   But other than having read the diary recently, you have no direct recollection?
A   No.

Q   And you do not know whether it was in the morning

or the afternoon?
A   No.

Q   I mentioned already that after that you went to a party at Methuen. Do you remember going to that party?
A   I remember it from the diary, yes.

Q   Independent of the diary, you have no recollection?
A   Oh yes. I mean - it's difficult to say which comes first. I remember it because I read about it in the diary and that jogged my recollection.

Q   Do you have any picture in your head of what happened during ---?
A   No.

Q   If you look at bundle D3 again and go to page 964 there is an entry for 28th November which we looked at a moment ago. I am interested in the end of the first paragraph. "Then over to John's for a script meeting. Our three large chunks of material all seemed to go down well, tho' John had more reservations than anyone else. Mark F was there." Do you remember that initially in relation to the script of *Holy Grail* there was going to be a modern section and a medieval section? Do you remember that in the script?
A   I remember that it was decided at some point there should be modern interpolations into the original script, yes.

Q   A modern setting for some of the script. So some of the film would take place in modern day and some of the film would take place in the medieval period?
A   Yes, it was a fine thing. It was actually

interpolation. There would be certain, yes, elements. A man in modern dress appearing at various points, yes.

Q That ended up being removed from the film, is that right?
A No, I do not think it was entirely removed.

Q Do you remember Mr. Forstater having any involvement in the script meeting that you have recorded in your diary on 28th November?
A No, I cannot remember his involvement.

Q We have talked about your concerns in relation to Mr. Gledhill being the producer. I would like to turn to talk about the concerns that you had with Mr. Gledhill as being your manager. What I would like to suggest to you is that by the end of 1973 you, as in all of the Pythons, were very dissatisfied with him and were considering sacking him entirely as being the manager.
A We were certainly very dissatisfied with him, yes. Whether the question of sacking him had come up at that point, I do not know. But we were unhappy with his performance at that time.

Q If you look at your diary entry for 23rd October 1973, which is at p.959, you deal with, in the first paragraph, some comings and goings in relation to what was being discussed and then you say in the second paragraph: "At last the attack develops. Gilliam rants and raves and expresses his frustration with Gledhill very forcibly, banging the chair".
A Excuse me, I am slightly -- It is on which page?

Q 959, 23rd October.

A   23rd October, I am with you.

Q   The second paragraph.
A   Yes.

Q   "At last the attack develops. Gilliam rants and raves and expresses his frustration with Gledhill very forcibly, banging the chair. Eric is very quiet. John wades in though not ruthlessly. I try to tell John why we are dissatisfied - that he has for far too long been giving us definite optimistic pronouncements which turn out to mean nothing. Graham gets angry again. John reacts, cleverly in retrospect, with injured aggression. He fights back, 'Then why not get yourselves another manager?', he says sweeping his glasses off with a flourish. You could have heard a pin drop in Waterloo Place this uncommonly mild October afternoon", and then cut down to about five lines from the bottom: "Only Terry J had reacted to Gledders' 'Why not get another manager?' speech. He had said, 'We might need to' but then had conditioned this. Still, the air of accusation and dissatisfaction was fairly thick and tho' the meeting had switched off John G and onto the stage show again, there was a feeling that he had been hit. We'll see what develops". Then on 5th November, 962, you deal with another Python meeting "chez Cleese". "When I arrived there at 1.00 John Gledhill was sitting on the arm of a sofa looking wide-eyed and uncomfortable. Also there were Mark, John C, Eric and Graham". The meeting then continued and one sees over the page, at 963, Mr. Forstater outlined criticisms of a contract that Mr. Gledhill had asked you to sign at the book launch party "last Thursday night". By this stage you were not, and this is you personally, Mr. Palin, keen to rely on advice

that Mr. Gledhill was giving to you. Is that right?
A   No, I think that is there.

Q   If you go on to the entry at 964 you see that on 27th November, the top entry: "I left about 6.15, collected the car and we drove over to Michael Henshaw's for a meeting with him and Anne generally about Python and our personal financial relationship with Python Productions but more specifically about the shortcomings of John Gledhill as a business manager. Henshaw and Anne both bullshit a bit but I do think that between them they're a lot more capable than John Gledhill". So at this stage you were discussing with the Henshaws the shortcomings of Mr. Gledhill as a business manager. Yes?
A   Apparently so, yes.

Q   Do you have any recollection of that meeting at all?
A   No.

Q   At that stage you were recording that Mr. and Mrs. Henshaw between them are a lot more capable than Mr. Gledhill. Yes? Do you recall having that view at that time?
A   I was thinking of alternatives to John Gledhill, not anything much more than that. Certainly considered that Anne Henshaw might be more competent.

Q   Mr. Henshaw is an accountant, is that right?
A   Yes, he was my accountant.

Q   Mrs. Henshaw was involved in the world of business management, artistic management, is that right?

A   I cannot quite remember. I think she was something involved in the legal world.

Q   So she was not an accountant?
A   No.

Q   So where you say "between them they are a lot more capable than JG", is it right that you were at that stage looking at Mr. Henshaw to provide the accountancy services and Mrs. Henshaw to provide the business manager type services?
A   No, that would not be true. Mr. Henshaw was already my accountant at the time. Anne was his wife. I did not know Anne particularly well at that time. The more I got to know her the more I thought she gave some very good advice, but there was no question of Michael Henshaw becoming the Pythons accountant.

Q   So from your perspective Henshaw Catty were not, and never became, the accountants for Python. Is that right? Is that what you are saying?
A   I cannot remember the exact details now.

Q   There then follow, in January, February, March and April, a number of meetings in relation to Python Productions that are attended by people from Henshaw Catty. I am sorry, not January. We have records for February, March and April. If you look at p.889A ----
A   Is this in my diary?

Q   I am sorry, no, Bundle D3. The very front of the bundle, Mr. Palin.
A   Yes, yes.

Q   889A. It is a Henshaw Catty invoice addressed to Python Productions Ltd., and you see the date is 19th January 1974 to 24th July 1974.
A   Yes.

Q   The first entry is "to attending various meetings with John Gledhill in order to take over the day-to-day running of Python Productions", then to meetings with yourselves, 21st February, 28th February, 6th March, 4th March, 11th March, 2nd April, 5th June, and preparing agenda and minutes for such meetings. Then visiting Mr. Smith's offices, general bookkeeping and then general correspondence and calls with third parties. What I suggest to you, Mr. Palin, is that shows that from 19th January 1974 Henshaw Catty were helping you out in relation to Python affairs. Would you agree with that?
A   Anne Henshaw was helping us out, yes.

Q   She was attending meetings with Mr. Gledhill in order to take over the day-to-day running of Python Productions? Is that right?
A   Yes, I assume she was.

Q   You say you assume she was but that is your recollection, is it not, Mr. Palin?
A   I am recollecting the mind nudged by what I see here but, yes, I am sure she did.

Q   She was someone who, we have seen, in November you had confidence in and during the early part of 1974 you had confidence in the advice that she gave you when she gave you advice. Is that right?
A   Yes.

Q   Given the dissatisfaction -- (After a pause): I will keep moving, my Lord! I meant physically rather than verbally. So she was someone who was, because of the dissatisfaction that we have seen with Mr. Gledhill, she begins in the early part of 1974, so January, February, March, April, she is beginning to take on functions that Mr. Gledhill, as the manager, had been performing prior to that date. Is that right?
A   Well, she has taken on what is written down here. I do not remember the exact details of what she did or would compare it with what John Gledhill was doing, but, yes, she was doing certain things that John would have done.

Q   Mr. Olswang says that he was liaising with Mrs. Henshaw in relation to matters about corporate matters, so the way in which the money would flow in relation to the film. I assume that you would be entirely happy that that is what Mrs. Henshaw was doing on your behalf?
A   I do not recollect that she was doing it.

Q   But if he says that that is what he recollects you would have no reason to think that he was wrong, would you?
A   Well, that is his recollection.

Q   But you would have no reason to think that he was wrong given your knowledge of what Mrs. Henshaw did and came to do for you, i.e. certainly by the middle to late part of 1974 she is your business manager, is that not right?
A   John Gledhill was officially our manager until, I think, I seem to recollect, the middle of 1974, so Anne Henshaw was not at that time our manager. She was

more of a coordinator. But after mid-1974, yes, she would be, I think, our business manager although I do not recollect ever drawing up any formal contract.

Q   If you look at your diary, Mr. Palin, at 966 of D3 you record on 4th March that you were due to meet with the Henshaws and Nancy [Lewis] and Ina before lunch. We finally got there at 1 [o'clock]. There were some sandwiches and white wine. Under discussion was Nancy's official future with Python. At a recent meeting we decided to put Nancy in charge of our new music publishing company, Kay-Gee-Bee ... and also to give her control of records and recordings and all future contracts." Now, do you remember that meeting?
A   Ah...

Q   Aside from your diary, do you have any independent recollection of the meeting?
A   I don't.

Q   What I suggest to you is that you are having the meeting at the Henshaws because you are wanting Anne Henshaw to be involved in the meeting itself. Is that right?
A   That would seem fair, yes.

Q   You were looking to her to give you advice in relation to the deal that was going to be done with Nancy Lewis in relation to Kay-Gee-Bee. Is that right?
A   Certainly we would have met there because that was the place where the Pythons mainly met together and Anne would have enabled them to come along as the obvious place to meet. And, yes, we would have discussed all these matters that are down here in the

entry.

Q   You would have been taking advice from Anne in relation to the position that you should be adopting vis-à-vis Nancy Lewis?
A   We would have discussed Nancy's' role with Anne, yes.

Q   You would have discussed it with her so that she could give you any advice that you might want to get?
A   Well, possibly, but we could tell her about what we knew of Nancy, which was a two-way thing. It wasn't saying "help us out".

Q   That is the normal situation for the manager, is it not? The manager gives advice and the artist gives information in relation to what he or she wants for any deal going forward?
A   Well, she was not our manager at the time. That is all I can say.

Q   I accept she was not your formal manager, but I am suggesting to you that she was operating like a manger in relation to this particular issue. Would you agree with that?
A   I don't agree actually, no. I think we were still on the edge of discussing with her and all the rest of the Pythons, I assume, possible ways of going forward.

Q   If you look at the next entry on 11th March you say "Another Python meeting at Henshaw's. Anne was there, smoking slightly nervously as usual, John C, Eric and myself and John Gledhill. John G had come to give us his reactions to our proposed 'Gledhilll Retirement

Scheme'..." Do you know what that is a reference to, Mr. Palin?

A   I assume it was a reference to our plan to dispense with Mr. Gledhill's services, I think.

Q   I have assumed that is the document we were looking at a moment ago at page 999. Would that be right?

A   999?

Q   Do you have that?
A   Yes.

Q   Was this a document that Mrs. Henshaw helped you draw up?

A   I have no recollection that she helped draw it up, but she would probably be consulted.

Q   Consulted to see whether she had any views on it?
A   Yes, I should think so.

Q   Back in your diary entry you then continue to deal with what John Gledhill's reaction was. We can see that at the bottom of 966?

A   Yes.

Q   Over the page at 967. "He's very difficult to pin down, tho' I detected almost visible discomfiture when Anne mentioned the figures for UK and Canada tours." So she was assisting you in your negotiations with Mr. Gledhill. Is that right?

A   When she was certainly collating information that we needed in order to understand Mr. Gledhill's position.

Q   And then presenting it to Mr. Gledhill to assist you in your negotiations/discussions with him?
A   Yes.

Q   Then you say, "I really could have ripped into him then, as he had promised me categorically that he would have copies of our expenses for the UK tour sent to everyone two months ago. But without the vociferous anti-Gledhill lobby [the two Terrys] there, he was let off the hook and all that was decided was that we should meet again in a couple of weeks and John would present a full and complete account of what he thought we owed him for back projects before starting on the 'retirement plan'. Full marks to Anne, who is working hard to try and sort us out. At least we are now meeting fare more regularly." Now, Mr. Palin, I suggest to you that that shows a realisation by you in early March that Anne Henshaw is providing you with useful manager-type services. Would you agree with that?
A   I don't know how you define "manager" exactly. I mean a manager to me is someone who you appoint as manager. She was providing us with information, certainly. She was providing us with views on how we should perhaps use that.

Q   So she was providing you with information. She was providing you with views, and so she was providing you with advice?
A   She was giving her opinion, I'm sure, yes.

Q   She was there to help read and review documents that were being produced as part of the film financing process. Are you aware of her doing that?
A   I'm not aware of the details of that, no.

Q   Not aware of the details, but do you believe that that is what she was doing at the time?
A   Sorry, can you ask that again?

Q   Was she reviewing, considering and reviewing, documents that were being generated as part of the film financing process?
A   I don't know.

Q   In any view she was doing more than a mere book-keeping role, was she not?
A   Well, she was certainly talking to us about her interpretation of figures she found and all that, yes. She was not forcing us into any particular course though.

Q   She was not forcing you to do anything. One would hope that no manager would ever force you to do anything, Mr. Palin, but she was providing you with services that were not just an accountant's services. In fact, you have said that she was not an accountant. But she was providing you with advice and assistance in relation to your position as the Pythons. Is that right?
A   Certainly yes, to me. I am not sure about all the Pythons at that particular time because we didn't always gather together at the same time, but....

Q   We have seen that she is assisting you in discussions with Mr. Goldstone and we have seen that she was giving you assistance in relation to Nancy Lewis. If Mr. Olswang was receiving information from Mrs. Henshaw, would you think that, given the position that Mrs. Henshaw was occupying, they would have been entitled to think that that was information that was coming from

you - the Pythons?
A   Not necessarily. Certainly not the Pythons because I can't talk about the Pythons as a united group. As you can see from some of these things, different people had different ideas of what should be done at a certain time.

Q   If she says the Pythons want X to, say, Mr. White, would you expect   Mr. White to think that Anne Henshaw says that that is what the Pythons want. I am going to work on the assumption that the Pythons want that. Do you think that that would have been the position that Anne Henshaw occupied at this time?
A   I can't really say for sure, to be honest, no.

Q   That is because you do not really remember precisely what role she was occupying at that time?
A   I can remember her giving us advice and talking to us, providing us, as I said, with figures, checking dates of things that had been done before. That I can remember very distinctly. As to her role with Mr. Olswang, I am less clear.

Q   I would like to look at some of the memos and agenda documents that appear from 966 and following. Can you turn to those in D3 please, Mr. Palin?
A   966?

Q   I am sorry, 996?
A   996. I have got up to 955 of the documents at the beginning.

Q   It is 996. There are quite a lot of ones that are 995, A, B, C and D. Do you have those?
A   I have that.

Q There is a 996 and your document may have the final digit obliterated?
A Oh I see. I think it comes later, yes. It comes after the diary extracts. So 996.

Q Yes, the last digit may have been obliterated?
A Yes.

Q That is a document that is dated 21st February 1974. Do you see that on the right-hand side?
A Yes.

Q You have no diary entry for that meeting, or indeed for the meeting that one sees on 28th February. You were clearly in attendance at the meeting. One looks at that at 997 because your name is on the memorandum. Do you have any independent recollection of that meeting at all?
A No.

Q Who would have prepared these documents, do you think? Mrs. Henshaw?
A I should think so, yes.

Q Do you know why you would not have made a diary entry for the meetings on 21st February? There seems to be another meeting on 28th Febraury, but we do now know whether you attended that meeting. Why would you not have made a diary entry?
A I really don't know. I didn't make a diary entry of everything that happened.

Q Then there is a memo on 6th March which we have looked at already, the Gledhill Retirement Plan at 999.

Do you have that?
A   Yes.

Q   According to Henshaw Catty there was a meeting on that day. Do you remember whether there was a meeting on that date or not?
A   I don't.

Q   If you then go to page 1000, there is a meeting on 11th March and this is an agenda item. If one looks at the notes to the agenda which start at page 1001 do you have any recollection of these documents - the agenda or the notes to the agenda which carry on for three pages after that? Do you know whose handwriting is on 1003?
A   No.

Q   And do you know whose writing is at 1004? It is the same document but it is a slightly different version.
A   I think it is Anne's writing though.

Q   The writing on 1004 looks like Anne's writing?
A   Yes.

Q   I would like to go back to 1001, and what is set out at the bottom of 1001 in typescript is in relation to item 3 on the agenda. "Obviously what Nancy has in mind for the US is business manager. What has to be borne in mind is that the base worked from is the company in London, and working on your previous budget, to give 15% of 80% would only allow 5% to cover overheads, commission to UK agent etc. Normally something would be paid to the negotiator or coordinator at the London end because whereas your US representative would not be involved in any UK contracts the London end would

at least be involved in coordinating and supplying information etc.", and the document continues: "In the area of records it may be feasible to pay 15% of 80%. Where other matters are concerned it may be better to view Nancy has a coordinator and pay a fee of, say, 5%". It carries on that sort of vein. Is that something that any of the Pythons would have said, either in advance of the meeting or at the meeting?
A   I really cannot be sure of that.

Q   It is likely, is it not, that that is material that comes from Mrs. Henshaw?
A   Well, that is your interpretation. I am not sure if it all comes from Mrs. Henshaw. She would have had an input clearly.

Q   If you look at the final paragraph under that item heading: "The next point is at what notice would you wish to terminate the agreement with Nancy Lewis if this became necessary. The company should perhaps use a lawyer to finalise the draft agreement". That suggests, does it not, Mr. Palin, that this is a document produced not by the Pythons but by someone, and what I suggest to you is that that someone is Anne Henshaw? Would you agree?
A   Possibly, yes.

Q   What I suggest to you is that by March 1974 she is very clearly providing you with advice in relation to business affairs and that is advice to all the Pythons in the form of this type of document. Would you agree?
A   Yes.

Q	Would you agree that the type of thing one sees at p.1001 to 1002 is the type of advice that a manager would give you?
A	Well, possibly but she is not our manager.

Q	But the type of advice that she is giving you is the advice that a manager would give?
A	Yes, I suppose you could say that.

Q	As you have said, Mr. Gledhill ceased to be your formal manager in the middle of 1974 and Mrs. Henshaw then became formally your manager. That is right, is it not?
A	I am not sure if she became formally our manager because I do not know if anything was signed at that particular time. All I know is that Mr. Gledhill ceased to be our manager in mid-1974.

Q	And Mrs. Henshaw then operated as your manager?
A	Yes.

Q	Until when?
A	Until about, I think, 1997. But there was a period in between, in about 1980, when she ceased to be our manager for a while and Sir Denis O'Brien of Euro Atlantic took over our management for a few years.

Q	So Euro Atlantic is not Mrs. Henshaw?
A	No.

Q	But Mayday Management is?
A	Yes.

Q	If you could go to the back of Bundle D3, Mr. Palin, and go to p.1107B, that is an extract from the Companies House register.
A	Yes.

Q	That relates to you. If you put your finger two pages on, at 1107D, you see the entry for Anne James and that is Mrs. Henshaw, is it not, under her new married name?
A	Yes.

Q	Looking at the two, the first company on your entry at 1107B is Prominent Palin Productions Ltd. If one looks at 1107D, Mrs. Henshaw is also a director of that company. What does that company do, Mr. Palin?
A	That produces my television travel programmes.

Q	If you then look to the penultimate entry on p.1107B which relates to a company called Prominent Television Ltd, do you see that?
A	Yes.

Q	Then look at 1107D, one sees in the fourth entry again Prominent Television Ltd. as being one of the companies that Mrs. Henshaw is a director of. What is Prominent Television Ltd., Mr. Palin?
A	My recollection is it was set up to deal with any television programmes that we might make independently outside of Python. I think I was the only one who used it.

Q	If you look back at 1107C, we see that you were a director of Mayday Production Services Ltd. between 29th December 1991 and 1st April 2005, and Mrs.

Henshaw is still a director and was for a time the secretary of that company. What did that company do, or what does that company do, Mr. Palin?
A   I do not know.

Q   What did the company do for the 14 years approximately that you were a director of it?
A   Mayday was a company that represented me as my agent and Production Services Ltd. is not a name I know, but certainly Mayday was a company run by Anne James and Steve Abbot, and Anne has ceased to be involved with the company apart from, as I say, just a name and a shareholder for about, I should think, almost 10 years.

Q   So you do not remember what that company was doing while you were a director of it?
A   Not specifically, no.

Q   You have no recollection at all?
A   I mean, just the name Mayday Production Services Ltd. is, I am afraid, not a name that I recognise. Mayday I recognise. It may have been a separate company involving others.

Q   It is a separate company, Mr. Palin. If you go to 1107D you will see that Mrs. Henshaw is a director of Mayday Management Ltd., the second company, which is the company that you were referring to a moment ago as ----
A   Yes.

Q   -- having been your manager, and one sees also that she is a director of Mayday Production Services Ltd. But you cannot help us as to what that company did or

does?
A   I cannot.

Q   Then over the page, at 1107E, the second full entry relates to Kay-Gee-Bee Music Ltd. Do you see that?
A   Yes.

Q   Then the next one is Python (Monty) Pictures Ltd. and the next one is Python Productions Ltd. What seems to have happened is that Mrs. Henshaw was a director of those three Python companies for about five months, six months, from 1997 to the middle of 1998. That coincided, as I understand it, with you beginning to retain FSM as your new manager. Is that right?
A   That would be the period, yes, that that took place, yes.

Q   Why was Mrs. Henshaw appointed to be a director of those three Python companies?
A   I have no idea.

Q   You are still a director of two companies with Mrs. Henshaw. When did you last see her?
A   I should think probably a year ago.

Q   You said that you have not talked about Mr. Forstater's claim to her at all. Is that right?
A   I have avoided talking to her about it because I felt it was a Python matter and not something I personally wanted to get into.

Q   So you did not ask her to give evidence in these proceedings?
A   I might have asked her if she had any views on

what was going on. That was all. That may have been a long time ago, but I always insisted that if she had anything she wanted to say she should go through the normal process and talk to our solicitor. I recollect that only came up once.

Q   I would like to talk to you very briefly about the position of Mr. Olswang.   I am sorry, one final question in relation to those documents I have just been showing you, Mr. Palin.
A   Yes.

Q   Both you and Mrs. Henshaw give an address at 34 Tavistock Street, WC2E 7PB. What is that address?
A   That was the address at which Prominent Television and Mayday have had their offices since 1998.

Q   For the purposes of Prominent Palin Productions Ltd., do you go and have meetings there?
A   Yes.

Q   Do you have meetings with Mrs. Henshaw in relation ----
A   No.

Q   -- to Prominent Palin Productions?
A   Well, not after she ceased to be involved in the regular running of Mayday, and I cannot remember exactly what that date was but I think, as I said, it must be seven or eight years ago. She has not been involved at all in the running of my affairs.

Q   Thank you, Mr. Palin. I would like to talk to you about Mr. Olswang very briefly. Do you recall ever

meeting Mr. Olswang?
A   No.

Q   I think you have already said you do not recall attending his offices in Brook Street.
A   I am afraid I do not, no.

Q   I would now like to talk about the terms that came to be agreed between Python (Monty) Pictures Ltd. and the investors and Michael White. Did you take a keen interest in what terms were being negotiated with Mr. White?
A   No.

Q   I would like you to take up bundle D2, please. You can put bundle D3 away and go to page 659. That is a letter on Chippenham Films notepaper dated 30th January 1974. It is unsigned but everyone has assumed that it comes from Mr. Forstater. Have you ever seen this document before?
A   Yes.

Q   When did you see it?
A   When it was presented in evidence.

Q   As part of these proceedings?
A   Yes.

Q   You did not see the document at the time?
A   I can't remember.

Q   What Mr. Forstater says in the first paragraph is, "I have given quite a lot of thought to your later proposal on the Monty Python film, and have spoken to some of the

Pythons about it." Do you remember having conversations with Mr. Forstater about the terms that were being offered by Mr. White?
A   I don't remember those conversations, no.

Q   You do not remember what proposal was being put by Mr. White at this stage?
A   I just can't recollect that, no.

Q   Is it right that you believe that you did discuss matters relating to the funding and the terms of the funding with Mr. Forstater at around with period?
A   I don't know.

Q   If Mr. Forstater is saying that he has spoken to some of the Pythons about it, would you not assume that he is telling the truth?
A   Yes, but I might not have been one of the Pythons. That's all I am saying.

Q   In terms of the structure of the deal and the taking forwards of the film, is it right that you, Mr. Gilliam and Mr. Jones, were the people who were driving the project forward?
A   Mr. Gilliam and Mr. Jones were both very keen to get the film made, wanted to direct the film. I was closely in touch with them at that time. You could put that view on it, yes. All the Pythons wanted to get the film going.

Q   I am sure all the Pythons wanted to get the film going, but in terms of who was driving it forward I suggest that it was much more you and the two Terrys rather than Mr. Idle, Dr. Chapman or Mr. Cleese. Would

you agree with that?
A   Not entirely, no.

Q   Given the support that you and the two Terrys were giving to Mr. Forstater, it is likely, is it not, and I accept you cannot recall, but it is likely that   Mr. Forstater would be discussing the financial terms of the Michael White deal with you and the two Terrys?
A   It's possible, yes. I'm sorry I can't give you memory. It's possible, yes.

Q   And in this letter one sees in the second paragraph, "We feel that the fairest division of profits between ourselves and Gladiole..." Do you know what Gladiole was?
A   I think that was Mr. Goldstone's company.

Q   ".... would be on an equal for all parties. This would split the 45½% remaining from our side into 8 shares, ([5] Pythons, Gladiole, myself) of approximately 5.7%." Do you remember Mr. Forstater raising with you the suggestion that he should get the same percentage as you and the other Pythons?
A   I don't recall that being raised, no.

Q   But do you assume that that is what happened?
A   I cannot say how it happened.

Q   Do you assume that it did? It is likely, is it not, that that was something that you knew about at the time. You knew that Mr. Forstater was getting the same percentage as you?
A   Likely.

Q But you do not recall?
A No.

Q Do you remember what fee Mr. Forstater was getting in relation to the film?
A I think it was £5,000.

Q Do you recall that his fee, part of his fee, was deferred. Do you remember that?
A Yes, I think that is true.

Q Do you recall who else had deferred fees?
A Again, from the papers which have been presented, I think that Terry Jones and Terry Gilliam were going to defer their fees.

Q Did you have a fee deferred?
A I can't remember.

Q So you cannot remember how the deferrals came to be agreed?
A No.

Q In fact, Mr. Palin, you did have a deferred fee. Part of your fee was deferred and the same amount of fee was deferred, £2,000, as Mr. Forstater was deferring, but you have no recollection of how that came about?
A No.

Q If you look in your witness statement at paragraph 26?
A Where are we?

Q   Bundle C, the slim bundle in front of you?
A   Yes.

Q   Can you look at paragraph 26. I am sorry, it is paragraph 26, the final three lines of that: "There were meetings and discussions in which we would be given updates, but I think I took no more part in this process than that. We left Mark to get on with sorting out the investors and the documentation." Do you see that, Mr. Palin?
A   Yes, I do.

Q   You have no recollection, particularly, of what those updates involved, do you?
A   No.

Q   If you look at the top of that paragraph you refer to to-ing and fro-ing -you can see that in the third line?
A   Yes.

Q   "I do recall that there followed much 'toing and froing' over the documents but we had Mark Forstater and Simon Olswang dealing with that." Again, I assume you do not have any recollection of what that toing and froing entailed?
A   No.

Q   If you look back where we started, "There were meetings and discussions in which we would be given updates...", those meetings would take place at the Henshaws, is that right?
A   I can't be sure, no. Possibly. Updates does not necessarily mean we would have to all be there, I suppose. If one could assume that we're all very busy.

We were rushing around preparing the film and doing our stage show. The updates may just have been provided for us to read.

Q You say that there were meetings. I was asking you where the meetings took place?
A Well, I don't know. I'm not quite sure what the meetings are. There might be meetings between other people, not necessarily the Pythons.

Q Mr. Palin, what you are saying is "There were meetings and discussions in which we would be given updates." That suggests to me that at that stage recalling that you had meetings "in which we would be given updates"?
A Yes. I am just not sure of the nature of those meetings, whether it was Python or whether we got together later to hear what had been said. I am just saying I'm not absolutely sure about those meetings and discussions or what they were about.

Q What I suggest to you, Mr. Palin, is that it is likely that Mrs. Henshaw attended meetings where you were given updates. Would you agree?
A I don't know.

Q It is likely, is it not, that that is what happened?
A It is likely that she would have been there possibly, yes.

Q At some point someone went to Mr. White and demanded a greater share of profits in relation to merchandising. So that I am clear, you have no idea who raised that issue with Mr. White and Mr. Goldstone?

A   No.

Q   I would like to discus with you the purpose of the top half as it was presented to investors. You have no recollection of what purpose was put forward to persuade the investors to allow for the creation of the top half?
A   No.

Q   In your witness statement at paragraph 34 you have assumed that it was put forward to reflect the work that you would do to create the merchandising. I am sorry, 35?
A   35, yes.

Q   "... this mechanism was intended to recompense the individual Pythons for the additional work/effort which would be involved in producing such merchandise/spin-offs." So that is what you assume to have been the reason put forward to investors. Is that right?
A   Yes.

Q   You have no direct memory one way or the other?
A   I don't have a direct memory but I can certainly remember there was a big issue that the Pythons should receive some recompense for work they had done themselves, which added value.

Q   And once that had been accepted by the investors an agreement is produced which allows for the creation of the top half - yes?
A   Yes.

Q   And an agreement is also produced which allows Mr. Forstater a share of the top half, yes?

A   So it would seem, yes.

Q   And that was the agreement that you came to initial?
A   Yes.

Q   You said that you assume that the reason for including the top half was because of the additional work that the Pythons would do. There are two particular bits of merchandising that are produced during the 1970s. There is an album and there is a book?
A   Yes.

Q   In relation to the album, a Python company, Kay-Gee-Bee, is inserted above Python (Monty) Pictures Limited to claim a revenue stream, before all the money trickles down to PMP. Do you accept that?
A   I can't remember.

Q   In relation to the book another Python company, Python Productions, was inserted above Python (Monty) Pictures Limited to receive its own share of the revenue stream that was being generated from the book. Do you have any recollection of that?
A   No.

Q   So if I asked you why were these two companies inserted above Python (Monty) Pictures Limited, you would have no idea at all. Is that right?
A   I would assume it was just created because we had created the majority of the work ourselves.

Q   But if only you were entitled to share in the top half, why do you need to have other Python companies above Python (Monty) Pictures Limited?

A   I can't answer that satisfactorily.

Q   What I suggest to you -and it may be that you simply do not recall - is that when those deals were structured it was known that Mr. Forstater had a share of the top half once it came to Python (Monty) Pictures Limited. Does that ring any bells?
A   No, it doesn't ring a bell.

Q   Those deals, done in 1975, 1976 and 1977 were deals that would have been done under the aegis of Mrs. Henshaw, is that not right? She was then your business manager?
A   She was our manager, yes.

Q   Do you remember discussing with her why Kay-Gee-Bee and Python Productions Limited were to be inserted into the structure?
A   I don't, no.

Q   Do you know whether when money that comes from the top half comes to Python (Monty) Pictures Ltd., at the moment money is paid to Mr. Forstater in respect of his share of the top half. Does the company seek to allocate the monies that are received to the Python who has done work on the particular bit of merchandise?
A   I cannot recall the exact details on that.

Q   You have no idea?
A   I am not sure. I am not sure what the procedure was.

Q   Because suppose Mr. Cleese decided that he was not going to do any work on the book at all in the mid-

1970s, but Mr. Gilliam worked very hard at producing new images, new material, on the basis of the way in which the top half is structured the money goes to PMP and falls to be divided, one would assume, equally between, after Mr. Forstater has had his share, the six Pythons? Is that, to your recollection, what happened?
A That is my recollection but I think obviously the idea of extra work that we had done, that was done by one Python particularly more than another, and we would then distribute it to the Python who needed it most.

Q Is that way Kay-Gee-Bee and Python Productions were doing? They were identifying which Python did the work and then distributing the revenue to the Python who did the work?
A I cannot be sure of that. I am just not sure of that particular structure, I am afraid.

Q I would like now to look at the agreement that you initialled, Mr. Palin, so if you take up Bundle D1 and turn to p.323. That is the third schedule to Mr. Forstater's agreement. One sees it says "profits of film" at the beginning. It then defines what profits of the film mean and one sees handwritten amendments in the fourth line, "less the merchandising rights hereinafter defined and", and then we have your initials and the initials of Mr. Forstater. Do you see that?
A Yes, I do.

Q You would accept that those are indeed your initials?
A Yes.

Q Then one reads down and one sees, about five lines

up from the bottom, "of exploitation of such rights", and then there are some more handwritten amendments, "such share being", and then again your initials and Mr. Forstater's initials. You have, as I understand it, no recollection whatsoever of putting your initials on this document. Is that right?
A I am afraid I have not, no.

Q What I would suggest to you, Mr. Palin, is that before you put your initials on the document you would have wanted to know what the document meant. Is that not right?
A It does not necessarily follow, I am afraid. ... something you should sign. It has all been agreed. All you have got to do is put your initials on there".   I hope I read it but I am not sure if I did read it. If I did read it I would not really have understood it.

Q You see in the penultimate line: "be entitled to receive 7.1429% of such merchandising profits in addition to his said shares of the profits of the film". What I suggest to you, Mr. Palin, is that at the very least you would have seen that there was, on one view, quite a large percentage being included in the document. I suggest to you that that is something that you would have paid attention to and seen.
A It is only 7%, not a large percentage. I am afraid I have no recollection of how I reacted to this when I saw it.

Q It is unlikely, is it not, Mr. Palin, that you would have signed the document without someone telling you in broad terms what the document meant?
A Well, all I can say is that I really do not, you know

-- I should have read all this maybe at the time. All I can remember is that I do not have a recollection of exactly what was said at the time. It did not make any impact on me at the time. I may have signed it very, very fast when we were rushing, say, to get through to the last base before we went up to Scotland or whatever. That is all I can say.

Q It is not a document that you signed in formal terms, because one sees at 325 that it is Mr. Jones who signed it, so again what I suggest to you is that the very fact that the document had been signed by someone else and you were being asked to initial a particular schedule of it that was being amended meant that you would have wanted to know what the document was doing. Do you accept that?
A Well, it is one interpretation but, as I say, at the time I just remember that we were in a rush. I do not remember asking much about this. Maybe I felt it had all already been agreed and I was just initialling it and I had no time to do anything more than that.

Q If Mr. Forstater had not agreed with you that he would take a share of the top half, it would have been a very odd thing to do, would it not, for him to have put a document to you that contained an amendment to that very provision and ask you to initial it? It would have been a very odd thing to do, is that not right?
A Possibly, yes.

Q If there had been no earlier agreement, he is raising with you and asking you to sign something that could have, on the basis of the evidence that we will come to look at in a moment, caused you some concern, because

you are giving   Mr. Forstater a share of the top half.
A   I did not see it as that at the time. I just thought it must be something generally to do with merchandising rights and I am afraid I was remiss. I should have perhaps checked more clearly but it was just general merchandising.

Q   So do you recall knowing that this was about merchandising when you signed it?
A   I do not recall that.

Q   Because, as we have already discussed, some of the Pythons had become very het up that Mr. Gledhill had got you to sign an agreement at a book launch. What I suggest to you is that it is very unlikely that you would have blindly signed something without being told what it was. Is that not right?
A   I do not think you understand quite how we operated at that time. I am afraid we were working very, very hard. It was a very last minute -- It is an inference you can draw but I would say that it was entirely possible that I could have just initialled something that was already there without taking in its full significance.

Q   You have no explanation, do you, as to why Mr. Forstater came to have a share in the top half?
A   No.

Q   You have no explanation as to why you came to make the manuscript amendments to his entitlement to the top half?
A   No.

Q   You have no recollection of agreeing to give Mr. Forstater a share of the top half?
A   No.

Q   So your position is, "I do not remember giving Mr. Forstater 5.6875%. I do not remember Mr. Forstater agreeing to defer part of his fee. I do not remember the fee that Mr. Forstater was going to be charging and I do not remember" ----

MR. JUSTICE NORRIS: That he did. He did remember that.

MR. WEISSELBERG: I am sorry. I apologise. And you do not remember the circumstances in which Mr. Forstater came to have a share in the top half?
A   No, I remember him asking for his share of what was the bottom half. I remembered there was some issue there. I do not dispute that. But I do not remember him wanting to get -- I do not remember him asking for a portion of the top half, no.

Q   So do you remember him saying, "I would like a share of the merchandising revenue"?
A   No.

Q   Because the top half and the bottom half only related to merchandising revenue, not a profit share in the film altogether.
A   I understand.

Q   Do you remember Mr. Forstater asking for a share of merchandising revenue in particular?
A   No.

Q You then seek to challenge Mr. Forstater's evidence as to the recollection that he has on the basis that now you say you would never have given him that share. In a nutshell that is the position, is it not?
A Say that again. Sorry.

Q Mr. Forstater says that he remembers a particular meeting.
A Yes.

Q And you do not remember a meeting. Mr. Forstater says that at the meeting there was you, possibly Dr. Chapman but certainly the two Terrys, and Anne Henshaw, and he made a proposal to you of taking a share in the top half. You do not remember that?
A I do not remember that.

Q Then after Mr. Forstater left he understands that you were considering the proposal and then Anne Henshaw told him what your decision was, and you do not remember that.
A I do not remember that at all.

Q You say that that did not happen, as I understand it, or do you say that you simply do not remember whether it happened.
A Well, I do not remember that it happened. I made no note of it happening. It was not sort of in my memory so all I can say is, no, as far as I am concerned it did not happen.

Q But, as we have seen, your memory is unsurprisingly very reliant on the diary and your diary does not record any of the detailed financial discussions

that take place in 1974 in relation to the terms of the deal. So what I suggest to you is, you may not recollect the meeting but it is possible, is it not, that the meeting took place and because you do not have a diary entry you are not in a position to say one way or the other whether the meeting took place?
A   I mean, it is possible but I have no memory of that meeting every taking place. There is no evidence of it anywhere else having taken place, so that is my position.

Q   I would like to look at the reasons that you now give as to why you think it would never have been possible for you to have agreed to give Mr. Forstater a share in the top half. You need to remember, Mr. Palin, that you give that evidence in circumstances where Mr. Forstater does in fact have a share in the top half, and you have no explanation as to why he has that entitlement. No position was put to Mr. Forstater as to why the top half was included?
A   I have no reason to know why he should have been included in the top half, which was reserved for Pythons.

Q   If you look then at paragraph 35 of your witness statement, page 277?
A   Are we on C?

Q   Yes, C, tab 15?
A   277, yes.

Q   In the third line you say: "Mark Forstater had never been and was never going to be a part of that extra work or effort." Mr. Palin, we have seen that you were saying to Mr. Gledhill that there was an intention of Mr. Forstater producing further films for Python?

A   This is what is said, yes.

Q   We have seen you describing, albeit with an exclamation mark, Mr. Forstater as being part of the film section?
A   Yes.

Q   I suggest to you that in circumstances where Mr. Forstater was the producer of the film, he had helped to make the film, he had been through the financing and production work, he had invested time and effort into it as part of the team, and he was someone who you thought there might be a future role for within the Python set-up, there was a possibility that he was going to be involved in extra work or effort in relation to merchandising. Would you agree?
A   No, I don't think there was any question in my mind that he would not be involved in merchandising. That was put together by the Python team. We put creative input into it, because that is what the Python team did. We always added an enormous amount of material to any sort of work that we did. So the added value was going to us, and not to Mark. Mark would not be a part of that.

Q   What Mr. Forstater says is that when he attended the meeting with you he explained his proposal to you and because of his involvement as the producer and creator of the film, not creatively making the film but the maker of the film, he was someone who should be entitled to share in all the merchandising revenue that came to be generated?
A   He wasn't the creator of the film. The film had been created by the Python team entirely. Mark came on board, became the producer, but I don't think that entitled

him to anything beyond that that we had put our own work into. Mark was not part of our team.

Q But he was part of the film section?
A With an exclamation mark.

Q Then I would like to look at paragraph 36 where you say, "I am sure that I would remember if there had been any such discussion or agreement to which I was a party." Mr. Palin, as we have established there is quite a lot that you do not recall. If it is not in your diary you have very little recollection of what was going on. Is that right?
A In most cases, yes.

Q What I suggest to you is that given the nature of merchandising revenue in the 1970s, i.e. it was not going to be a golden egg, and Mr. Forstater is at this stage someone who is trusted by you, and if he asked to have a share in the revenue stream and you did not think it to be outlandish, you would not put it in your diary at all. Is that not right?
A I can't say.

Q In paragraph 38 you say that in the second line, second sentence, "There is no note of any such meeting in my personal diary for that period, and nor is there any mention in the notes of many such meetings which Anne James prepared at the time." Now, Mr. Palin, I will not take you through the meeting notes and diary entries. As we have established, I think, some of the minutes do not have corresponding diary entries for you. What I suggest to you is that the mere fact that there is no entry in your diary does not mean that it did not happen. Is

that right? The fact that you do not have a diary entry for a particular meeting with Mr. Forstater does not say one way or the other whether a meeting in fact took place?
A   No. I have no evidence to say absolutely it did not take place, nor do I have any memory of it ever taking place at all. So as far as I'm concerned, it didn't happen. It wasn't written down - and I've got a feeling it would have been written down if it was a significant apportioning of our income to somebody else who had not done the work we were paying them for.

Q   You say that, Mr. Palin, but there is no record anywhere of the fact of you all agreeing that you would get 5.6875% of the profits of the film, other than the agreements themselves. There is no document other than the agreement itself, kept by the Pythons, which shows the discussion or agreeing of the deferral. So what I suggest to you is that you cannot rely on the absence of any entry in relation to the share of the top half given to Mr. Forstater from any document as being evidence that no such discussion took place.

MR. JUSTICE NORRIS: Is this not really a forensic point rather than something for the witness.

MR. WEISSELBERG: Yes. I am happy to move on. (To the witness) I would like to look at paragraph 39 of your witness statement, Mr. Palin, where you say that in the second line, "Python normally operated by consensus..." You appeared to be suggesting that without Mr. Cleese and Mr. Idle being there you would not have agreed anything. Is that what you are saying?
A   I am saying that we wouldn't have agreed some adjustment of our percentage without the agreement of

all of us.

Q   You and the two Terrys agreed to get Mr. Forstater to work as a producer and do work for you without a consensus. That is right, is it not?
A   Well, we had to get the consensus. That is why I had to speak to Mr. Cleese to try and get everyone behind it.

Q   What Mr. Forstater says happened is that he presents to you - maybe four of you, maybe three of you - in the presence of Mrs. Henshaw and you take some time to think about it, and then the decision comes to Mr. Forstater thereafter. At that stage there was nothing binding, was there? There was no "sign on the dotted line" and therefore a deal was done?
A   I mean, I don't know. That is Mr. Forstater's interpretation of how this was all done and how the meetings took place. As I can't remember any of this meeting ever taking place, I can't give you any detail.

Q   What I suggest to you is that you would have felt able to reach a conclusion in relation to a payment or a share in circumstances where it is clear that no formal written agreement will yet be concluded?
A   I can't answer that. I was aware all the time John Cleese was not happy so I don't think we would have agreed to anything like this, without at least talking it through to him and Mr. Idle.

Q   We have seen Mr. Cleese not being happy in January but your diary has no reflection on any criticism of Mr. Forstater from Mr. Cleese for the periods of February, March or April. What I suggest to you is that

you would at that stage, in circumstances where you trusted Mr. Forstater, have been willing to agree in principle for him to share in the top half without Mr. Cleese and Mr. Idle being physically present?
A   I don't think we would have made such an agreement because I think we would have had to refer it back to the two other Pythons, and particularly to John. It was two months since I recorded him being unhappy with Mark, but that is not that long in terms of people's feelings.

Q   Then in paragraph 40 you deal with the suggestion that Mr. Forstater's position of being treated as if he were the seventh Python is incorrect. Now, I am not interested in any suggestion that Mr. Forstater was being treated as a creative Python. What I suggest to you is that the terms of his deal were very similar to the terms of the deal that you, the Pythons, all had. You had the same percentage. You all had deferrals and he was given a share of the top half. What I suggest to you is that he was seeking to be treated like a Python and not like Mr. Goldstone. Do you accept that?
A   That might have been what he was seeking but it was never going to be accepted by the Pythons. The idea of a seventh Python is - just doesn't happen. It's never been like that. So if it's a purely technical thing maybe but certainly I don't think there is ever any question that this man was a seventh Python.

Q   But from a financial perspective he was wanting to be treated in the same manner as you and the other five Pythons. Do you remember him saying that to you?
A   I don't remember him saying that, but purely financially that might be the case. He may have asked to

be considered the seventh Python, but I don't think it ever came up in our discussions that we had a seventh Python.

Q What I suggest to you, Mr. Palin, is that there was no mistake in relation to Mr. Forstater having a share in the top half. The only mistake that may have arisen arises out of the amount of that share. The mistake arises out of the manuscript amendments that you initialled. Do you accept that that is the mistake, as to the amount of the share, not his entitlement to the share?
A I don't think his - I don't think he was entitled to the share.

Q I am just going to summarise where we have got to. What I suggest to you is that there was a meeting at which you and the Pythons other than Mr. Idle and Mr. Chapman were present. Mrs. Henshaw had arranged the meeting. Mark Forstater wanted to be treated equally with all of you. He attended the meeting; he made the proposal; you considered it and then Mrs. Henshaw gave him the answer that you agreed in principle to the proposal that he put, i.e. he should have a seventh share of the top half. Do you accept that that is the true position?
A No.

MR. WEISSELBERG: My Lord, I am about to move on to a different topic.

MR. JUSTICE NORRIS: I think that might be a convenient moment. Mr. Palin, I say this to all witnesses: please do not discuss your evidence over lunch with anyone, either the evidence you have given

this morning or what you might say this afternoon?
A   Okay.

MR. JUSTICE NORRIS: 2 o'clock.

(Adjourned for a short time)

MR. WEISSELBERG: There is one matter to pick up from this morning. I know that you do not accept that a meeting took place at which Mr. Forstater made a proposal in relation to the top half, but assume that you had that meeting for the purpose of my question, and assume that Anne Henshaw, after the meeting, told Mr. Forstater that his proposal was agreed. In your view, would Mr. Forstater have been entitled to think that that was the decision of the Pythons?
A   No, I think he probably should have realised that all the Pythons should have been party to such a decision.

Q   Do you think that Anne Henshaw would have communicated the decision without knowing that everyone agreed?
A   I can't say.

Q   In circumstances where Anne Henshaw is giving that information, do you think she would do it not believing that it was agreed? Is that the type of thing that she would do?

MR. SPEARMAN: My Lord, I do not want to interrupt my learned friend, but it does seem a little bit hypothetical.

MR. JUSTICE NORRIS: It is hypothesis founded on hypothesis, but let there be an answer and I will give whatever weight is due.
A   Could you repeat the last question?

MR. WEISSELBERG: If Miss Henshaw did give that information, would you think that Miss Henshaw would give that information without believing the truth of what she was saying?
A   I really can't say.

Q   Thank you, Mr. Palin. In the middle of 1974 do you remember that Mr. Forstater asked Mr. Idle for the director's percentage to be reduced and for him to be able to distribute that to Mr. Doyle? Do you remember that?
A   I don't recall it.

Q   Do you remember Mr. Forstater asking for the deferred amount, the £2,000 that was deferred, being released to him, even though the film had gone over budget?
A   I can't tell whether I recall it or whether I have read it in the documents. It seems familiar.

Q   Is that because at that stage you were still willing to deal with Mr. Forstater in a way that was sympathetic? Do you know why you agreed to the deferral?
A   I don't know why we agreed.

Q   If you look in bundle D2, please Mr. Palin, and turn to p.666, that is a letter dated 17th February 1975 from Mr. Forstater to the Pythons. Do you remember receiving the letter at the time?

A   I must have received the letter at the time. I don't remember the exact reception of the letter, no.

Q   Do you remember discussing it with anybody?
A   I don't remember discussing it with anybody in particular, no.

Q   Do you remember discussing it with Mr. Gilliam or Mrs. Henshaw?
A   No, I don't remember.

Q   Keep that bundle open but turn to bundle D3 p.977. It is the entry for 4th April. The paragraph at the second hole punch:

"In the evening Mr. Gilliam, who has taken on a new lease of life as Python chief organiser or chief liaison officer with Anne H, certainly, came round and stayed to supper. We talked about a letter just received by us all from Mark F, in which he asked for an extra £1,000 to cover the extra work he's done on the film, and in addition he asks each of us to accept a cut in our percentage ... Now, it's always been part of the deal that Julian and Mark were to share their profit percentages, this was between the two of them, and Mark is now trying to use us. Mark has scraped the barrel of our sympathy and there is nothing left for him. It's a pity everything has to happen like this but as soon as money is involved the knives come out."

Does that refresh your memory at all as to how you received Mr. Forstater's request.

A   Yes. When you say "do you remember" I'm really not sure. I don't recall talking about it with anyone, but that reassures me that I did talk to somebody about it.

Q   So you talked to Mrs. Henshaw, and the decision was that no payment would be made, is that right? Do you remember that?
A   I'm just having a quick look just to refresh my memory here. (Pause) Yes, I think that must be right.

Q   I would like now to ask you, Mr. Palin, about the book deal that was done in 1997. In the same bundle, D2, could you turn to p.682a. This is a letter from the NFTC dated 29th March 1997 to Mrs. Henshaw which refers to discussions that have taken place in relation to the book deal. As we have discussed this morning, Python Productions ends up being involved in this particular transaction. One sees that, if you cut on in the bundle, at p.694 in the middle just by the second hole punch. What is then being proposed is that Python Productions will take 15% of the publisher's gross receipts and then certain other percentages, and then the NFTC will take 10% and 5% of the retail price. This is the proposal that is being put. What happens is that Mr. Forstater raises a concern. One sees this in 697. It is in relation to the particular form of the deal. Page 697 is Mr. Forstater writing to Mrs. Henshaw. He has received the letters from Python Productions and the NFTC. "It seems that the deal being offered by Python Productions is a fair one for the investors and has been justly managed by the Pythons." What he then says is: "However, this new deal does affect me directly since in the original deal negotiated I was allocated 1/7th of the Pythons' share of any spin-offs. Under this proposed

deal I will lose that share. Would the Pythons be willing to bring me in on the Python Production side so that this 1/7th share remains the same?" Mrs. Henshaw's response to that is at p.698: "Thanks for your letter of 23rd June. I will bring this question up with the Pythons when they meet, hopefully next week." I will tell you, and I will show you it if you need to see it, but what the minutes of a meeting on 22nd July then record (p.1020 D3) was that Mark Forstater's letter was not brought up at the meeting but Michael Palin, Terry Jones and Eric Idle have already approved Anne writing a letter to say no, he could not have a share in Python Productions royalties. Do you remember having a discussion with Anne Henshaw about Mr. Forstater's request?
A   No.

Q   But you have no reason to believe that she did not have that conversation with you?
A   No.

Q   In D2, the response that she then sends, at p.701, is to refuse the request and, in the last four lines, she says: "You will after all be receiving your investor's share plus 1/7th of 50% of the amount paid to the NFTC which will be Python (Monty) Pictures' share". Do you remember seeing that letter in 1977?
A   I do not remember seeing it, no.

Q   Is that the type of letter that Mrs. Henshaw would show you?
A   Not necessarily, no.

Q   It suggests that, from our perspective, Mrs. Henshaw knew that Mr. Forstater was entitled to 1/7th of

the top half. What I suggest to you is when Mrs. Henshaw discussed with you the request from Mr. Forstater she must have discussed the fact of Mr. Forstater's $1/7^{th}$ share with you at that time. Do you recall any of that at all?
A   I do not recall it, no, but it may have been discussed.

Q   So you have no recollection of any discussion about the $1/7^{th}$ share with Mrs. Henshaw in 1977?
A   I am afraid not, no.

Q   When did you first see that letter, Mr. Palin?
A   What, the letter ----

Q   That we are looking at at 701.
A   -- at 701? Well, I have just seen it now.

Q   Had you seen it before?
A   No.

Q   So the first time you have seen this letter is in the witness box?
A   Yes, I think so.

Q   So throughout these proceedings this letter has never been shown to you?
A   Not as far as I remember, no.

Q   Just for your Lordship's note, the letter is pleaded at para.22.3 of the particulars of claim. Mr. Palin, if you could turn to p.709. This is a letter from Mrs. Henshaw to Anton. Do you know who Anton was?
A   No, I am not sure who Anton was.

Q Might you have had an accountant or an auditor who was called Anton at any point?
A I cannot remember.

Q I would like to turn then on to the circumstances in which a decision is taken not to pay Mr. Forstater his 1/7th share or what he says to be his share of the top half. Did you know that Mr. Forstater had been invoicing for many years for 1/7th share of book and album royalties?
A I cannot recall that I knew, I am afraid. It may have been accounted for.   It may have been something that we never picked up.

Q If you look in Bundle D3 and turn, for example, to p.930, you have got an invoice raised in June 2004 and there is an entry for a 1/7th of the record album. It is a zero figure. But the same entry for the 1/7th of the record album appears on numerous invoices, which you did not know? You have not seen these invoices before, have you?
A No.

Q Have you seen any of these invoices before appearing in the witness box?
A Not that I remember, no.

Q As *Spamalot* becomes successful and an income stream begins to be generated, Mr. Forstater challenges the basis on which that money is not being paid to him. Do you remember that happening?
A I remember being aware that he challenged it, yes.

Q Is it fair to say that there was a division of view

within the Pythons as to whether or not payment should be made of the 1/7th share that he was claiming?
A   This is when? In 2005?

Q   From 2005 onwards.
A   I do not remember there being any division amongst the Pythons about it.

Q   What was the position that your agent was adopting - Mr. Saunders?
A   Mr. Saunders, as far as I remember, questioned the right of Mr. Forstater to have the 1/7th share.

Q   Was it he who first suggested that Mr. Forstater should not have a 1/7th share?
A   He suggested he should not have it. He was not entitled to it.

Q   Was he the first person to suggest that?
A   Yes, I think so.

Q   What Mr. Forstater does is he then writes to you. One sees the letter in Bundle D2, p.732. Would you turn that up, please?
A   Yes.

Q   Do you remember receiving that letter?
A   No, I do not remember receiving it but I obviously have received it.

Q   If you look at the bottom of 732, what Mr. Forstater is saying is: "Roger Saunders and Anne James now claim there was an allowance made that I could invoice for 1/7th because other Python companies, Kay-

Gee-Bee Music etc., were taking so much of the merchandising revenue off the top before my share was applied. Their current argument is that since the Spamalot revenue does not have any monies coming off the top to other Python companies that I need to reduce my share to what is written in the appendix. In response I have to say that this is the first time I have ever heard of this allowance argument and was certainly not aware of it at the time. I do not know if your memory bank goes back this far, but I believe that the true nature of our agreement at the time was that I should be treated as a seventh Python to this revenue which I did help to create". Mr. Palin, if one looks back at 732, is the explanation being given or being said by Mr. Forstater to have been given by Mr. Saunders and Miss James a correct one? Do you recall whether there was an allowance made that Mr. Forstater should invoice for a 1/7th because other Python companies were taking so much of the merchandising off the top?

A   I am sorry, I do not recall that arrangement.

Q   In your witness statement you say, at para.31, that you do not recall whether you replied to him directly. If you go to p.738, there is a letter from you: "Dear Mark, I am afraid I am lost in all this. Roger Saunders is now our manager and should know all the contact details. We barely get together these days to discuss our own future plans so I am only being realistic to say that it may take quite a while to get the group to consider this. But the most I can do is to query the situation with Roger Saunders and try to make sense of it all". You expected Mr. Saunders, did you, to find out what had been agreed in 1974?

A   Well, he had raised the whole issue in 2005 so I

felt that it meant very little to me. The figure did not mean anything. I had not followed up the figures. I was probably doing lots of other things at the time and so my obvious reply was to put Mark in touch with Roger Saunders.

Q   Did you discuss with the other Pythons what they recalled having occurred in 1974?
A   No.

Q   Have you ever discussed with them what they recall?
A   Well, only recently.

Q   Did you exchange emails with any of the Pythons as to what they recalled?
A   Not as far as I remember, no.

Q   Did you exchange emails with Mr. Saunders as to what you recalled?
A   Again not as far as I remember.

Q   Did Mr. Saunders ask you what you recalled about the top half?
A   I am sorry to say, I do not remember him asking me that, no.

Q   Then if you go on to p.746, there is a letter from Mr. Forstater to you referring to an earlier letter from you which I do not think I need to show you.
A   Is that the one we have just looked at?

Q   No, it is a different letter. 742. Why not just see it very briefly?

A   Okay.

Q   742. "Dear Mark, Thanks for your letter. I've raised the question of your royalty with the Pythons, well, all but Cleese who has been inaccessible for a while in New Zealand. They said that they would like Roger Saunders to investigate the situation and after your letter arrived I contacted him to see how things were going. He has a lawyer looking into things who should report back in a week or so. All the best".
A   Yes.

Q   So you were leaving it to Mr. Saunders and the lawyers to find out what had gone on in 1974. Is that right?
A   Yes, the whole question of the share and what happened there, yes, was going to be looked into by somebody else because I do not think the Pythons could remember anything about it really.

Q   What Mr. Forstater then says at 746 is that over 30 years ago he had agreed with Anne "approved by the group that I should receive equal shares of the merchandising revenue with the six Pythons". He is saying that he agreed with Anne (that is Anne Henshaw). Why, when you got that letter, did you not go and ask Anne Henshaw what agreement, if any, she understood to have been entered into?
A   I can only think there was just too much going on at the time and I did not actually follow this one up.

Q   Because what you reply to Mr. Forstater, at 747, is: "I have been away filming the Eastern European series and have rather small windows in between each shoot.

The general feeling amongst the Pythons was that the lawyers should examine the detail and come to some conclusion as to the share of merchandising revenue to which you are entitled". Did you tell the lawyers to go and talk to Anne Henshaw?
A   No.

Q   If you look at 748, Mr. Forstater says - and one sees this at the bottom by the second hole-punch - "It is now down to the lawyers but I am not certain they will find the objective truth. Often they find what they are asked to look for and fit the facts to a preconceived notion. It is easy for Roger to try to re-write history because he wasn't around 30 years ago. However, Anne was and she knows where the bodies are buried. Have you ever asked her frankly to tell you the truth in this matter?" So again you received that letter but you did not ask Mr. Saunders or the lawyers to ask Anne Henshaw for what had been agreed. Is that right?
A   That seems to be right, yes. Yes. There were many, many other things going on. This is a pursuance of an issue which I felt should have been sorted out and did not really want to have a sort of hands-on involvement with.

Q   What you hoped would happen Mr. Palin, is this right, is that the lawyers and Mr. Saunders would investigate what had happened 30 years ago and would ask Anne Henshaw for what had happened?
A   Well, I wanted them to investigate what had happened all those years ago, yes. Whether they asked was obviously up to them, but yes ...

Q Do you know what Anne Henshaw would say happened in relation to the 1/7th? Do you know what her position is?
A I'm afraid I don't, no.

Q So you have decided to defend these proceedings, you are a director of PMP and you do not know what Mrs. Henshaw might think was agreed back in 1974?
A Well, at this time Roger Saunders was dealing with it. It had been our management for a few years. I was leaving it to him to discuss with whoever he wanted to discuss it with. I didn't have much contact with Anne James at this time about any business matters at all because Python had dismissed her as manager in 1997.

Q So if Mr. Saunders wanted to be a hawk, he should be a hawk and you would allow him to do whatever he wanted to do, is that right?
A I believed he would get to the facts of the matter. He had raised something which seemed to be a problem.

Q Sorry, there is one more letter I need to show you, Mr. Palin, which is at 852. That is a letter from Mr. Forstater to you dated 4th December 2008. He notes that he has just received a letter from your solicitors rejecting your proposal for an equal share of the merchandising in *Spamalot* revenue. "As you know, I put this proposal forward in an attempt to avoid going to court. However, this response leaves me with no alternative. Before I do that I want to explain to you directly about my proposal." Three claims, the first claim he sets out in paras.1 to 5. Those are the allegations that we have discussed in some detail. What I would like to draw your attention to is para.5 over the page at 853. What Mr. Forstater says is:

"To back up my original claim I cite correspondence between Anne Henshaw and myself regarding the proposed publication of a book of the film. In that correspondence I wrote to Anne on June 23 1977 seeking to clarify how my merchandising share would work with the book. I wrote to her [and this is in the bundle]. In the original deal negotiated I was allocated 1/7th of the Pythons share of any spin-offs. Under this proposed deal I lose that share. Would the Pythons be willing to bring me in on the Python Production side so that my 1/7th share remains the same?" That is the document I showed you a moment ago. Then "Anne wrote back to me on July 28th 1977 confirming: "You will after all be receiving your investors' share plus 1/7th of 50% of the amount paid to the NFTC which will be Python (Monty) Pictures' share." He says at the end of that paragraph: "I attach the letters for you". The second quotation comes from the document that we looked at earlier on: p.701 of D2 which, as I told his Lordship, was a pleaded document. I think your evidence, Mr. Palin, was that the first time you had seen it was in the box?
A I am sorry, what are you referring to? I am slightly lost.

Q Sorry, Mr. Palin. You see the words in bold?
A Yes.

Q "You will after all be receiving your".
A Yes, I understand.

Q That comes from the letter I showed you a moment ago from Anne Henshaw dated 28th July 1977. What Mr. Forstater says is "I attach the letters for you". Do you want to have one more look at the letter that he attached,

which is at 701. I think you told his Lordship that the first time you had seen it was today in the witness box. In light of Mr. Forstater's letter do you want to reconsider that answer? Do you recall seeing that letter?
A   I don't recall reading the attached letters that Mark sent to me on 4th December 2008 I'm afraid, I just don't recall it.

Q   My Lord, that is all the questions that I have for Mr. Palin.

BOOKS AND AUDIOS
BY MARK FORSTATER

I Survived A Secret Nazi Extermination Camp
The Spiritual Teachings Of Yoga (with Jo Manuel)
The Living Wisdom of Socrates
The Spiritual Teachings Of Marcus Aurelius
The Spiritual Teachings Of Seneca (with V. Radin)
The Spiritual Teachings of the Tao

AUDIO ONLY

The Tao Te Ching
The Age of Anxiety

All audios available on Audible.com

Mark Forstater blogs at www.theageofanxiety.me

Printed in Great Britain
by Amazon